SAINT LOUIS:

The Story of Catholic Evangelization of America's Heartland

A four-volume series

SAINT LOUIS:
The Story of Catholic Evangelization of
America's Heartland

Volume 1: From Canoe to Cathedral
Volume 2: The Lion and the Fourth City
Volume 3: The Age of Cardinals
Volume 4: Contemporary Challenges

SAINT LOUIS:
The Story of Catholic Evangelization of America's Heartland

Volume 4: Contemporary Challenges

Monsignor Michael John Witt

The Miriam Press
Saint Louis, Missouri

The Miriam Press
4120 West Pine Blvd.
St. Louis, MO 63108
www.hebrewcatholic.net

ISBN: 978-0-939409-11-2
Library of Congress Control Number: 2016904014

DEDICATION

To the men and women who animate this fourth volume. While multitudes fled from convents, rectories, and monasteries, these joined religious orders and founded new ones. When their comrades abandoned their vocations, and still others sullied the priesthood with despicable acts, these served as faithful priests and disciples. When others turned cold and abandoned the practice of their faith, these enlivened the faith by Eucharistic Adoration and enriched sacred liturgy, and they followed the promptings of the Holy Spirit, spread the word of God by new initiatives in radio and print, and explored the rich heritage of the Jewish roots of Catholicism.

In a world jaded by militant secularism, bloodied by war and murder and untethered abortion, drunk with apostasy and abuse, these men and women, religious, clerical, and lay were exemplars of the words Saint Paul wrote to Timothy: "I have run the good race. I have fought the good fight. I have kept the faith." These met the contemporary challenges and have prevailed.

TABLE OF CONTENTS

Preface   ix

Chapter 1.   A Poseidon Adventure   1

Chapter 2.   I Kept the Faith   39

Chapter 3.   I Fought the Good Fight   68

Chapter 4.   The Hermeneutics of Rupture   96

Chapter 5.   The Hermeneutics of Continuity   124

Chapter 6.   Quid Putas? The John L. May Years   152

Chapter 7.   John L. May and the NCCB   192

Chapter 8.   Justin Rigali   214

Chapter 9.   Crises   248

Chapter 10. Raymond Leo Burke and a Pride of Lions   258

Chapter 11. The Long View   294

Bibliography   304

Index   308

PREFACE

A prime role of an historian, when studying contemporary history, is to put into perspective events which shape our lives.

Sadly, the failure to present this perspective objectively has led to the institutional amnesia which poisons the citizens of our republic and, as Catholics, that of our Church. As Americans, too many of us do not know the facts of our nation's founding. The words of de Tocqueville do not ring in our ears as they should. As Catholics, too many of us cannot even grasp the Real Presence of Christ in the Eucharist, among other bedrock tenets of our Faith. Are we a people adrift, as some have argued?[1]

How did we come to this state of affairs? And how are we addressing these challenges and crises? That is the story of this fourth volume of the history of Catholic evangelization of America's heartland. It is a story of despair, abandonment, hardship, sorrow, and challenge. It is also a story of faith, commitment, encouragement, and loyalty.

Not all clergy are heroes; some are mindless villains. Others are walking saints. Not all religious are tepid; some are inspiring evangelists. Not all laity are passive in the pews; some have stepped up to bring Catholic evangelization to the fore in media; others have addressed the Hebrew roots of our Faith. Some have embraced education which is unabashedly Catholic. Some have discovered the richness of Catholic liturgy in "the reform of the reform," either embracing the highest quality of the Novus Ordo as envisioned by Vatican II, or rediscovering the sacred beauty of the ancient Gregorian Mass.

This "people adrift" is not adrift. While we seem to be without context and even without content, contemporary history of the Catholic Church can show how the Holy Spirit still leads us in surprising ways.

The role of the contemporary Church historian is to tell the story, as Leopold von Ranke once said, "wie es eigentlich gewesen war," as it actually happened. The historian thus motivated might also point to the ways *Deus absconditus,* the hidden God, is indeed not obscure, but is even now with us, guiding Catholics of America's heartland.

Further thanks go to the proof-readers and editors of this volume, Kathleen Moss, Mary Ann Aubin, Pam Nickels, Rena Schergen, and Mary Agnew. A big thank you goes to Archbishop Robert Carlson, who has encouraged me in this task.—MJW

---

1 Peter Steinfels. *A People Adrift: The Crisis of the Roman Catholic Church in America.* New York: Simon & Schuster. 2003.

Chapter One

A POSEIDON ADVENTURE WHEN EVERYTHING WAS TURNED UPSIDE DOWN

The tumultuous 1970s, with its assault on human life and the nuclear family, with its anti-war protests and its displays of radical feminism and militant homosexuality, with its presidential scandal and its crippled economy, began on August 28, 1968 in Grant Park, Chicago.

On that night there was a national spectacle, a violent clash between militant anti-war protesters and the Chicago Police Department. The struggle for the Democratic presidential candidacy had been a brutal one. Senator Eugene McCarthy drove President Lyndon Baines Johnson out of the primaries. Robert Kennedy was assassinated in California immediately after winning that primary. Vice President Hubert Horatio Humphrey was the anointed candidate in a convention controlled by back room politics, of which Mayor Richard Daley was a glaring example.

Four protest groups descended on Chicago to disrupt the convention. David Dellinger and Rennie Davis brought the National Mobilization to End the War in Vietnam. The Yippies were organized by Abbie Hoffman and Jerry Rubin. Tom Hayden's Students for a Democratic Society came, along with the Coalition for an Open Convention. Senator McCarthy cautioned the crowd and urged them to leave Chicago, but these groups were there for a fight.

After a day of peaceful protests and marches, some 7,000 people gathered in Grant Park across from the Hilton Hotel where many Democratic delegates were lodged. The protesters confronted the police line. Vulgarities were flung at the police, along with spit and bags of human feces. Television, newspaper, and radio media were present, ready to record the events.

Suddenly, the police went into action, clubbing and stomping on anyone in their way, bystanders as well as protesters. Just as suddenly, TV cameras were turned on, and the spectacle of a police riot was flashed all around the nation and around the world.

Civility was a casualty that night and would be again and again over the decade of the 70s. Another casualty would be objective journalism. Not for the first time, but certainly with an intensity seldom seen before, the media went on a campaign in 1968 to save America from itself. They found a villain in a third-party candidate, and they honed the tools needed to destroy him, tools they would use on others who became their targets.

Governor George Wallace was an unlikely national candidate. He had been governor of Alabama and made a national spectacle of himself trying to prevent the integration of the University of Alabama in 1963. He seemed like a regional candidate at best, only popular in the Deep South, endorsed by the Ku Klux Klan. But there was another side to George Wallace which touched the pulse of many Americans, especially the struggling working class. He was a populist.

Wallace spoke out against the establishment elites who were making policy decisions which many people resented, decisions common people felt they had no control over. He railed, "It is the trend of pseudointellectual government where a select elite group have written guidelines in bureaus and court decisions, have spoken from some pulpits, some college campus, some newspaper offices, looking down their noses at the average man on the street... saying to him that you do not know how to get up in the morning and go to bed at night unless we write you a guideline ..."[2]

This rhetoric was raw meat for Americans who resented federal interference in their local schools, who wanted law and order in the streets, and were appalled by what they saw at the Chicago Democratic convention. They resented that much of the largess doled out by the Johnson administration went to minorities. Even as neutral an observer as Theodore H. White noted, "Out of cynicism and despair, the new avant-garde has come to despise its own country and its traditions as has rarely happened in any community in the world."[3] Wallace tapped into all that.

As the presidential race entered the fall, Wallace polled as high as 21 percent in mid-September, just seven points behind Humphrey. What political pundits, as well as Nixon and Humphrey, thought a farce, a Wallace run for the White House was becoming a real threat.

---

2 Richard M. Scammon and Ben J. Wattenberg, *The Real Majority* as cited in Beth Bailey and David Farber, ed., *America in the 70s*. Lawrence: University of Kansas Press. 2004. P. 86.

3 Theodore H. White. *The Making of the President, 1968*. New York: Simon & Schuster. 1970. P. 243.

That's when Wallace got squeezed in the middle. Richard Nixon began to adopt the same populist verbiage. Union organizers in the north pointed to the dismal treatment of unions in Wallace's Alabama. Humphrey made speeches, promising to end the war in Vietnam. This alienated him from President Johnson, but he began to make peace with the McCarthy camp.

In October, the national press turned its guns on George Wallace. They acted as a bullhorn for the Humphrey campaign as he blasted, "George Wallace's pitch is racism. If you want to feel damn mean and ornery, find some other way to do it, but don't sacrifice your country. George Wallace has engaged in union-busting whenever he's had the chance ... and any union man who votes for him is not a good union man."[4] The AFL/CIO began a campaign to bring their workers back to the Democratic fold.

Headlines turned bitter on the Alabaman. The press was sour. "Tennessee Mob Beats Boy Who Sassed Wallace." "Hecklers Throw Eggs, Apple Core at Wallace in Oshkosh." "Clashes Mar Wallace Rally in Detroit." "Police Club Leftists after Wallace Rally."[5] Wallace poll numbers shrank from 21 percent to 13 percent.

In the election of 1968, George Wallace received more than 13 million votes. He had tapped a raw nerve in America, but the very establishment he railed against beat him.

A new form of journalism/entertainment was introduced in 1968. It premiered with a television weekly called *60 Minutes*. The program made no attempt at objectivity. It was sensational news reporting, pure muckraking in modern garb. And the style caught on and spread to other channels and local formats. In the process, it cast doubt on the integrity of institutions like government and big corporations.

A new low in television entertainment came two years later when Phil Donahue's interview programs went national. Each program highlighted families or individuals who aired their problems to millions of viewers and to a live audience which booed or cheered them on.

Turmoil was not unique to America in 1968, as the Chicago riot was one of many civil disturbances which had rocked American cities for four years in a row. In Paris, mobs of leftist students shut down the university and clashed with police. In Czechoslovakia, Prague was still smarting from the protests of a few months earlier

---

4 Ibid. P. 451.
5 Ibid.

which ushered in the brief Prague Spring, brutally crushed by Soviet tanks.

Further violence visited the United States with the assassination of Dr. Martin Luther King and the riots which followed. Columbia University was closed down by radical students. Final exams had to be cancelled, and the spring semester was abruptly ended.

A similar incident happened at Washington University in Saint Louis. After campus police arrested a student for a parking violation, and allegedly beat him, the chancellor's office was occupied by some 200 students. This was on December 5, 1968. The next day a group calling itself the Association of Black Collegians took over the University Finance Office and held it for nine days. White students joined them until Chancellor Thomas Eliot agreed to their demands and instituted a Black Studies program at Washington University.

If all these protests and civil disobedience displays needed a single icon, it could be found in a 1967 *Time* magazine photo. It showed a handsome young man in a protest line. He was placing a flower in the rifle barrel of a national guardsman. The act was pure theater, and George Harris III was an actor. He used the moment to contrast the militarism of the Vietnam War with the anti-war peace movement. That photo became one of the best-known images of the era. Lesser known is the life and career of George Harris. That life and career show us another seedier side of the 1970s.

George Harris moved to San Francisco and changed his name to Hibiscus. He joined a commune and began to abuse hard-core drugs. He grew a beard and joined other men who cross-dressed as women, using the Palace Theatre to create a drag performance. It was so well-received by the audience that a second performance was held in February 1970, and he became a fixture in San Francisco's gay scene. George Harris III died of AIDS at the age of 33.

The Catholic Church struggled to find a voice in the midst of the turmoil of the 1970s. If the goal of John XXIII and Paul VI was to implement the decrees of the Second Vatican Council, to bring aggiornamento (updating) to the Church and her structures, and to relate the message of Jesus Christ to the modern world, the first years after the Council were stumbling years. In 1967, Pope Paul issued *Populorum Progressio*, his only social encyclical, which spoke of equitable distribution of the world's wealth. It no doubt was prompted by the pope's eye-opening visit to India earlier. It was well-received by the laity, though criticized by the *Wall Street Journal*.

Less well-received was *Sacerdotalis Coelibatus*, an encyclical reconfirming mandatory celibacy for priests in the Western Church. The Dutch bishops met in synod at Noordwijkerhout in April 1969 to discuss, among other things, clerical celibacy. They put forth a four-point plan of action, but then hesitated to act. First, they called for voluntary celibacy for clergy, and second, that priests who had abandoned the priesthood to marry might be readmitted to the clerical state. A third point was that married men might be ordained, and the fourth point was that celibacy no longer be considered necessary for priestly ministry. Two weeks later, the Dutch bishops issued a letter watering down their proposals. Nonetheless, Pope Paul reacted bitterly to these proposals and to the flood of priests abandoning priestly ministry. On December 15, he spoke to the College of Cardinals and called it his "crown of thorns," adding that "such desertions cause so much bitterness and scandal in the People of God."[6]

Some got around the restriction by being ordained in the Ukrainian Catholic Church. Though this Church had been unincorporated and was forced to merge with the Moscow Patriarchate in 1946, it still existed in the United States, Canada, and Australia as a Church in exile. However, Ukrainian priests in the west were held to celibacy. Regardless, Cardinal Josef Slipyi, freed from a Siberian labor camp, took up residence in Rome where he ordained married men. Since they could not be sent to Ukraine which was under Communist control, he assigned them to dioceses in the U. S., Canada, or Australia as "missionaries."

Pope Paul introduced the practice of having priests renew their promise of celibacy at the Holy Thursday Chrism Mass each year. This act elevated the question of clerical celibacy beyond a mere Church discipline. Celibacy was seen as a sign of total dedication of the priest to Christ and to his Church. The priest, as *alter Christus*, another Christ, was in a sacramental and mystical way, married to Christ's bride, the Church.

Neither encyclical caused the uproar which came with the publication of the 1968 encyclical *Humanae Vitae*, a strong condemnation of birth control and a strong defense of family life and love. That theologians might dissent, and many did, should not have come as a surprise. Father Charles Curran, at Catholic University of America, gath-

---

6 Insegnamenti di Paolo VI. Tipographia Poliglotta Vaticana. 1969. P. 799.

ered some fifty-one other theologians to denounce the encyclical. Cardinal Patrick O'Boyle of Washington, D. C. had his hands full with dissenting theologians and disobedient priests. Many seminaries used the popular moral theology textbook of Father Bernard Häring, CSSR in their classes. Häring, as well as American Father Richard McCormack, SJ, had been advocating a change in Catholic teachings about birth control.

What was surprising was the tepid acceptance that several bishops' conferences made regarding the encyclical. In Canada, Cardinal Paul-Emile Léger of Montreal openly questioned it, and the Canadian conference issued the Winnipeg Statement, which recognized the legitimacy of Catholics using birth control under extraordinary circumstances. Similar statements came from conferences in France, Germany, Austria, the Netherlands, and Scandinavia. Cardinal Léon-Joseph Suenens became a thorn in the side of the pope when he complained that *Humanae Vitae* was a singular act by Paul VI, and this violated the sense of collegiality as expressed in the spirit of the Second Vatican Council.

The bishops' conference in the United States issued a statement which supported the pope, but it then watered down the statement by recognizing "Norms of Licit Theological Dissent." Already, the American opinion was shifting. The Johnson administration made birth control part of its Great Society programs, and the Nixon administration, especially internationally, made population control a priority. The day after Christmas, 1970, President Nixon signed the Family Planning Services and Population Research Act which provided family planning services to low-income Americans. The measure had passed with strong bi-partisan support.

It was in 1968 that Paul Ehrlich's *Population Bomb* appeared. It was a doomsday prediction. Ehrlich saw the end as early as 1974 when Asia, Latin America, and Africa would be written off as unredeemable, descending into chaos, food riots, and famine. The Stanford University professor, specializing in the study of butterflies, even predicted that the pope would reverse course on birth control, even advocating abortion as a way to reduce the human population.

Population Bomb made such a sensation that it influenced the American Friends Service Committee to publish its own study in 1970 entitled *"Who Shall Live?"* which advocated the repealing of abortion laws. The Quaker group argued that these laws violated the privacy of married couples, another theme which would frame the 1970s.

The sanctity of life, the stability of the nuclear family, and the expression of human sexuality were all hot button issues as the '60s morphed into the '70s, each issue challenging those with traditional Christian convictions.

In 1969, the Supreme Court of the United States set the tone in *Stanley v. Georgia*. Here the court ruled unanimously in favor of an individual who was in possession of pornographic material. The Georgia law which made possession illegal was struck down by the court, the majority arguing that the law violated the privacy rights of an individual.

And there was plenty of pornographic material available. And plenty of places to view it. Parts of New York City were notorious for their "peek shows," porn theaters, and bathhouses. There was open street prostitution, and other big cities began to experience the same patterns, too.

In August 1970 the federal Commission on Obscenity and Pornography published its findings and found that smut had no effect on its viewers. The Nixon administration immediately rejected the report and hoped that Nixon's two new Supreme Court appointees, Warren Burger and Harry Blackmun, might swing the court to more conservative stands when new test cases came to the Supreme Court.

But massive, irreversible changes had already begun. In 1965, the Supreme Court ruled in *Griswold v. Connecticut* that states could not regulate the use of birth control methods. Griswold was Estelle Griswold, head of Planned Parenthood in Connecticut. In a 7-2 decision, the court ruled that the right to privacy is implied in several amendments to the Constitution and that states could not regulate contraception by married couples. In his dissent, Justice Potter Stewart argued that he could not find any implied privacy rights but added that the Connecticut law was "uncommonly stupid."

This decoupling of the sex act and its potential biological consequences set in motion the many exploratory expressions of sex. Women, men, and children would each be devastated by these expressions.

In 1969 California revised its divorce laws, removing the preference for maternal custody of children. This ushered in the era of "no-fault" divorces. As one historian of the period commented, "A society in which people are encouraged to put themselves first is not likely to be a society in which many people celebrate their golden wedding anniversaries."[7] Divorce rates for American couples went from 9.2 per thousand in 1960 to 22.6 per thousand in 1980.

There were radical voices which heralded these statistics as liberating. Kate Millett in her *Sexual Politics* and Shulamith Firestone in her *The Dialectic of Sex* saw contraception and no-fault divorce as freeing women from "the tyranny of their reproductive biology" and smashing the patriarch of the nuclear and "bourgeois" family structures. These books joined the earlier work of Betty Friedan with her 1963 *The Feminine Mystique* which had sold over two million copies. Helen Andelin developed a course entitled "Fascinating Womanhood" and claimed to have trained eleven thousand teachers.

Some of these works were Christianity-based; others were purely secular. But each caused a self-consciousness in millions of women who read them and caused many to rethink the traditional relationships in the nuclear family.

Other voices came from the Frankfurt School, a group of scholars at Columbia University who had fled Nazi Germany. These scholars taught and wrote books, combining the ideas of Sigmund Freud and Karl Marx into what they referred to as critical social theory. They encouraged the liberation of women and men from the paternalistic family. For them, marriage was a farce; sex was recreational and could be performed in many forms—heterosexual, homosexual, with individuals as well as in groups.

Adding fuel to the fire was the life work of Alfred Kinsey. Though he was trained as a zoologist, Kinsey became famous for founding the Bloomington Institute for Sex Research. Kinsey was militantly anti-Catholic, often claiming without any evidence that the largest collection of pornography in the world was hidden away in the Vatican archives. His papers and books were full of extraordinary exaggerations. He claimed that eighty-five percent of men had intercourse before marriage and that at least thirty-seven percent had had homosexual encounters. He further claimed that twenty percent of pregnancies of white, middle class women ended in abortion.

There were serious scholars who were studying human sexuality. William Masters and his assistant Virginia Johnson, in Washington University's Department of Obstetrics and Gynecology, studied the

---

7 David Fromm. *How We Got Here: The 70s.* New York: Basic Books. 2000. P. 73.

nature of human sexual behavior and published two important books on the topic. But Alfred Kinsey skewed his findings by purposefully interviewing male prostitutes and sex offenders and then extrapolating the findings to the general population. As one writer observed, "He subverted moral standards by demonstrating 'scientifically' that they weren't observed in practice. He legitimized deviance by exaggerating its frequency."[8]

In an era where people were acting out in the public arena, emboldened by the civil rights movement and the anti-war movement, one might expect people to act out over sexual liberation. And they did.

On September 7, 1968 there was a protest in Atlantic City, New Jersey objecting to the Miss America Pageant. The New York Radical Women organization staged a bra burning, destroying what they called an instrument of torture. Actually, it was a symbolic burning. There was no fire for fear of setting the famed boardwalk aflame.

A radical feminist group calling itself SCUM, Society for Cutting Up Men, released the Redstockings Manifesto in 1969 declaring that "Women are an oppressed class... Our oppression is total, affecting every facet of our lives. We are exploited as sex objects, breeders, domestic servants, and cheap labor."[9]

The most brazen display of militant sexual liberation happened in New York City in the early morning of June 28, 1969. A bar called The Stonewall was a hang-out for homosexual men. It was owned by the Mafia, which routinely bribed police to look the other way. This time was different.

The police entered The Stonewall, ordering most of the patrons to leave immediately. They arrested a few of the employees and a few transvestites, as cross-dressing was illegal in New York at the time. On the street, the crowd attacked the police rather than disperse. The police were outnumbered and were pelted with bottles and rocks. So, they retreated into the building and locked the doors. There was an unsuccessful attempt to set the building on fire. Some of the crowd formed a chorus line and did a can-can until reinforcements arrived, driving off the revelers and rescuing the trapped police.

Though the Stonewall event was bizarre, it marked a turning point

---

8 Tom Bethell. "Sex, Lies and Kinsey." *The American Spectator*. May 1999. P. 16.
9 "Redstockings Manifesto" as cited in Bruce J. Schulman. *The Seventies: The Great Shift in American Culture, Society, and Politics*. New York: Da Capo Press. 2002. P. 165.

in gay pride and encouraged like behavior. Of greater importance was the 1970 convention of the American Medical Association held in Chicago. The doctors were targeted by the Gay Activists Alliance and the Chicago Gay Liberation Front. The objective was to get the AMA to declare that there is no link between homosexuality and a sickness, as was previously assumed. By the end of the convention, the AMA declared that there was no link between homosexuality and pathology.[10]

Also in Chicago in July, a group labeling itself Rise Up Angry was making itself known. While advocating against slum housing and lead poisoning, it also engaged in community organizing, building relationships with street gangs and giving them alternatives to violence such as softball games and barbeques. But there was another side to RUA. It opened a clinic which, supported by Chicago's Women's Liberation Movement, operated a clandestine abortion facility.

Abortion was illegal in all states, but attitudes were beginning to change. Lawrence Lader published a book in 1966 entitled *Abortion*. There he described illegal abortions taking place across the land. The book helped to move lawmakers in New York State to liberalize their abortion laws, making it legal for doctors to perform elective abortions. Previously, abortions were restricted to cases of rape, incest, and severe deformities in the baby. Hawaii, Alaska, and Washington followed immediately. Then thirteen other states liberalized their abortion laws.

By 1966, there were voices in Missouri which advocated the liberalization of state abortion law. *The Saint Louis County Medical Society Bulletin* counseled, "The decision to perform therapeutic abortion should be medical and not 'theological' or political." It argued, "Countless illegal abortions were performed each year," adding, "by unofficial estimates more than forty thousand women die each year from illegal abortions in Italy."[11] Neither observation was based on factual statistics.

In a Page One article for the *St. Louis Review*, writer Robert. J. Byrne cited the *Medical Society Bulletin* article by Dr. Melvin Schwartz which favored a change in Missouri's abortion law. Schwartz, an obstetrician,

---

10 Dan Berger, Ed. *The Hidden 1970s: Histories of Radicalism*. New Brunswick: Rutgers University Press. 2010. P. 185.

11 "Law to Permit Therapeutic Abortion Urged." *St. Louis Post-Dispatch*, 1966. Saint Louis Archdiocesan Archives. File: Abortion #1.

was the president-elect of the Society but wrote as a private doctor, not as an officer of the Society. Byrne countered with a quote from Dr. Eugene G. Hamilton, chief of obstetrics at Saint Mary's Hospital in Richmond Heights. He noted, "In legislative reform, we must guard against providing a latitude which would make it possible for the unethical to exploit the new freedom under a cloak of legality."

Then Dr. Hamilton seemed to hesitate, adding, "There is no doubt embryologically that the fetus is human from the time of conception so, if its destruction is to be sanctioned, let's be sure there is good cause."

Other doctors, quoted anonymously, also seemed to hesitate. One noted, "Change is inevitable," and added for the Church, "There's no reason for us to jump up and down and stamp our feet." Another doctor was quoted, "Rather than a theological outburst, I think Catholics should just present the facts." Yet another doctor said, "Life begins at conception but that such a life could be sacrificed, if it were absolutely necessary."

Byrne ended his article on a note of comity. "Those interviewed by the *Review* expressed the hope that the discussion, wherever it takes place, will be 'pertinent and temperate.'"[12]

Other sad news filled the evening airwaves. The war in Vietnam continued to rage, despite the Nixon campaign promise to end the war. In November 1969, investigative reporter Seymour Hersh revealed information about a massacre of the villagers of My Lai. The slaughter conducted by U. S. troops under the command of Lieutenant William Calley happened on March 16, 1968 but had been covered up by Pentagon brass.

The trial, which resulted in a 1971 conviction for the murder of twenty-two innocent civilians and a sentence of life imprisonment for Calley, split the nation apart. Anti-war elements saw this as justification for their cause. But there was a strong counter-reaction too. Twenty-four hours after the verdict was announced, the White House received five hundred telegrams and fifteen hundred phone calls, ninety-nine percent favoring clemency for Calley.

Georgia's governor, Jimmy Carter, declared "American Fighting Man's Day," and encouraged his fellow Georgians to drive with their headlights lit as a sign of support for Lieutenant Calley. George Wallace visited the soldier in the Fort Benning stockade. An oft-repeated

---

12 Robert J. Byrne. "Is Abortion the Next Great Public Issue?" *St. Louis Review*. March 3, 1967.

observation was that Calley was "just another victim of a war nobody wanted to fight."[13]

When the Army sent Lieutenant Calley to prison at Fort Leavenworth, Kansas, President Nixon had him returned to Fort Benning, Georgia for house arrest. In 1974, he was released by a judge who argued the trial had been prejudiced in several ways. However, three months later an appeals court upheld the conviction and dismissal from the army, though he was freed from any further jail time.

The Calley trial showed how divided the country was, even by economic status and class. Calley was from a lower middle-class family. He had dropped out of junior college to work as a dishwasher and bellhop. He joined the army and scored well enough to enter Officer Candidate School. While he was one of 1.6 million men to serve in the Vietnam War, he was also one of some 27 million American men of draft-age eligibility. These numbers show the disparity between those who could have served and those who were called up to serve. The draft exemptions were so generous that those who served came disproportionately from the lower classes and minorities.

The fracturing of American society could also be witnessed in many other facets. Daniel Patrick Moynihan, serving as assistant secretary of labor in the Johnson administration, commissioned a study entitled *The Negro Family: The Case for National Action*. It showed that the successes of the civil rights movement over the past decades had not produced the expected economic and social results. It argued that much of black urban poverty was due to the recent migrations out of the rural South with a sort of "social disorganization" which left the next generation of urban blacks disadvantaged in education, in social skills, in employable talents.

The study, in its most controversial section, argued that black families were disadvantaged in that they tended to be matriarchal, and the solution was to get good-paying jobs for black men. This solution suggested an all-out assault on illiteracy.

The Moynihan Report stirred controversy. President Johnson used it in a speech at Howard University to declare that he wanted "not just equality as a right and a theory but equality as a fact and as a result."[14] At the same time, the *Wall Street Journal* used the Report

13 David Frum. *The 70s. How We Got Here*. New York: Basic Books. 2000. P. 85.
14 Andrew Hartman. *A War for the Soul of America*. Chicago: University of Chicago Press. 2016. P. 44.

to explain the black rage exhibited in the Watts Riots of Los Angeles. Others accused Moynihan of blaming the victim, "justifying inequality by finding defects in the victims of inequality."[15] In time, Moynihan would temper his own enthusiasm for government solutions to black inequality. He would serve in the Nixon administration as counselor to the president for Urban Affairs, U. S. ambassador to the United Nations, and later was elected senator from New York.

In Saint Louis, the dilemma of inner-city poverty was as real as any government report. The traditionally black enclave, The Ville, had been devastated by the Great Depression, and the census tract there changed considerably in the years following. In 1940, a slight majority of whites of the 11,000 residents there changed by 1970, so that the population of 8,000 was almost entirely African American. By 2000, the same tract was occupied by just 1,900 black residents.[16]

With whites fleeing to the suburbs, plus zoning restrictions and construction of subdivisions along with their regulations, all of this acted as a "white noose around the city." One exception was University City. There the city officials tried to make integration work. A 1962 renewal proposal tried to manage the influx of underprivileged blacks into its neighborhoods. The city passed a fair housing ordinance, forbad the use of "for sale" signs, and tried to counter "block-busting" and other activities of unscrupulous realtors. Decades later, it would be a marvelous success story, making University City one of the best integrated communities in the nation. But in 1970, the *St. Louis Post-Dispatch* lamented that University City was "no longer one of the more desirable areas of St. Louis County."[17]

After peaking with an enrollment of 1,200, Mercy High School in University City began a decline in the early 1970s which precipitated its closure in 1984. Mercy was just one of the casualties of changing demographics and changing attitudes about Catholic education. Despite the best efforts of University City, realtors refused to show houses north of Olive Boulevard to prospective white buyers. When Cunningham Park, a subdivision in All Saints parish made up of working-class Catholic families, was seized by eminent domain and

---

15 Andrew Hartman. *A War for the Soul of America.* Chicago: University of Chicago Press. 2016. P. 45.

16 Colin Gordon. *Mapping Decline: St. Louis and the Fate of the American City.* Philadelphia: University of Pennsylvania Press. 2008. P. 4.

17 Ibid. P. 87.

turned into an industrial park, the parish suffered a significant blow. In 1968, All Saints became the first parish to close its school, sending its children to Saint Patrick's to the west or Saint Roch's to the east. Four years later, Saint Patrick's closed its school, too.

On April 30, 1970, Cardinal Joseph Carberry sent a letter to the pastors of his archdiocese. He requested that pastors with troubled school enrollment should contact the archdiocesan school board for review and a final recommendation. He also wrote superiors of religious congregations engaged in the educational apostolate, expecting that many of them would be withdrawing their communities due to declining numbers of religious vocations. He recognized their service in the past and lamented that their replacements would be lay teachers who would require higher salaries, thus boosting tuition, thus further reducing the population of students.

This letter anticipated what happened just two years later. In January 1972 the Sisters of St. Joseph, the Sisters of the Most Precious Blood, and the Notre Dame Sisters announced that eighteen schools would no longer have women religious on staff. Some parishes scrambled to find lay teachers to replace the Sisters. Others consolidated their schools with other local Catholic parishes.

On October 7, 1970 Cardinal Carberry met with four thousand Catholic educators at their annual institute. There he reported on the Commission on Religious Education which he had founded a year earlier. The Commission had four committees. The first committee was chaired by Father John T. Byrne, who held a Ph. D. in theology. The scope of that committee dealt with matters of faith and morals. The second committee, chaired by an Ursuline nun, Sister Mary Margaret Vitt, concerned itself with the state of religious education in the Archdiocese. A third committee studied religious textbooks and was chaired by a Jesuit from Saint Louis University High School, Father Edward O'Brien, S. J. The fourth committee, the Liaison Committee, was co-chaired by Mrs. John Horgan and Mr. Earl Werth. Its task was to survey the attitudes regarding Catholic education throughout the archdiocese.

Eyebrows were raised when the textbook committee refused to approve the texts published by the Daughters of Saint Paul. The October 1971 act was taken because the texts were judged to be "pre-conciliar," but Cardinal Carberry reversed the decision the next February.

The Daughters of Saint Paul was founded in 1915 by Father James Alberione and Teresa Merlo in Italy. Originally, a community of just a half dozen women, the congregation grew as it developed an apostolic outreach through media, first in writing and publishing Catholic literature. By 1955, they had spread to the British Isles where they opened up bookstores. Earlier in 1932, Mother Paula Cordero brought the sisters to New York City. It was the depths of the Great Depression, but undeterred, the sisters published and stored their books in an abandoned barn.

The arrival of the Daughters of Saint Paul and their bookstore in downtown Saint Louis would be one of the bright spots in local Church development in the 1970s.

In the midst of a nation coming apart, a city in decline, and a Church in confusion and diminishment, Cardinal Carberry tried to hold the center together. In January 1970 he gave a keynote address in Wichita, Kansas regarding Christian Unity at that city's centennial celebration. He found solace in his devotion to the Blessed Virgin Mary. Carberry had always had a strong Marian attachment. After his ordination in Rome, he joined his parents in a pilgrimage to Lourdes, where he celebrated Mass in the high chapel. His episcopal motto was "Maria, Regina Mater," Mary, Queen Mother.

In May 1970 Cardinal Carberry led a pilgrimage to Fatima. There he offered Mass, preached, and was so moved by the experience that he commissioned a statue of Our Lady of Fatima to be placed in the Old Cathedral and recommended the devotion for his whole archdiocese.

Challenges awaited the cardinal upon his return to Saint Louis. Before leaving for Fatima, Carberry penned a letter to his pastors. While complimenting them on the way the liturgical reforms were being implemented, he also warned of aberrations. "Some deviations from the Pastoral Guidelines issued with my prior approval to the Liturgical Commission have been brought to my attention... the use of unauthorized eucharistic prayers, the granting of general absolution at communal celebrations of penance, the reception of Holy Communion in the hand, and the use of non-biblical readings."[18]

The mention of general absolution at penance services stood in stark contrast to events which were taking place in the diocese of Memphis. There, on two occasions, Bishop Carroll Dozier celebrated a Mass of Reconciliation in which he dispensed general absolution to

---

18 John Joseph Carberry to Priests and Religious of the Archdiocese of Saint Louis. May 8, 1970. Saint Louis Archdiocesan Archives. RGIG 10. Chancery/ Pastoral 1970-71.

auditorium-filling crowds. This brought a rebuke from Pope Paul VI, but no further discipline was applied.

A former provincial of the Christian Brothers, Brother I. Philip Matthews, had launched his own general absolution campaign within Carberry's archdiocese. Brother Philip wrote letters to Cardinal Ritter during the Second Vatican Council urging adoption of general absolution but received a non-committal reply. Brother Philip penned letters to the *Saint Louis Review* and the *National Catholic Reporter.* He was quoted three times in an article on confession in *Time Magazine.* Reaction was widespread, both positive and negative. One critical letter came from Brother Philip's blood brother, then-current provincial of the Saint Louis Province, Brother Lambert Thomas Matthews.

Brother Philip's last attempt to encourage general absolution came in a 1968 article in *Homiletic and Pastoral Review*, with a readership of some 35,000 priests and religious. After this publication, the retired Brother seemed to have lost interest in the topic, though by Cardinal Carberry's admonition to his priests, others were continuing to carry the torch.

The cardinal's letter mentioned also the prohibition of receiving Holy Communion in the hand. The reception of Communion was undergoing changes. Select religious and laity were authorized as extraordinary ministers to distribute Communion. These individuals would be required to undergo training, and there would have to be a significant reason that a parish or institution would need non-clerical ministers.

As to receiving Communion in the hand, a poll of laity was taken in November and found that over two-to-one the notion was rejected, with over 80,000 voicing their opinion. This flew in the face of a recommendation by the Liturgy Committee of the National Conference of Catholic Bishops to allow the practice. But when the proposal came to the full body of bishops, it failed to receive the required two-thirds vote. It would take seven years before the NCCB approved by two-thirds vote a request to Pope Paul VI to allow the reception of Communion in the hand to American Catholics.

On December 17, 1970, Cardinal Carberry took a momentous step into a national issue which would be the most divisive for decades to come, the protection of unborn babies. He joined the other bishops of the Missouri province in designating that day as "Right-to-Life Sunday" and in a pastoral letter quoted the NCCB. "The child in the womb is human. Abortion is an unjust destruction of a human life and morally that is murder. Neither the expectant mother nor society has a right to destroy this life."[19]

Reacting to the American Medical Association vote encouraging the liberalization of abortion laws, Dr. Andre E. Hellegers, on the faculty of John Hopkins University School of Medicine, and a member of the papal birth control commission, noted, "For the first time the medical profession has gotten into the business of deciding or being concerned with which people shall live and which ones shall not." He added that this is not about health, but rather "a eugenic matter."

Father James McHugh noted that the proposal "presages a decided change in the philosophy of medicine and a whole new era in American medical practice."[20]

Robert J. Byrne, writing in the *Saint Louis Review*, returned to the question of abortion as a local issue in a May 5, 1967 article as the Missouri Senatorial committee on Criminal Jurisprudence drafted legislation to liberalize Missouri's abortion law. The committee chairman, Maurice Schechter, Democrat from Creve Coeur, stated, "I was surprised that no one appeared in opposition to the bill." That would change. Norbert Plassmeyer, an engineer from Florissant, organized Missourians Opposed to the Liberalization of Abortion Laws. His little group of eight included a few doctors and a few engineers and one Catholic newspaper editor, yet by mid-April they had mailed out 1,700 petitions and gathered nearly 1,500 signatures. They sought to rally Catholic and Lutheran pastors, Baptist and Episcopalian congregations, the Lutheran Laymen's League and the Knights of Columbus.[21]

The abortion bill became Senate Bill 206 and, by 1969, opposition had jelled. Witnesses testified powerfully. Dr. Denis Cavanagh, chair of gynecology and obstetrics at Saint Louis University Medical School, targeted the claims of deaths due to illegal abortions, noting, "There is no evidence that a woman's life has been lost because of the current abortion law." Missouri permitted abortions only in the case of saving the mother's life.

---

19 John Joseph Carberry to Priests of the Archdiocese of Saint Louis. December 7, 1970. Saint Louis Archdiocesan Archives. RGIG 10. Chancery/Pastoral 1970-71.
20 "Dr. Hellegers Criticizes AMA Support for Abortion." *St. Louis Review.* June 30, 1967.
21 Robert J. Byrne. "Opposition Group: Abortion Bill Passes Committee without Fight." *St. Louis Review.* May 5, 1967.

The next witness was Dr. Dermott Smith, associate professor of psychiatry at Saint Louis University. He criticized the exception for the mental health of the mother, saying that the ability to determine the mental state of a pregnant woman was "beyond the scope of the science." Dr. Matt Backer of the Saint Louis Gynecological Society called the aborting of deformed or defective fetuses "a throwback to barbaric practices." Dr. William Drake, Jr., associate clinical pathologist at Deaconess Hospital, the most graphic to testify, showed slides of embryonic development and abortion procedures. Finally, a non-doctor, Rev. Alfred Evans, of the Trinity Church of God and Christ, a black Pentecostal congregation, argued for the sacredness of life."[22]

When pro-abortion Robert Pranger, Republican of Saint Louis County, argued that the law should be liberalized because illegal abortions were now being performed, Lawrence J. Lee, Democrat from the city, responded, "If that is the case all criminal violations should be made legal." In the end, the Missouri senate killed the abortion bill 11 to 17.[23]

Other voices were late to take up the pro-life cause. It was not until 1978 that the world heard Rev. Jerry Falwell preach against abortion, five years after *Roe v. Wade*. Indeed, the National Conference of Catholic Bishops did not publish *The Pastoral Plan for Pro-Life Activities* until November 1975. Carberry had already established the Archdiocesan Pro-Life Commission in 1969.

The Right-to-Life movement perhaps has its origins in the mind of Father James McHugh, director of the U. S. Catholic Conference Family Division. In 1970 he called the first National Right to Life Committee meeting and encouraged the formation of other associations nationwide. Dozens of such organizations sprang up in Catholic circles. Political action had consequences. In Michigan, a referendum was placed on the ballot to allow for physician-assisted abortions in early pregnancy. Proposal B had widespread support, 59 percent, until Voice of the Unborn began a two-week campaign against it. It was voted down by 60 to 40 percent.[24]

In New York, when the state legislature repealed a two-year-old

---

22 "Physicians Testify against Liberalized Abortion Laws." *St. Louis Review*. June 3, 1969.

23 *St. Louis Globe-Democrat*. June 3, 1969.

24 Robert O. Self. *All in the Family: The Realignment of American Democracy Since the 1960's*. New York: Hill and Wang. 2012. P. 155.

liberalizing abortion law, Governor Nelson Rockefeller vetoed it, causing him to be marginalized within the Republican Party. Pro-lifers in his party as well as in the Democratic Party struggled for the heart and soul of their respective parties. It proved to be an uphill battle for Republicans and a lost cause for Democrats.

Polls showed that Americans were open to relaxing abortion laws. In 1971 Opinion Research Corporation found that 60 percent favored legalization, and a full 50 percent thought abortion was an issue between a woman and her doctor.[25] A 1972 Gallup poll showed support among Catholics, 56 percent, despite the vocal opposition of the hierarchy and the tradition of opposing abortion traced back to the earliest days of the Church.

Even before *Roe v. Wade*, there was plenty to divide the nation as it entered the 1970s. On April 22, 1970, America celebrated its first Earth Day. While the day was a festival of concerts and teach-ins, it planted seeds of environmental sensitivity and potentially significant legislation. A direct result was the Endangered Species Act of 1973 which came to protect even the most obscure animals and plants at the cost of development and economic vitality. Most famous was the protection of the tiny Tennessee snail-darter, whose discovery in 1973 halted the construction of the Tellico dam until a Supreme Court decision in 1977.

On May 8, a clash took place in the streets of New York. Thousands of anti-war protesters had gathered to decry the killing of college students on the campus of Kent State University in Ohio just days before. The deaths had been a terrible accident when raw, barely-trained Ohio state militia fired on a crowd of student protesters. Now all of a sudden, hundreds of New York City construction workers donning hard hats swarmed out of their worksites armed with clubs and tools. More than seventy protesters were injured. The construction workers drove the protesters from the financial district and won the praise of President Nixon, who exclaimed, "The workers were with us when some of the elitist crowd were running away from us. Thank God for the hard hats!"[26]

There seems to be some evidence that the hard hat action was not spontaneous. One historian of the period points out that Charles

---

25 Ibid. P. 156.
26 Beth Bailey & David Farber, ed. *America in the 70's*. Lawrence: University of Kansas Press. 2004. P. 87.

W. Colson, a White House counsel, had placed a call to the offices of Peter J. Brennan, head of the New York City construction union council.[27] Colson had a reputation for getting things done for the president and would later be swallowed up in the Watergate scandal.

The Kent State affair was precipitated by a perceived expansion of the war in Vietnam by the Nixon administration. There had been a coup d'état in Cambodia, and an anti-communist government came to power. The Cambodians resented the Vietnamese and especially the Ho Chi Minh Trail that brought supplies from the north through Laos and Cambodia to feed the war in South Vietnam.

Nixon and his adviser, Henry Kissinger, saw this as an opportunity to strike at the communist supply lines. The U. S. gathered some 15,000 captured AK-47 rifles to supply the Cambodian army. On April 30 President Nixon went on national television to announce, "This is not an invasion of Cambodia," and then went on to outline what could only be called an invasion. It was later revealed that the U. S. dropped over 2,700,000 tons of bombs on Cambodia between March 1969 and August 1973.[28]

Direct military aid to the Cambodian Lon Nol government went from $8.9 million in 1970 to $185 million in 1971.[29] This precipitated massive demonstrations, including the one at Kent State.

The American Indian Movement was active in those days also. In 1969, and into 1970, AIM members occupied the island of Alcatraz in San Francisco harbor, claiming it as Indian land. On Thanksgiving Day, 1970, others spilt red paint on Plymouth Rock as a protest against white expansion across the continent. Inspired by Dee Brown's 1970 *Bury My Heart at Wounded Knee: An Indian History of the American West*, a protest lasted for ten weeks at Wounded Knee in the Pine Ridge Reservation. There were many shootings and several deaths recorded there until federal troops finally cleared the area.

The state of the union in 1970 was summed up by a memo sent to President Nixon from Daniel Patrick Moynihan. In a broad critique of the state of affairs, he stated, "No doubt there is a struggle going on in this country of the kind the Germans used to call a *Kulturkampf.* The adversary culture which dominates almost all channels of infor-

27 Tim Weiner. *One Man against the World: The Tragedy of Richard Nixon*. New York: Henry Holt and Company. 2015. P. 91.
28 Ibid. P. 42.
29 Ibid. P. 100.

mation transfer and opinion formation has never been stronger, and as best I can tell it has come near silencing the representatives of traditional America."[30]

The midterm elections of 1970 caused Nixon to ponder his political future. While the Republicans gained two seats in the Senate, they were still in the minority. In the House of Representatives, the Democrats gained twelve more seats, strengthening their majority. With his eye on the presidential election just two years away, Nixon convinced John Mitchell to give up his post as U. S. Attorney General to oversee Nixon's reelection campaign. This included constant surveillance of Senators Ted Kennedy of Massachusetts and Ed Muskie of Maine, considered potential rivals.

Worse, the President agreed to create a secret intelligence unit within the White House called the Plumbers. Their initial task was to stop leaks which were constant in his presidency, but soon their role expanded into illegal activity which would finally bring Nixon down as the first president in U. S. history to resign.

In 1971 there was no respite from the frenetic activity of the past few years. On February 9, South Vietnamese troops entered Laos in an attack called Lam Son 719. The objective was to drive back elements of the North Vietnamese army. The invasion began with a disaster. U. S. air support accidentally struck an ARVN unit, killing six and wounding fifty-one. Sixty thousand troops from the north, armed to the teeth, repulsed the South Vietnamese. In the end, South Vietnam lost 102 dead and 215 wounded in this failed assault. It also lost face. The U. S. lost any illusion that the war could be won on the ground, using the strategy of Vietnamization. Instead, it could only be ended by diplomacy or bombing the north into the stone ages.

Before the year was out, the world witnessed the signing of an Indian-Soviet treaty which was a thumb in the eye to the communist Chinese who had fought a war with India some eight years earlier. Two years before that, there had been a quick firefight on the Ussuri River between Soviet and Chinese troops. The treaty also upended U. S. relations with India and caused Nixon to resort to profanities on more than one occasion. Nixon retaliated by supplying arms to Pakistan when it entered into a brief war with India toward the end of the year.

---

30 Andrew Hartman. *A War for the Soul of America: A History of the Culture Wars.* Chicago: University of Chicago Press. 2015. P. 51.

What upset President Nixon most was a leak by columnist Jack Anderson in which he intimated a U. S. turn toward Pakistan. This leak endangered one of Nixon's most important international initiatives, an imminent visit to China. It also revealed a spy very deep in the administration. Later, it was proven that the spy was Yeoman Charles Radford, working for none other than the Joint Chiefs of Staff![31]

Other leaks came from a raid on an FBI office in Media, Pennsylvania. Thousands of files were stolen and, drip by drip, were given to the press, including the *Harvard Crimson*. The files showed domestic surveillance by the FBI on various anti-war groups and on individuals. The revelations became fuel for flames against the war, including in Congress.

These leaks frustrated the administration already trying to deal with the worst leak of the century, the Pentagon Papers. These documents were given to the *New York Times* by former Defense Department consultant Daniel Ellsberg. They represented forty-seven volumes of documents, 7,000 pages, commissioned by then-Secretary of Defense Robert McNamara. His intention was to document the way the U. S. became involved in the war and was damning of Democratic administrations: Kennedy for pressuring to send ground troops, for involvement in the 1963 coup which led to the murder of President Diem; Johnson for faking the attack on the *U. S. Maddox* and expanding the war through the Tonkin Gulf resolution.

Instead of seeing the Pentagon Papers leaks as a vindication of Republican administrations, Nixon saw it as a threat to the presidency itself. Failing to silence the *New York Times* after losing a case in the Supreme Court six-to-three, he authorized the break-in of the office of Daniel Ellsberg's psychiatrist. They found nothing. Things were spinning out of control.

A group calling itself Movement for a New Society was formed in early 1971. It had Quaker roots which abhorred the war in Vietnam, as well as capitalism, racism, sexism, and ecological exploitation. Founded in Philadelphia, MNS never counted for more than one hundred members but sought to influence beyond its number by taking strident direct action.

In July, members climbed into canoes and kayaks in Baltimore harbor to block a Pakistani ship on-loading military supplies. The same

---

31 Tim Weiner. *One Man against the World: The Tragedy of Richard Nixon*. New York: Henry Holt and Company. 2015. P. 148.

thing happened in Philadelphia, where police boats rounded up the protesters. Regardless, longshoremen sided with MNS and refused to load the ship, which departed empty twenty-four hours later. MNS would also participate in the Wounded Knee occupation.

MNS was also engaged in draft dodging. Their efforts and those of other resisters were not inconsequential, as it is estimated that as many as 70,000 young men had fled the U. S. to avoid the draft.[32]

If things were not bad enough, a prison riot broke out in August 1971 at San Quentin State Prison in California in which guards killed a Black Panther. In New York, three weeks of riots broke out at Attica State Correctional Facility. Before it was over, twenty-nine prisoners and ten New York State Troopers lost their lives.

If all of these activities needed a handbook, they got it when Saul Alinsky published *Rules for Radicals* in 1971. He advocated direct action and organization building to bring about social change. While Alinsky was lionized by the far Left, many of his ideas found favor within elements of the Catholic hierarchy, particularly in his hometown, Chicago.

Alinsky got his start by organizing the Back of the Yards Council in 1939. The object was to use pressure to bring about social change. Over ninety percent of the targeted neighborhood was second-generation Catholic immigrants. Parishes, along with labor unions, were natural allies in the movement of community organizing. Alinsky, a secular Jew, worked closely with Catholic clergy, including auxiliary bishop Bernard Sheil, who acted as honorary chairman of the Back of the Yards Council. Successful threats of a nation-wide strike against meat packing giants such as Armour and Swift brought Alinsky fame and invitations to community organizing in many cities. He was also influential in establishing the Campaign for Human Development in November 1969 by the National Conference of Catholic Bishops.

Wars, riots, and radical organizing all took their toll on the American spirit, but it was court actions which set the tone for decades to come. In 1971, the Supreme Court ruled in favor of court-ordered busing to desegregate schools. *Swann v. Charlotte-Mecklenburg Board of Education* separated white, blue-collar families from upper middle-class liberals and African Americans, each important elements in the New Deal Democratic Party.

---

32 Dan Berger, Ed. *The Hidden 1970s: Histories of Radicalism*. New Brunswick: Rutgers University Press. 2010. P. 254.

The dramatic application of court-ordered busing was expanded two years later in another Supreme Court decision which extended the measures to northern cities when it was found that segregation was just as prevalent there. Then in 1974, in *Milliken v. Bradley*, the court limited busing by decoupling the suburbs from the cities, setting off even more white flight. Wealthier families abandoned the cities or sought private education for their children. The end result was poorer cities and worse educational opportunities for minority children.

Blue-collar angst and elite smugness were most on display in what developed in Boston in 1974. Bean City was a federation of ethnic neighborhoods which had come to live in more or less peaceful coexistence with one another. The Irish dominated Charleston and South Boston. Italians reigned supreme in the North. Roxbury was black. Boston schools reflected this ethnicity.

On June 21, 1974, federal judge, W. Arthur Garrity, Jr. changed all of that. Garrity was from the elite. A Harvard law school graduate and a friend of the Kennedy family, he had little in common with the people whose lives he was about to upturn. In *Morgan v. Hennigan*, Garrity targeted an Irish Catholic South Boston high school and black Roxbury High. While the seniors in both schools could choose which to attend, the entire junior class from South Boston was transferred to Roxbury and the other classes were mixed. Tony neighborhoods of old Boston wealth—Brookline, Wellesley, Newton—were all excluded from the order.

The results were disastrous. On the first day of school, only one hundred of the expected thirteen hundred black students came to South Boston High. A mere thirteen of the expected five hundred and fifty whites came to Roxbury. Both sides had to run angry gauntlets. By October, food fights broke out in cafeterias, brawls were common in corridors and classrooms. One hundred and fifty state troopers had to be assigned to the schools to maintain peace. South Boston High's student population plummeted to four hundred, protected by five hundred police!

Before Garrity acted, the Boston school system educated 80,000 children. Afterwards, that number bottomed out at 57,000, 42,000 of whom were black. Many white children used the suburban addresses of relatives to enroll in schools away from the Boston system. Regardless, Judge Garrity pressed the issue even further by applying desegregation plans all the way to first graders. When events spiraled out of control, with fights breaking out even in the grade schools, Garrity ousted the principal at South Boston High School and took over supervision of the school himself.

The Boston busing dilemma was played out in hundreds of communities across America. The stark divide between a small elite who made the rules but did not apply them to themselves, and the rest of the nation, was on display in Boston. Judge Garrity's children were not affected. His family lived in Wellesley. Senator Ted Kennedy sent his children to an elite, private school. Governor Michael Dukakis and his family lived in Brookline.

But the most egregious of all instances of court activism, a case which would forever shatter civic comity in America, came in 1973 in the Supreme Court decision of *Roe v. Wade.*

The morality and legality of abortion had been a hotly debated topic for over a hundred years. The Catholic position was defined by Pope Pius IX in an 1869 papal bull. Any abortion from the moment of conception was considered murder and carried a penalty of excommunication. Prior to 1869, Catholic opinion was divided between life beginning at conception or at the time of "ensoulment," also termed "quickening."

In 1930, Pope Pius XI published *Casti Connubii*, an encyclical which admonished Catholics who used birth control. He grounded his teaching in the very incarnation of Jesus Christ and what it meant to chaste marriages. "How great is the dignity of chaste wedlock, Venerable Brethren, may be judged best from this that Christ Our Lord, Son of the Eternal Father, having assumed the nature of fallen man, not only, with His loving desire of compassing the redemption of our race, ordained it in an especial manner as the principle and foundation of domestic society and therefore of all human intercourse, but also raised it to the rank of a truly and great sacrament of the New Law, restored it to the original purity of its divine institution, and accordingly entrusted all its discipline and care to His spouse the Church."[33]

Catholic arguments against abortion and contraception were generally based on natural law principles. The natural outcome of sexual relations in a marriage was the possibility of new life. Birth control would block this. It takes out of the hands of God, the author of life, His authority to create new life.

---

33 *Casti Connubii*, Paragraph 1. December 31, 1930.

Reacting to the news of fetal deformation due to the use of Thalidomide, Boston's Auxiliary Bishop Thomas J. Riley commented, "Efforts to deprive the unborn child of its right to live on the ground that it is likely to be born in a condition of deformity must meet the objective that the same reasoning would justify not only what is commonly known as euthanasia, or mercy killing, but also the taking of the life of any human being who would be judged to be lacking in normal physical integrity."

Bishop Riley grounded his argument in natural moral law. In fact, while some 20,000 women received Thalidomide before the drug was pulled, and several hundred were pregnant at the time, only seventeen children were born with defects nationwide.[34]

The Catholic position was not helped by an awkwardly composed statement by Cardinal Richard Cushing of Boston. When a scientist, a Catholic, developed the pill Enovid as a form of contraception, the Cardinal criticized him in the diocesan newspaper, *The Pilot*. He stated, "The Church is not opposed to birth control as such, but the artificial means to control birth."[35]Unfortunately, the second part of the sentence was immediately forgotten.

The "truly and great sacrament of the New Law" was not on the minds of most Protestant denominations. The Anglican Lambeth Conference of 1920 condemned the use of contraception and warned that the decoupling of sex and procreation would debase Christian marriage. It counseled "deliberate and thoughtful self-control."

Ten years later, the Conference reversed itself and declared that a couple who had a "clearly felt moral obligation to limit or avoid parenthood" could use artificial birth control. Of the three hundred and seven Anglican bishops attending the Conference, one hundred and ninety-three voted for the proposition. Passage of the measure so enraged Bishop Walter Carey of Bloemfontein that he left the assembly and wrote a letter of protest to King Edward VII. It was to no avail.

The Lambeth Conference of 1930 opened the flood gates for other denominations. Within a few years, the American Episcopal, United Methodist, United Presbyterian, and Congregational Christian Churches had all passed similar measures.

---

34 "Thalidomide Case Held Suggestion No Change in Catholic Stand." Religious News Service. August 2, 1962. Saint Louis Archdiocesan Archives. File: Abortion #1.
35 "Cardinal Cushing Denies Contention Church May Approve Contraception." *The Harvard Crimson*. April 23, 1963.

Regardless, most states had laws on their books which forbad the sale of contraception drugs or devices, even to married couples. That changed with *Griswold v. Connecticut* in 1965, when the Supreme Court declared that the decision for married couples to use birth control was a privacy issue, a right found within the Constitution, though such a right is not mentioned in that document.

Public opinion paralleled the Court's decision. Between 1963 and 1965, Gallup polls found approval of the dissemination of birth control information went from fifty-three percent to seventy-eight percent.[36]

It was just a small hop to extend this same privacy right to non-married couples, as was enshrined in *Eisenstadt v. Baird* (1972).

These events revealed a fundamental disagreement on the nature of human beings, their interaction regarding sexual union, the family, society, and the sanctity of human life. In 1937 the National Federation of Catholic Physicians' Guilds accurately described the other side as fostering the notion that humans have the right "to improve society by deciding who should live and who should die."[37] This utilitarian, eugenic, and relativistic position contrasted with the Catholic view that human life is God-given and sacred. Married couples are co-creators with God.

By the 1940s, the introduction of penicillin, anesthetics, and surgery procedures like Caesarean sections made giving birth much safer for mothers. This failed to dissuade the utilitarian secularists who not only wanted contraception, but therapeutic abortions. Key among these was New York gynecologist, Alan Guttmacher. He and others found a way around the New York law forbidding abortions. The law allowed for a therapeutic abortion if the life of the mother was in danger, though this was becoming more and more rare.

As an example, Margaret Hague Maternity Hospital performed only four abortions in twelve years, among 67,000 live births. In contrast, Johns Hopkins University Hospital aborted three out of every one hundred deliveries. The pretext was based on the mental stability of the mother, upon the certification of a psychiatrist. Guttmacher admitted to a friend his dodge. "The reason that psychiatric indications have become increasingly common, and form more than 60 per-

---

36 Daniel K. Williams. *Defenders of the Unborn: The Pro-Life Movement before* Roe v. Wade. New York: Oxford University Press. 2016. P. 59.
37 Ibid. P. 26.

cent of the abortions done in my own institution is that we physicians are trying to find a way to do more legal abortions."[38]

The debate about changing abortion laws took a turn in 1959 when the American Law Institute called for liberalization. No longer was this a heated discussion between medical professionals; lawyers were now getting involved. Catholic lawyers took up the argument that the unborn child has certain inalienable rights, particularly life. The courts seemed to agree. In cases where a fetus was killed, as in an automobile accident or homicide of the mother, victims had the right to sue for wrongful death of the unborn baby. In *Smith v. Brennan* (1960), a New Jersey supreme court stated, "medical authority recognizes that an unborn child is a distinct biological entity from the time of conception, and many branches of the law afford the unborn child protection throughout the period of gestation."[39]

The journey of what seems perfectly obvious, that the unborn child is a child deserving of protection, to legal disregard for this life, via *Roe v. Wade*, is fascinating and tragic. Battles took place in state legislatures, in media coverage, and in direct action by citizens on both sides of the debate.

The American Law Institute pressed for liberalizing state abortion laws. It called for legal abortions in the case of rape, fetal deformity, and "women's health." The last criteria were extraordinarily expandable, as in the case of mental health. Yet in 1962-63, every bill in state legislatures meant to liberalize abortion laws failed to be voted out of committees.

In April 1965 *Life Magazine* published an issue with color photographs of the stages of fetal development. It sold eight million copies in just a few days. The pictures showed an eight-week- old baby in the womb with clearly discernable eyes, fingers, and toes. Any doubt that this was a human person was wiped away. Pro-abortionists would have to find another argument, and they did, based on a balancing of rights.

This approach was played out in the California Supreme Court ruling *People v. Belous*. Dr. Leon Philip Belous had helped a California woman obtain an abortion because she was distraught and intending to get an abortion in Tijuana, Mexico. Belous did not perform the abortion but referred the woman and her boyfriend to an abortion-

---

38 Daniel K. Williams. *Defenders of the Unborn: The Pro-Life Movement before* Roe v. Wade. New York: Oxford University Press. 2016. P. 35.
39 Ibid. P. 48.

ist licensed in Mexico, but not California. Police found out about the abortionist, arrested him, and traced the referral trail back to Dr. Belous, who was also arrested. The abortionist pleaded guilty and implicated Dr. Belous. Belous pleaded the case to the California Supreme Court which ruled in his favor. Based on *Griswold v. Connecticut*, the court ruled, "The fundamental right of the woman to choose whether to bear children follows from the Supreme Court's and this court's repeated acknowledgment of a 'right of privacy' or 'liberty' in matters related to marriage, family, and sex."[40]

This was a huge blow to the pro-life movement, and a new strategy had to be found to convince the public that abortion is wrong. The National Conference of Catholic Bishops voted to spend $50,000 in an educational campaign promoting the dignity and sanctity of human life. This would be an ongoing effort. Head of the Family Life Bureau, Father James McHugh, brought sex education programs into Catholic schools. He wanted to decouple the issues of contraception and abortion, to concentrate on what he saw as the greater of the two evils. Philosophers like Georgetown's Germain Grisez opposed him, arguing that both issues were tied together by natural law.

McHugh forged ahead and created the National Right to Life Committee. The NRLC would be powered by the laity, would have Chapters in every state, and would seek to reestablish abortion restrictions through state legislation.

Others got involved, too. Mildred Jefferson, the first woman to graduate from Harvard Medical School and an African American, was repulsed by the vote of the American Medical Association to liberalize abortion laws. She spoke out loud and clear about taking personal responsibility. She showed that medical science clearly pointed to the fetus as a human person and hinted that abortion was being used as a form of genocide against the poor and against blacks.

Another approach was pioneered by Father Paul Marx at Saint John's University in Minnesota. He discovered while lecturing on embryology that graphic images of abortions appalled his students. He found that nurses who were forced to witness and participate in abortions were horrified and opposed the procedure by almost nine-to-one. While this approach was effective, it put a hard edge on the pro-life movement and would radicalize some like Randell Terry's

---

40 *People v. Belous*. 71 Cal. 2d 954 (September 5, 1969)

Operation Rescue, where civil disobedience was the rule. Pro-abortion groups countered with their own graphic campaign, using the coat hanger as a reminder of the danger of illegal abortions, though they failed to produce evidence that coat hangers had been used for such a purpose.

Another voice on the pro-life side who used explicit images was Jack Willke and his wife, Barbara. They sold one-and-a-half million copies of their 1971 book *Handbook on Abortion*. Using photographs of fetuses, they illustrated that these were human beings. The couple took to the road, developing a large following in Saint Louis, and spoke to over seventy thousand people in just one year.[41]

On a more genteel level, a lay woman, Mary Winter, gathered a dozen women in her home in 1970 and founded Women Concerned for the Unborn Child. Winter was a mother of seven children, married to an optometrist, a college graduate, and former grade-school teacher. She saw the abortion issue as an outgrowth of radical feminism which tended to neuter or even masculinize women. Her voice, and that of the WCUC, would seek to appreciate the natural gender differences, to see mothers who abort their babies as victims of avaricious doctors.

Similarly, Patricia Gotz, a member of National Organization of Women, began to argue that abortions harmed women and was expelled from NOW in 1974. She went on to found Feminists for Life. Bolstering her argument was the fact that during the first three weeks of legal abortion in New York, three women died during the procedure.

Another grass-roots movement had been founded in Toronto by a mother of seven, Louise Summerhill. Calling her group Birthright, she sought to aid women in crisis pregnancies and to convince women to give birth to their children by offering them counsel and aid. When several states legalized elective abortion in 1970, her organization grew rapidly in the United States. By 1973, there were over one hundred Chapters of Birthright in America, and the Archdiocese of Boston adopted the movement when it declared December 30 of that year as "Birthright Sunday."

Soon, Birthright would come to Saint Louis and become a bright beacon of the local pro-life movement.

The early 1970s saw great pro-life victories in state legislatures. In 1971, when twenty-five state houses took up legislation to liber-

---

41 Daniel K. Williams. *Defenders of the Unborn: The Pro-Life Movement before* Roe v. Wade. New York: Oxford University Press. 2016. P. 138.

alize abortion laws, every one of them was defeated. It was in the courts that the pro-life movement had setbacks. California, Vermont, Florida, and New Jersey struck down state abortion laws. Michigan showed the trend best. Pro-abortionists had been defeated in the state legislature. When they took the issue to a referendum, the people of Michigan rebuked their cause. They then went into the courts and won. As in the issue of busing, we find the courts thwarting the will of the people.

Realizing that the next battle would be in the courts, and pro-abortion victories there would undo everything the pro-life forces had accomplished in public opinion and in state legislatures, two congressmen proposed a Human Life Amendment to the constitution. In the summer of 1972, Congressmen Lawrence Hogan of Maryland and John Schmitz of California, both Republicans, simply proposed, "An individual, from the moment that he is conceived, shall not be deprived of life, liberty, or property, without due process of law."[42]

After *Roe v. Wade*, the Human Life Amendment would be the only viable way forward for the pro-life movement.

Two cases were decided on January 22, 1973 by the Supreme Court of the United States. Both silenced the public debate over life and death and set the stage for rancor and discord in America. The first case was *Doe v. Bolton*.

Sandra Cano, known in the case as "Doe," sought an abortion in Georgia where the law was very strict. Arthur Bolton was the attorney general of the state. The Supreme Court ruled seven to two that the Georgia law was too restrictive, and that Doe had a constitutional right to privacy.

Writing for the majority, Nixon-appointee Warren Burger declared, "the medical judgment may be exercised in the light of all factors – physical, emotional, psychological, familial, and the woman's age – relevant to the well-being of the patient. All these factors may relate to health. This allows the attending physician the room he needs to make his best medical judgment. And it is room that operates for the benefit, not the disadvantage of the pregnant woman."[43]

In *Roe v. Wade*, the Texas lawyers were clumsy in arguing the state's case. In both the Georgia and Texas cases, their cases rested on

---

42 Daniel K. Williams. *Defenders of the Unborn: The Pro-Life Movement before* Roe v. Wade. New York: Oxford University Press. 2016. P. 196.
43 *Doe v. Bolton.* 410. U. S. 179 (1973)

right-to-life of the fetus. Past cases had assured the protection of the unborn. But the justices asked questions to which the lawyers could not give clear answers. Why does Texas not prosecute a woman who self-aborts if the state protected the unborn? In *Doe*, the assistant attorney general could not answer the question of why Georgia permits abortions in cases of rape, deformation, and the health of the mother if the fetus had a right to life.

In *Roe*, the Texas attorney stumbled on his own argument, questioning ensoulment. "There are unanswerable questions in this field... When does the soul come into the unborn – if a person believes in a soul? I don't know."[44]

Texas and Georgia were given something of a reprieve when the Supreme Court decided to hear the cases again after William Rehnquist and Lewis Powell were sworn in. This time the plaintiff's lawyer was asked tough questions. Sarah Weddington was asked directly, "Would you lose your case if the fetus was a person?" Her answer was unclear, arguing that there was a balance of rights, that the fetus as a person could have statutory rights, but the mother had constitutional rights, rights assumed in the constitution, as ruled in *Griswold v. Connecticut* (1965) and *Eisenstadt v. Baird* (1972).

It was on that issue, the personhood of the fetus, that *Roe v. Wade* would be decided. Was the unborn child a person and citizen, protected by the Fourteenth Amendment? But that amendment specifically said, "All persons born or naturalized in the United States..." The fetus did not qualify; he was not yet born, and therefore did not qualify for Fourteenth Amendment protection!

Justice Blackmun wrote for the majority, trying unsuccessfully to split the difference. The fetus was not "a person" in the sense which is found in the Constitution. He noted that anti-abortion laws were only developed in the late nineteenth century when scientific knowledge of fetal development was better understood, and that even these laws equivocated on fetal protection, as most of them allowed for abortions in the case of endangerment of the life of the mother.

Blackmun stated, "It should be stressed that the Court does not today hold that the Constitution compels abortion on demand. It does not today pronounce that a pregnant woman has an absolute right to an abortion. It does, for the first trimester of pregnancy, cast

---

44 Transcript of Oral Arguments in *Roe v. Wade* (1973), December 13, 1971 as cited in Daniel K. Williams. *Defender of the Unborn*. P. 198.

the abortion decision and the responsibility for it upon the attending physician."[45]

The ruling upended abortion laws in forty-six states, yet Blackmun told a friend, "I suspect, however, that the furor will die down before too long. At least I hope so." A former Blackmun clerk, Edward Lazarus, thought differently. He noted "as a matter of constitutional interpretation and judicial method, *Roe* borders on the indefensible...Justice Blackmun's opinion provides essentially no reasoning in support of its holding. And in the almost 30 years since *Roe*'s announcement, no one has produced a convincing defense of *Roe* on its own terms."[46]

In four-and-a-half years, America experienced a Poseidon Adventure. It seemed like the cinema genre of the age was disaster films. Early on, audiences were excited by *Airport* (1970) depicting a snowstorm paralyzing an airport, a Boeing 707 getting stuck, and a mad bomber terrorizing the passengers. The next year, *Andromeda Strain* told us of the evils of the military-industrial complex and a disaster involving germ warfare. *Towering Inferno* (1974) dealt with corruption in the construction industry while *Earthquake* came out the same year. The year 1976 gave us *The Cassandra Crossing* about bio-terrorism. But it was the 1972 *Poseidon Adventure* which was most emblematic of the era.

A cruise ship was hit by a giant tsunami and turned upside down. Everything was topsy-turvy, chaotic. At fault for this disaster is an evil elite, the ship's owners, who put at risk their passengers to maximize profit. One historian of the period noted, "Americans lamented the decline of heroism and the heroic, defining themselves as survivors..."[47]

Gene Hackman played a priest whose leadership caused some of the passengers to seek a way out, while others went the wrong way or despaired. In the end, only a few survived.

As much as disaster films frightened and entertained audiences, reality outside the movie house was even scarier. The Vietnam War, seemingly without end, anti-war demonstrations, White House leaks, radical feminism, attacks on the nuclear family, and attacks on human

---

45 *Roe v. Wade* (1973)

46 Edward Lazarus. "The Lingering Problems with *Roe v. Wade*..." *FindLaw*, October 3, 2002 as cited in Ramesh Ponnuru. *The Party of Death*. Washington, D. C.: Regnery Publishing. 2006. P. 14.

47 William Graebner. "America's Poseidon Adventure: A Nation in Existential Despair as cited in Beth Bailey and David Farber, ed., *America in the 70's*. Lawrence: University of Kansas Press. 2004. P. 158.

life swirled all around the nation. And another dark secret was about to burst into the news cycle: Watergate and the fall of a president.

Despite all of this, there were those who soldiered on and struggled to keep the faith.

Representatives of the priests of the Archdiocese renewed pledges of priestly dedication and celibacy at the Holy Thursday Chrism Mass at the Cathedral Basilica in 1972. Photographer Richard Finke. From the Archdiocese of St. Louis Archives and Records.

Cardinal Carberry commissioned this statue of Our Lady of Fatima after his return from his pilgrimage to Fatima, Portugal in 1970. Arteaga Photographers. From the Archdiocese of St. Louis Archives and Records.

Daniel Moynihan spoke to Saint Louis University graduates in a commencement speech in 1968 about American racial tension with the federal government. Photographer Richard Finke. From the Archdiocese of St. Louis Archives and Records.

Cardinal Carberry outlines the goals of the Archdiocesan Commission for Religious Education at its first meeting at the chancery on November 4, 1969. Thirty-five priests, religious and lay people were appointed to the commission. Bishops Joseph McNicholas and George Gottwald sit on either side of Cardinal Carberry. Photographer Richard Finke. From the Archdiocese of St. Louis Archives and Records.

Rev. John H. Byrne was appointed by Cardinal Carberry to the Commission on Religious Education in 1970. Photographer Richard Finke, 1972. From the Archdiocese of St. Louis Archives and Records.

Mother Mary Margaret Vitt, OSU, was prioress of the house of studies for Ursuline Sisters. Mother Vitt was appointed to the Commission on Religious Education by Cardinal Carberry in 1970. Photographer Richard Finke, 1966. From the Archdiocese of St. Louis Archives and Records.

Eugene Walsh and Mary Fran Horgan were co-chairmen of the Archdiocesan Pro-Life Committee in 1975. Photographer Richard Finke. From the Archdiocese of St. Louis Archives and Records.

As leaders in the pro-life movement in the U.S., John and Barbara Willke came to St. Louis in 1974 to conduct lectures and workshops on abortion and the pro-life cause, indicating that St. Louis was in the forefront of the movement. Photographer Richard Finke. From the Archdiocese of St. Louis Archives and Records.

Audrey O'Neil of Birthright Counseling in St. Louis looks at the baby clothing donated by students at St. Francis of Assisi Parish School in Oakville. The school held a "baby shower" donation drive in 1985. Pictured from left to right are Jamie Donnelly, Stephanie Moll, Ellen McDermott, Audrey O'Neil, Lori Peters, and Cindy Foushee. Photographer Richard Finke. From the Archdiocese of St. Louis Archives and Records.

At the 1975 award ceremonies for the Archdiocesan Campaign for Human Development, Cardinal Carberry speaks with Maria Rangel of the American Indian Cultural Center of Mid-America in Festus and Mrs. Rasber Wharton of St. Martin's Child Care Center in Kinloch. Photographer Richard Finke. From the Archdiocese of St. Louis Archives and Records.

Chapter Two

I HAVE KEPT THE FAITH

THE CARMELITES AT SAINT AGNES HOME

While life in the Catholic Church and in America between 1968 and 1973 seemed like a Poseidon Adventure where everything turned up-side down, many positive developments took place that ran counter to the trends of chaos and disintegration.

In Saint Louis, on September 20, 1977, the Carmelite Sisters of the Divine Heart of Jesus made plans to convert their convent's third floor into more room for their novitiate. Bucking the downward trends in religious vocations, these sisters needed to expand to make room for more applicants. The year before, the sisters put an extension to the Memorial Wing of St. Agnes Home, adding a dining room and a full-care activity area.

The Carmelite Sisters of the Divine Heart of Jesus were one of the brighter spots in the Archdiocese of Saint Louis as it adjusted to the new reality of the Post-Vatican Church. The congregation was founded in Germany by Mother Mary Teresa of Saint Joseph, a strong-willed Prussian, living in a hostile land dominated by Protestants and secularists who teamed up with the Iron Chancellor, Otto von Bismarck, to torment the Catholic Church.

Anna Maria Tauscher van den Bosch was born on June 19, 1855. Her family was Lutheran. Indeed, her father was an official in the Lutheran Church. Sorrow struck her early, as her mother died at the age of forty-five. In her early twenties, Anna Marie was shocked and disgusted at the government's persecution of the Catholic Church. Her own grandfather, a Lutheran minister, was hounded from his congregation by the government for failing to assent to the demands of King Frederick III. She turned to daily readings from scripture and from *The Imitation of Christ* by Thomas à Kempis. Her faith deepened, and she developed a devotion to the Blessed Virgin Mary.

A chance conversation with a priest led to her conversion three years later. For that she was fired from her job. Shortly after, Anna Maria was given work at a convent which cared for elderly women. While doing needlework one day, an inspiration came to her, not to join a religious order, but to found one herself. In 1891, she moved to Berlin and, with the aid of a priest and some friends, founded Saint Joseph's Home and took in three children.

Life was difficult. Once, she expected a donation of 10,000 marks from a wealthy woman. Instead, she got 10 marks. Later, she received another gift of 15,000 marks, but the family kept the money for three years, giving her only the interest. In 1894, the bequest was honored. Thereafter, a new building was constructed, candidates came to join her, and they began to live according to the Carmelite rule. A small hospice was occupied in the western part of Berlin, all this with the silent approval of Cardinal Georg von Kopp, prince-bishop of Breslau.

On a visit to Rome, Anne Maria, assuming the name Mother Mary Teresa of Saint Joseph, was formally received into the Carmelite Order. Her community was called "Carmelite Sisters, Servants of the Divine Heart of Jesus." Regardless, Mother Mary Teresa suffered continual setbacks and trials. Her strong will and determination to serve God saw her through it all, and saw expansion into the Netherlands, Switzerland, Hungary, and the United States.

The sisters' first attempts in America were met with rebuffs in Cleveland and in Chicago. In Milwaukee, they were graciously received in late 1912. More professed sisters and postulants arrived, and in 1913 an invitation came from the Archbishop of Toronto to work among the Italian immigrants there. In 1915, they were invited to open a house in Calumet, East Chicago, Indiana. It was sparsely populated but had a promise of growth, as seven railroad lines passed through.

A motherhouse was established in Wauwatosa, near Milwaukee. Other houses were opened in South Kenosha, Detroit, and in 1920, Saint Charles, Missouri. Taking the train to San Antonio, Mother Mary Teresa stopped in Saint Louis and was struck by the poverty of the surrounding neighborhood. Urged by the Carmelite nuns in Saint Louis to open a house there, Mother Mary Teresa and another sister visited with Archbishop John Glennon, who received them enthusiastically. He suggested several suburban locations.

The sisters settled on Saint Charles, coming to know Monsignor Francis Willmes, long-time pastor of Saint Peter's parish, and his assistant, Father Winkelmann. A perfect house was located, but the sisters had to wait nearly two years for it to be vacated.

In her autobiography, Mother Mary Teresa speculated, "I saw in this foundation only a small beginning. I hoped that here, like in Wisconsin, one establishment after another would arise, and especially the house mission work in St. Louis itself would flourish. Unfortunately, my wish has not been fulfilled in the past five years; but who knows what will develop out of the Carmel of the Divine Heart of Jesus in St. Louis."[48]

The foundress died September 30, 1938 in the Netherlands. Her premonition about future development in Saint Louis proved prescient.

In October 1929, the sisters got word that a friend and benefactor, Elizabeth Moehring, was dying. Two sisters left Saint Charles to be with her as she quietly passed away on October 19th. Much to their surprise, Miss Moehring left most of her estate to the sisters with a request that they use the money to build a home for the elderly. Included in the bequest was a patent Elizabeth Moehring had secured for a cure-all lotion called St. Agnes Wonder Salve.

The property willed to the sisters was unsuitable for an old-folks home. It was sold, and property was purchased in Kirkwood on the corner of Manchester and Woodlawn. It had been a dairy farm owned by the Geders family. The purchase was aided by the sisters' lawyer, Edward Scheiderhahn, who also served on the building committee. Maritz, Young and Dusard, Inc. was engaged as the architectural firm. This firm was responsible for many stately homes in the Saint Louis area. These included the Eugene Nims residence, home of the founder of Southwestern Bell, and the Orthwein residence, home of the founder of D'Arcy Advertising.

The purchase was a bold move, as the nation was in the throes of the Great Depression. Regardless, Archbishop John Glennon sought permission from the Sacred Congregation of Religious for the sisters to float a loan for $100,000. Eventually, the building, called St. Agnes Wing, cost $142,000.[49]

The construction company was Seldon-Breck. They were a well-known firm which had built Bessey Hall, University of Nebraska, Lincoln. They were also responsible for the eight-story concrete Clint Wood Bank building in Wichita Falls, Texas as well as First Presbyterian Church, Richmond, Kentucky. The construction was completed by May 1935. The building was blessed on June 16 by Auxiliary Bish-

---

48 *The Servant of God Mother Mary Teresa of St. Joseph: An Autobiography*. Trans. Rev. Berchmans Bittle, O.F.M. Cap. Wauwatosa: Carmelite Convent. 2000.
49 *A History of St. Agnes Home: Prepared for the Jubilee Year September 2009 – September 2010*. Privately Published. P. 8.

op Christian Winkelmann, who had known the work of the sisters while he was assigned to a parish in Saint Charles. The first resident moved in the day before the dedication.

The community consisted of five Carmelite nuns, with Mother M. Cecilia of Jesus as superior. By August, three more sisters joined the Saint Agnes community.

In April 1937 the community received another large bequest, this from Katherene Fruin Colnon. The instructions were that a three-story wing would be added to St. Agnes Home on the southeast. It was to be named the Fruin Colnon Memorial Wing. Maritz, Young and Dusard were again engaged as architects, though the construction company was Fruin-Colnon, the firm founded by Mrs. Colnon's husband and his father. The new wing included a library furnished from the Colnon estate. The building would accommodate fifty residents, and provisions were made for as many as twenty "who are wholly unable to pay for any portion of their care and comfort in said institution."[50]

As St. Agnes Home continued to grow, it became apparent that the accommodations for the sisters' community were inadequate. They were housed on the third floor of the original building, as well as in the basement. A convent was needed. With a convent, St. Agnes Home could add another fourteen residents. The superior, Mother Mary Agnes of the Immaculate Conception, wanted the convent to be warm and "home-like."

Again, Maritz, Young and Dusard was engaged. The first floor held a reception room, a small conference room and a large community room with a glassed-in porch. Several small bedrooms were set aside for visiting sisters. The second floor was for residential cells and included an infirmary and another glassed-in porch. The third floor held a dormitory and more cells. It was this floor which saw the renovations in 1977 to accommodate the formation of more novices.

By the end of World War Two, St. Agnes Home was staffed by nineteen sisters and had over one hundred residents, with a waiting list of fifty. With the arrival of Archbishop Joseph Ritter, a request was made to accommodate retired or infirm priests. A new wing as well as a chapel were planned. However, the new wing would not be made

---

50 "Agreement Between Carmelite Sisters and Trustees" as cited in *A History of St. Agnes Home: Prepared for the Jubilee Year September 2009 – September 2010*. Privately Published. P. 17.

available for priests until 2006. By 1952 the Fruin-Colnon Wing was deeded to the sisters for one dollar.

Two delays slowed the progress of the new construction. One involved a strike, though the union gave permission for the workers to continue. The other caused a nation-wide sensation. During construction, a robin chose the site to build a nest and bear her young. Joseph Vollmar, Jr., the construction firm owner, halted work until the birds were able to fly away. When asked about the delay, Vollmar quipped, "I'm no bird lover – I just respect a fellow contractor!"[51]

In 1964 St. Agnes Home was designated Provincial Headquarters for the new Central U.S.A. province. A novitiate was added.

The phenomenon of the rapid decline of religious vocations in most Catholic congregations is made the more puzzling by the growth, or at least stability, of other societies. Church historian Michael Zöller sees outside factors at work. Careers in teaching and nursing, traditionally mainstays for women's religious congregations, became viable career paths for lay women, as compensation came closer to a living wage. Also, after the Second Vatican Council, the prestige of having a daughter as a nun or a son as a priest seemed to lessen in most families.

If these trends were real, the pool of potential vocations would shrink. As many congregations gave up distinctive habits, a communal prayer life, and a single dedicated apostolic work, the difference between the daily life of a sister-teacher and a lay teacher blurred. Only those Catholics serious about following a vocation by giving up independence, property, and a chance for exclusive love would still be attracted to religious life. And naturally, they would turn to congregations which preserved their distinctiveness.

The Carmelites saw a surge in religious vocations during a time when others began closing novitiates, turning them into retreat centers or nursing homes. The habit was distinctive. Contemplative life was paramount, as was daily Mass and Eucharistic Adoration. But even then, reasons for joining were mixed and complex. Some came searching for security in life. They lacked true commitment. Many withdrew during the eight formation years before being invited to make final profession of vows. In a candid observation, one sister who experienced those years commented, "We were not the poorer

---

51 *A History of St. Agnes Home: Prepared for the Jubilee Year September 2009 – September 2010.* P. 29.

for losing them."[52] Sister Benedicta saw the decline in family life as another factor for instability. Regardless, the Carmelites continued to attract significant numbers of women willing to test the waters of religious life.

THE BENEDICTINES AT PRIORY

In 1973, celebrating the Solemnity of All Saints with the monks at the Priory of Saint Mary and Saint Louis, Cardinal Joseph Carberry commented after Mass how pleased he was to have the Priory "solidified with the Archdiocese of Saint Louis."[53] The Cardinal was referring to the fact that just over three months earlier, on 25 July, the monks at the Priory had received approval of independence from the mother abbey at Ampleforth.

Events leading to the independence of the Priory flowed rapidly after the election of Father Luke Rigby as Prior in 1967 and the visit of Abbot Basil Hume in 1969. A crisis had been brewing over vocations and staffing. For fourteen years, Ampleforth Abbey had supplied monks for the endeavor in west Saint Louis County. The community consisted of thirteen monks, only two of whom were Americans. Many young men had joined the community and experienced Benedictine formation but had left before taking solemn profession of vows.

Abbot Basil observed, "We were, like virtually every other religious house, in some disagreement over the way in which the changes made by the Second Vatican Council should be put into practice, especially in our liturgy."[54]

His assessment was bleak, and he told Prior Luke that without novices going forward, he would give the monks in Saint Louis five years to find another entity to take over the school, at which time the community would be returned to England.

Father Luke protested vigorously. "You can't do that to us; we have too much invested. Rather than that, we'll go independent." Abbot Basil retorted, "It's a deal."[55]

The story of the coming of the English Benedictines to Saint Louis

---

52 Interview with Sister M. Benedicta, DCJ March 26, 2019.
53 Timothy Horner, OSB. *In Good Soil: The Founding of Saint Louis Priory and School, 1954 – 1973*. Saint Louis: Saint Louis Abbey Press. 2001. P. 414.
54 Ibid. P. 408.
55 Ibid. P. 409.

and the rich contributions in education, in parochial leadership, and in sharing Benedictine spirituality were yet another example of positive developments in the post-conciliar Saint Louis archdiocese.

The first inklings of the adventure are found in the imaginations of three laymen, William Garneau Weld, Samuel J. Mitchell, and Fred M. Switzer, as well as others. Many of them had experience in boys' college preparatory schools, and although there were several Catholic high schools run by religious congregations, each preparing boys for colleges according to the charisms of their orders, these men felt Saint Louis would be enriched by introducing the Benedictine tradition.

Failing to interest a local Benedictine community, as well as failing to attract Portsmouth Priory School in Rhode Island, the men, simply known as "Inc," looked abroad. At Ampleforth Abbey, England, they found a community bursting at the seams. In 1952, there were 140 monks, plus novices, teaching some 650 boys. On May 13, 1954, a committee was formed to search out available property in West Saint Louis County and to test the interests of Ampleforth.

The Abbey was interested. Two monks, Fathers Richard and Robert, travelled to Saint Louis to meet Inc and to visit the fifty acres already purchased to establish a school. They found welcome not only from the committee and from Archbishop Ritter, but surprisingly from the other religious congregations which ran schools.

More acreage was added, another thirty-two contiguous to the original property, then another one, giving the school an eighty-four-acre campus. Impressive as this sounds, Ampleforth was built on two thousand acres. Later, more purchases would expand the campus to one hundred and fifty acres.

On the property was an impressive two-story brick house and adjoining garage. The Stannard House would be the monks' home for the next three years. Arriving to spearhead the project were Father Columba, fifty-one years old, Father Timothy, thirty-four years old, a former artillery man who served in the British army in Burma during the Second World War, and thirty-two-year-old Father Luke, who had studied under C. S. Lewis at Oxford.

Later, Father Timothy noted, "They had asked for a school, but were receiving instead a monastery which would run a school."[56]

---

56 Timothy Horner, OSB. *In Good Soil: The Founding of Saint Louis Priory and School, 1954 – 1973.* P. 34.

The early days required some adjustment in attitude on the part of the monks, too. When the County building inspector arrived just days before the school was slated to open to the freshman class on Thursday, 6 September 1956, he refused an occupancy permit. There was no covered walkway between the school and the lavatory, which was in a remodeled barn. The issue was addressed immediately.

Later, when the desks arrived, the monks discovered that they had to be assembled. While working late into the night, the crew was startled when a large tarantula crawled out of a carton. Father Timothy whisked it away to roam the property.

Perhaps one of the most humorous events took place when the monks applied for driver's licenses. Each passed the written portion of the exam, but when Father Columba got behind the wheel of the old Cadillac which had been left them, he was stymied when asked to turn on the lights. He had practiced driving before the exam, but always during daylight.

Undeterred, the monk promptly pulled one of the knobs on the dashboard. The hood popped up! After the officer secured the hood, Father Columba tried again. The windshield-wipers started to move. A third knob set off the washer fluid across the windshield. Perhaps bemused, the officer found the right knob and turned on the lights for Father Columba. The driving portion of the exam was, thereafter, successful. The monks had been advised to take their exam at a station which would be favorable to priests. The advice seemed to have worked.

The question of architecture came up, and the monks found themselves at odds with Inc. The Americans were considering a neo-colonial style, much like some of the private academies in Saint Louis. This would have easily incorporated the Stannard House. The monks had other ideas. "… we were fully determined not to try to turn Missouri boys into Little Lord Fauntleroys."[57]

Indeed, the chapel, built in 1962, became an iconic landmark of a most modern design. The project was given to a relatively new architectural firm, Hellmuth-Obata-Kassabaum. Gyo Obata was inspired by the recently constructed Lambert Airport Terminal, with its airy three-dome design which admitted lots of light. Obata created a three-tier building of thin, concrete parabolic vaults. It was only the

---

57 Timothy Horner, OSB. *In Good Soil: The Founding of Saint Louis Priory and School, 1954 – 1973.* P. 80.

third major project of H-O-K. The first two were the Bristol Primary School, 1956, for the Webster Groves school district, and the Southern Illinois University Edwardsville building, 1961. Both buildings were contemporary, but unremarkable. The Priory chapel was a bold, ultra-modern statement.

Previous experiences in building had been jarring. In 1956, bids had arrived for the construction of the monastery. Until then, the monks lived wherever there was room at the Stannard House. Indeed, when Father Ian Petit arrived, he was assigned the cedar closet.

The monks had hoped the bids would come in at around $60,000. The lowest bid was closer to $174,000. Yet events moved forward. In March 1956, the monastery received recognition from the Vatican as an established house under the title of the Priory of Saint Mary and Saint Louis. Later that month, the Priory received its charter from the State of Missouri. Classes began that next September.

Finding its place among the other private schools in Saint Louis proved challenging. While the monks sought to offer educational quality on a par with Country Day School, they could not charge that same high tuition. The tuition standard would be set by the other private Catholic schools in competition. The monks worked hard, especially with archdiocesan clergy, to dispel the notion that theirs was "an elite" school. Father Timothy served on the Priests' Council. They made available their auditorium for several years for the Archdiocesan Clergy days. The monks took over pastoral care of newly-formed Saint Anselm's parish.

In the summer of 1966, Cardinal Ritter decided to split Saint Monica parish in two. Founded in 1871, Saint Monica was for most of a century a rural parish, filled with truck farms and wheat fields. By the early 1960's, subdivisions began to pop up everywhere. There was an exodus out of the City of St. Louis and even out of the inner suburbs of University City and Olivette.

The archdiocese owned property north of the Priory and intended to build a church and rectory there. In conversation between the new pastor, Father Robert Slattery, and Father Columba, it was agreed that until the church was built, Saint Anselm's Parish could use the monastery chapel. But it became clear early on that the Priory chapel could easily accommodate the parish permanently. This decision was ratified by the new archbishop of Saint Louis, Joseph Carberry.

The parish and the monastery entered into a formal, legal agreement. The parish would pay the monastery for expenses and for services rendered by the monks, $850 for the use of the church and $250 for the services. Parish buildings would be erected on the grounds. The naming of any future pastor would have to have the monks' approval, but it was implied that someday the monks themselves would provide a pastor, which took place in 1981.

Before the coming of Saint Anselm Parish, the highlight of those early days was a 1958 visit by the renowned British historian, Arnold Toynbee. He had been a colleague of Father Columba when they both served on a think-tank for international affairs.

The school grew rapidly and outpaced the buildings available. The year 1958 became known as The Year of the Sardine. The enrollment reached 105 in the school's third year of existence. The faculty numbered six monks and seven laymen. The monastery was completed that year. The chapel was ready in 1962, and the high school was available by 1970.

The first high school graduation came in 1960. There were twenty-eight graduates. Two stayed local, one to Saint Louis University, the other to Washington University. The largest number, eight, enrolled at Georgetown. The ceremonies were held outdoors, and Archbishop Ritter who was soon to be named a Cardinal, spoke glowingly of the new school.

Reflecting upon this milestone, Father Timothy Horner comments in his history of the early days of Priory School and the Benedictine community, perhaps alluding to the Obata chapel: "But we were also in a position like that of a good architect who turns from a traditional style to thin shell concrete. He may be pleased with his first building in the new style, but at the same time may recognize that he still has much to learn and that he can make many improvements to future buildings. But when all is said and done, these seniors and their teachers, especially those who had taught them for all four years, had grown up together in the school and bonded in an unrepeatable way. They had and have a unique place in our hearts. Other classes may have surpassed their achievements, but they can never supplant these men. There can be only one First Graduating Class."[58]

---

58 Timothy Horner, OSB. *In Good Soil: The Founding of Saint Louis Priory and School, 1954 – 1973.* P.206.

THE SOCIETY OF OUR MOTHER OF PEACE

The Archdiocese of Saint Louis soon became home to another congregation, newly formed and eager to enter apostolic work, the Society of Our Mother of Peace.

On May 18, 1971, Cardinal Joseph Carberry gave permission to Father Placid Guste to establish Maria Fonte Solitude near High Ridge, Missouri. Nearly two months later, four sisters took up residence there. A chapel, library, two kitchen-dining room buildings, one for the Brothers and one for the Sisters, and thirty-eight hermitages were constructed. A new religious congregation was introduced to the archdiocese of Saint Louis, and despite its small size, its charism would enrich the spiritual life of many people and would bring vital evangelization to some of the most depressed parts of the city of Saint Louis.

The Society of Our Mother of Peace was the brainchild of Father Placid. It was conceived in his own spiritual journey and born in the many travails and challenges that he faced.

Placid Guste was born in New Orleans on October 5, 1932. He entered the minor seminary for the Archdiocese of New Orleans but never felt at ease there. By the end of his sophomore year, he spoke with his spiritual director about a more intense life of prayer, briefly considering the Trappists. Regardless, he continued his studies as a diocesan seminarian at Notre Dame Seminary, conducted by the Marist Fathers at that time.

Life in the major seminary gave Placid the time for long hours of mental prayer, sometimes up to six hours a day. Here he came to realize that such contemplative solitude was key to his spiritual life. But he also felt an urge for some apostolic life, though limited. These two forces steered him away from secular priesthood, which would have necessitated long hours of apostolic contact with people but would have limited his opportunities for hours of solitude. A third element of his spirituality was a recognition of radical poverty in his life.

Where to turn? What religious order combined long hours of private prayer, limited apostolic exposure, and radical detachment from material things? He sought out the Carthusians. That necessitated leaving the seminary and moving to the Grande Chartreuse, deep in the French Alps. The stay lasted only nine months.

Carthusian life did not fit well with Placid's three-fold spirituality. While prayer was essential, and quiet solitude was a must, the Carthusians had no opportunity to perform apostolic works. At first, he returned to Notre Dame Seminary and then joined the Discalced Carmelites in 1956. There, Placid made solemn vows in 1960 and was ordained a priest in 1961.

Father Placid spoke of surrendering his will and his three-fold spirituality to the Carmelite life. He did so successfully for six years. Then the yearnings returned, and for the next two years he felt "his desires… were still very much unfulfilled."[59]

In conversations with his Provincial, Father Placid made known his continued desire to live his three-fold spirituality. He was transferred to a Carmelite parish in Oklahoma City for one year, giving him an opportunity to work with a Tertiary group, some of whom felt attracted to his vision.

Father Placid met with the bishop of Oklahoma City/Tulsa, Victor Reed, and secured from him eighty acres of diocesan land outside Oklahoma City. His dream was to establish a diocesan congregation. Bishop Reed was known for being open to new ideas, enthusiastic about the changes the Church was experiencing after the close of the Second Vatican Council. He even established a "Little Council" to engage the laity in these changes. Father Placid's ideas would have intrigued him even more when two lay women joined the monk and began doing evangelizing work among blacks in Jones, Oklahoma. It was part of metropolitan Oklahoma City with a population of fewer than one thousand.

At the time, Saint Robert Bellarmine Parish was a mission parish and had just built a new church after the old one was destroyed by fire. Despite the best efforts of Bishop Reed to improve inter-racial relations, there was a deep gap between blacks and whites in Oklahoma City. This changed in Jones when the two women visited black households to take a census of religious membership. When they found people open to learning about Catholicism, they invited them to experience a Catholic Mass. Eventually, four members of a black family were baptized at Saint Robert Bellarmine, and the attitude of the congregation became one of warm embraces.

At the hermitage, if one could call it that, Father Placid cleared

59 Placid Guste. *History of the Society of Our Mother of Peace: Written for Cardinal Carberry.* Unpublished. As cited in Br. Peter Sirangelo, SMP. *Why African Converts to Catholicism in Saint Louis, Mo: The Experiences of the Society of Our Mother of Peace.* Master's Thesis. Kenrick-Glennon Seminary. 2005.

roads and began to build simple hermitages made of aluminum siding. Soon he had six join him, three seeking to become sisters. By June 1967 his community comprised twenty individuals and was dubbed Bella Maria Monastery. Five years later, Father Placid's community created a second foundation, this in High Ridge, Missouri.

It was from Maria Fonte Solitude that the brothers and sisters would leave each day and drive to parishes in north Saint Louis city and county. Eventually, they served at twenty-seven parishes, one extended-care facility, Northview Nursing Home, housed in the dilapidated former De Paul Hospital, and the Saint Louis Correctional Facility.

The three-fold spirituality of Father Placid was evidenced in the lives of these evangelists. Their day included six or more hours of mental prayer in solitude. They drove hand-me-down vehicles with high mileage, wore simple, dark blue habits, and ate simple meals.

One Brother reflected on this spirituality: "Fr. Placid envisioned the community that he founded to be first and foremost contemplative in nature with more time for solitary contact with God, accompanied by a limited time for direct spiritual apostolate, and supported by material simplicity which he understood to be poverty in spirit and in fact. These three elements of the SMP charism are the external structure and the chief cornerstone of the Society. These elements are enhanced by the spirit of our charism, the two underlying tones, namely, the victim-call and childlikeness, and fortified by the three *interiority strengtheners* which are solitude, silence, and austerity of life."[60]

The evangelization began much as it was done in Jones, Oklahoma. Households were visited. If no one answered, they moved on. If someone came to the door, he or she was asked to take a census regarding religious membership. If he were unchurched or showed some openness to Catholicism, he was given some literature and invited to visit a local church on Sunday.

The surveys produced some very interesting results. The reasons given for not being open to Catholicism included the sense that blacks were not welcomed in the Catholic Church, which was perceived as a white Church. Eighty-two percent of those surveyed said that.[61] This flew in the face of reality. Most of the twenty-seven parishes served

---

60 Bro. Xavier Ronnie Maldo, Lorilla, S.M.P. *The Shaping of the Charism of the Society of Our Mother of Peace*. Master's Thesis. Kenrick-Glennon Seminary. 2014.
61 Br. Peter Sirangelo, SMP. *Why African Converts to Catholicism in Saint Louis, Mo: The Experiences of the Society of Our Mother of Peace*. P. 49.

by the Society of Our Mother of Peace had predominately African American parishioners, though served by white priests, except Visitation/Holy Ghost which had a black pastor for several years. Most of the permanent deacons in north city and some in North County were also black.

Typically, the congregation made it a point to visit every household in a parish every two years. In some cases, the results were remarkable. For Saint Elizabeth, Mother of John the Baptist Parish, 497 conversions took place. There were several conversions at Northview Nursing Home when the practice of distributing Holy Communion to non-Catholics was stopped. Many of the elderly were upset with the change, but when the sisters explained that the sacrament was reserved for practicing Catholics in the state of grace, they experienced a flood of conversions!

The door-to-door evangelization had its dangers. Not infrequently, there was gunfire within earshot. Once, a brother drove up to a drive-up window to get some coffee. A man approached and stuck a revolver in his open window, demanding money. Typically, SMP members carry only two dollars on them. The brother surrendered what he had, which did not appease the thief. The brother replied that God would not allow the man to fire his gun. He pulled the trigger, but nothing happened. The brother drove off, confident in the miracle, for he had noticed that the safety was on!

The biggest challenge was dogs. In that part of Saint Louis, dogs were more for protection than fuzzy companion pets.

Once, Brother Peter Sirangelo climbed the porch of a home and rang the doorbell. The owner was away. As he turned to leave, he saw a large German Shepherd at the bottom of the porch. The brother retreated behind the screen door and was pinned there for nearly an hour before the owner returned and called off his dog.

On another occasion, one of the sisters was caught by a dog and pinned to a fence. She resorted to higher powers when she took a small bottle of holy water out of her habit and sprinkled the dog. The dog was so stunned that he lay down and let her get away.

A crisis came to the Society of Our Mother of Peace with the sudden death of Bishop Reed in September 1971. His successor was John R. Quinn of San Diego. The young bishop, just 42, turned his attention to his priests, holding hearing sessions around the state. He made it a point to visit as many parishes as he could in the first two years of his episcopacy. Soon, he would have to oversee the separation of his diocese into the Archdiocese of Oklahoma City and the Diocese of Tulsa. Negotiations were tense. The Tulsa Catholic community was comparatively wealthy, and many tended to be conservative in both politics and Church affairs. Many had the impression that the Tulsa Catholics had bankrolled the Oklahoma diocese for years, but most of the funds were spent on the western part of the state. Early in 1973 the diocese was split. Oklahoma City became an archdiocese, and Tulsa received its own bishop, 44-year old Bernard Ganter. Quinn had little time for, or interest in, Father Placid and his community.

The hammer fell on February 24, 1976, when Archbishop Quinn told Father Placid that the Society of Our Mother of Peace would have to leave his archdiocese. He also indicated that, as Father Placid was still a Carmelite, he would be under the obedience of his Carmelite superiors. Unless he could find another bishop to sponsor him, Father Placid and his dream were about to expire.

The Carmelites gave Father Placid until May 6, 1976 to find a new bishop or return to the Carmelite community. An outreach to Bishop Joseph McNicholas, former vicar general in Saint Louis but newly-appointed as bishop of Springfield, Illinois, was not satisfactory. Bishop McNicholas demanded that the entire community relocate to his diocese, not just the Oklahoma part. Father Placid did not want to lose his Saint Louis connections.

Next, he turned to Bishop Bernard Law of Springfield-Cape Girardeau diocese. Time was running out. It was May 2nd. Fearing the worst, Father Placid called for the election of a superior for the sisters. They elected Sister M. Perpetua.

On May 4th Bishop Law contacted Father Placid. He needed more time to talk with the diocesan consulters. He asked Father Placid to call his Carmelite superior and ask for more time. With grave concern, he did. To his surprise, Father Placid was told that no decision would be made until the provincial had returned from Rome, giving him more time to find a home.

In the end, the Carmelites agreed to establish a separate Carmelite province for the Society, and Bishop Law invited them to his diocese, without requiring them to leave Saint Louis. In the meantime, Cardinal Carberry met with the priests of the parishes being served by SMP, and they eagerly encouraged him to embrace the Society. In 1976 sisters took up residence at Maryville, Missouri, near Springfield.

On August 9, 1979, two pious unions, the Sons and the Daughters of the Society of Our Mother of Peace, were given constitutions by Bishop Law. In 1981 two brothers were ordained priests by Bishop Law. Over time, the Society would spread to the Philippines and Nigeria. Baltimore and Newark became interested in bringing the Society to their dioceses. While challenges continued, Father Placid's Society of Our Mother of Peace brought many blessings to those with whom they came in contact.

THE DAUGHTERS OF SAINT PAUL

On June 16, 1972, Cardinal John Joseph Carberry wrote a congratulatory letter to Sister Concetta, D.S.P., the provincial for the Daughters of Saint Paul. It was the fortieth anniversary of this Congregation's arrival in the United States. He wrote, "Your admirable work over these years has been a source of enlightenment and inspiration to us all."

In another paragraph the Cardinal wrote of his hopes for the future. "May He (God) extend your apostolate of communications down through the years and over farther horizons."[62]

Within a year, the Daughters of Saint Paul came to Saint Louis. A board of active Catholic laity formed to welcome the sisters. These included Martin Duggan, head of the editorial board for the *Saint Louis Globe-Democrat*, Leonard Lipic, president of the Joseph Lipic Pen Company, Gabriel Alberici, president of the J. S. Alberici Construction Corporation which he had inherited from his father, and Joseph Badaracco, president of the Board of Alderman for the City of Saint Louis.

They established an annual fundraiser at the Cedars, a banquet hall owned and operated by Saint Raymond's Maronite church.

A convent and bookstore were opened in downtown Saint Louis on the corner of 10th and Pine Streets. The four sisters who began the apostolate attended daily Mass at the Alverne Hotel which was staffed by Franciscan sisters and Capuchin Franciscan monks. Located near 10th and Locust Streets, the Alverne began life in 1924 as the Hotel De Soto but was converted into a retirement home in 1956 by the Archdiocese of Saint Louis. In the Eucharistic Shrine of Our Lady of the Angels, Mass was celebrated as many as five times a day.

---

62 Appendix. Daughters of St. Paul. *Communicators for Christ*. St. Paul Editions. 1972.

On Sundays, the sisters attended Mass either at the old Cathedral, the new Cathedral, or Saint Raymond's. This introduced the new congregation to Saint Louis Catholics. In addition, the sisters regularly spoke at various parish grade schools about vocations. They introduced book fairs and even outfitted a van as a bookmobile. The first trip was southward to Saint Agnes school in Bloomsdale, around sixty miles south of Saint Louis.

Once a chapel was opened in the 10th and Pine location, it became a virtual spiritual home for the many Catholic employees of Southwestern Bell. Eventually, Ma Bell purchased the building which housed convent and bookstore, allowing the sisters to relocate Pauline Books and Media to a brand-new facility in Crestwood.

The Daughters of Saint Paul is a member of a larger federation called the Pauline Family consisting of five Religious congregations, four institutes of secular consecration, and a lay association. All were founded by Blessed James Alberione, a diocesan priest of Alba, Italy. The co-foundress of the Daughters was Mother Thecla Merlo.

The congregation began in Italy and arrived in the United States in 1932 in the depths of the Great Depression. The sisters were led by Sister Paula Cordero, only twenty-three years old. The funds they brought with them included her portion of the family inheritance given to her by her brothers.

Life was difficult and began as soon as they arrived. Meeting the sisters at the dock was Father Borrano, who exclaimed, "You were not supposed to come now!" Even more discouraging was a visit to the chancery of the Archdiocese of New York. The Daughters had continued the tradition of handing out Catholic literature which caused some to think they were Protestant.

Meeting at the chancery, Sister Paula was told to stop disseminating literature. In halting English, she tried to explain that this was part of the mission of the Daughters but got nowhere. The conversation ended with a warning that a letter would be sent soon, forbidding them from giving out literature. Sister Paula and her companion returned to their convent and dropped a religious medal into the mailbox and prayed, "O Mary, O St. Paul, help us. Guard this mailbox and don't let any news which would stop our mission ever be left here." The promised letter never arrived, and the Daughters continued their work.[63]

---

63 Daughters of St. Paul. *Communicators for Christ*. St. Paul Editions. 1972. P. 102

By 1945, the community grew with three American postulants. In 1953, Cardinal Richard Cushing invited the Daughters to Boston. There, as would happen later in Saint Louis, a group of devout Catholic men supported their work. These included John Volpe, president of Volpe Construction Company and later secretary of transportation under President Richard M. Nixon. It was in Boston that they established their novitiate and provincial headquarters in 1956.

As the Daughters began to publish their own works, a humorous incident happened while visiting the vice-president of a large Connecticut printing firm. The officer was quite impressed with the sisters' work and commented, "If you are ever out of work, I'll hire you myself!"

The sisters smiled and replied, "No, thank you. Our boss is in heaven, and we are quite satisfied with his pay!"[64]

The reputation of the Daughters of Saint Paul spread rapidly, and invitations to expand came as quickly. Youngstown, Ohio in 1944, Alexandria, Louisiana in 1952, San Antonio, Texas in 1953, San Diego in 1956, Miami, Florida in 1960, Bridgeport, Connecticut in 1962, the Bronx in 1963, Oakland, California in 1966, New Orleans, Louisiana in 1968, San Francisco and Saint Louis in 1971, though the Saint Louis offer had to wait nearly two years.

The media apostolate of the Daughters of Saint Paul was supported by Popes Pius XI and Pius XII. Regarding film, founder Father Alberione took a forward-thinking view. "The film apostolate comprises and heightens the effects of the press apostolate. A film is a kind of edition which adds a vivid, visual image and sound. It joins art to thought, action to idea, enjoyment to truth, relaxation to learning, and example to doctrine. Science, moral teachings, history, liturgy – they all appear before the gaze of the viewers in the form of episodes, pictures, happenings. The evil spread by films is immense, but so, too, is the good they do. The Pope wants the film apostolate! Priests and teachers make use of it. The Daughters of St. Paul have committed themselves to it with intelligence and love."[65]

All this became more vital with the promulgation of the Second Vatican document, *Inter Mirifica*, The Decree on the Means of Social Communication. The 1963 document began, "Man's genius with

---

64 Daughters of St. Paul. *Communicators for Christ*. P. 155.
65 Ibid. P 295.

God's help produced marvelous technical inventions from creation, especially in our times."

Paragraph 15 calls on "priests, religious and laity ... to acquire the competence needed to use these media for the apostolate" and suggested that each bishop set aside a day "on which the faithful will be reminded of their duties in this domain."[66] This became World Communication Day.

Father Alberione wrote to the Daughters: "Daughters of St. Paul, do you realize what this council document means for you? It organically inserts your specific apostolate in the great new horizon of the Church. It will open wide to you the doors of the whole world, through which you can and must launch yourselves to carry out a concrete and efficient activity."[67]

On June 28, 1968, a thousand members of the Pauline Family were joined at the Vatican by Pope Paul VI. They celebrated the fifty-fifth anniversary of the founding of the first institute. The pope noted that the Pauline Family had been carrying out the wishes of the Council long before the Council was called. He praised Father James Alberione, though the priest had always shied away from honors.

Perhaps reflecting on the theological and ecclesial disruptions which came even before the Council had finished its work, the pontiff added, "May particular opinions departing from professional and ecclesial loyalty, interests having nothing to do with the cause of the apostolate, reasons of prestige, or anything else, never be allowed to prevail over your upright apostolic service."[68]

Of this, Pope Paul VI had nothing to fear. In Saint Louis, the Archdiocesan Commission on Textbooks did not approve of Pauline textbooks, calling them "Pre-Vatican" until it was overruled by Cardinal Carberry.

Addressing their reputation, Father Aloysius Zanoni, successor to Father Alberione, who died in November 1971, said, "From far away we sometimes hear it said that the Daughters of St. Paul of the United States – I would say especially of Boston – are a little 'conservative.' I have been asking myself in these days just what was meant by that term, 'conservative.' And I answered myself: if being 'conservative' means keeping the good spirit of one's congregation and the spirit of

---

66 Austin Flannery, O. P. *Vatican Council II: The Conciliar and Post-Conciliar Documents.* "Inter Mirifica." Wilmington: Scholarly Resources. 1975. P. 290.
67 Daughters of St. Paul. *Communicators for Christ.* P. 304.
68 Ibid. P. 330.

the Founder; if being 'conservative' means nourishing prayer and the interior spirit (it is evident on entering, dear Sisters, that there is a very different atmosphere here from what we find outside or in other communities) – if being 'conservative' means having fully grasped the charism of our Founder, his apostolic idealism, and having sought to carry it out in the most effective way possible, then I say to you: continue to be 'conservative'![69]

CHANGES IN CATHOLIC HIGH SCHOOLS

The academic landscape of the archdiocese was also shifting. The Jesuits opened a new high school in West County, De Smet Jesuit High School in Creve Coeur. A large wheat field was purchased on New Ballas Road in 1966, and construction began on the 28-acre campus, opening in September 1967. While De Smet did not affect the enrollments at Priory or the new archdiocesan high school, Kennedy in Manchester, it created an instant rivalry with the other long-established Jesuit high school in the city, Saint Louis University High School.

De Smet proved to be a challenge to another all-boys private high school, CBC. Christian Brothers College High School, located in Clayton, had been struggling for several years. A major campaign to build a new gymnasium failed, enrollment was trending downward, and the faculty was torn over the issue of the school's Junior R.O.T.C. The school went military in the 1930s when a significant number of Brothers faculty were transferred there from Cretan High School in Saint Paul, Minnesota. Cretan had had an R.O.T.C. program for years, and the brothers thought the student body would save money on clothes if they all wore uniforms. Other benefits flowed from the army. The athletic teams retired their old name, Hi-Pointers, and became The Cadets.

In the late 60's and early 70's, the Vietnam War was raging. The military personnel at the school was supportive of the war, but several younger brothers were openly critical and demanded that the school end its relationship with the army. The lay faculty were torn also, though most parents wanted to keep the program. They had chosen CBC specifically because it was military. Some brothers feared that for that very reason, many other Catholic boys opted to go to oth-

---

69 Daughters of St. Paul. *Communicators for Christ*. P. 356.

er schools, causing a serious dip in enrollment. One Brothers administrator quipped, "Do you know where to find the largest gathering of CBC alumni? The De Smet Fathers' Club!"

The graduation ceremonies of 1972 were marked with rancor when the valedictorian launched into an anti-military diatribe, causing the military instructors to exit the stage.

Augustinian Academy closed in 1972. Xavier High School, an all-girls school on the campus of Saint Louis University, closed in 1974. There were fears that CBC was next. To dispel these doom prophesies, the brothers' community was changed in a two-year period, 1976 and 1977. Twelve of the thirteen brothers were transferred, and new, young, energetic blood was infused. The new administrator was no-nonsense Brother Augustine Kossuth.

Brother Augustine had served in the United States Marine Corps. He had a keen financial acumen, taking the meagre resources of the school and investing them in overnight accounts at low risk, but high interest rates. He tapped the energy of his new young faculty and gave them positions of responsibility. Key among these was his new principal, Brother Michael Jordan.

Renovation of the Clayton campus got underway, signaling that the school was there to stay. Property which had been purchased in west county was sold. The enrollment was stabilized, and the school accepted free uniforms from the army, trading in the blue and grey which had become shabby hand-me downs. The R.O.T.C. program became revitalized under the direction of Lt. Col. Pat Patton. But the R.O.T.C. dilemma would not go away. Was CBC's enrollment hampered by the program or saved by it?

Things came to a head in October 1976 when the administration unilaterally announced the termination of the R.O.T.C. program at the end of the academic year. A hasty meeting was held in the packed cafeteria with angry parents and students. Shouting and incriminations filled the room, and at one point a parent called for a walk-out, which would have shuttered the school. Col. Patton stepped up and restored order. Brother Augustine then offered to keep the military program, but as an option for students, no longer mandatory. In the end, that was the way forward, with the military program slowly dying over time. When the enrollment fell under the mandatory 100 several years in a row, the program was quietly dropped. All that was left was the mascot name, The Cadets.

THE RELIGIOUS OF THE SACRED HEART

Another Congregation to undergo massive changes was the Religious of the Sacred Heart. Their roots go back to the very founding of Catholic Saint Louis, with the arrival of Saint Rose Philippine Duchesne and her sisters in 1818.

After 154 years of existence, Sacred Heart Academy in Saint Charles announced it was closing its high school department with the graduating class of 1972. The reasons given were three-fold. There were too few sisters to staff the faculty. Enrollment declined severely, with only forty-nine girls in the last graduating class. And costs were rising prohibitively.

Extra efforts were put into the grade school. There would be a three-year commitment on the part of the Religious of the Sacred Heart; after that, the school would have to stand on its own. The project was put into the able hands of Sister Patricia Steppe. She announced that a boys' component would be added, a first for the school, calling it "Perier Elementary," after the maternal family of Saint Rose Philippine. Sister Patricia explained, "In choosing the name 'Perier' for the boys' school, we did not only hope to give honor to a family very dear to Philippine, but also to hold up to our boys strong Christian ideals and leadership."[70]

A further challenge came with inheriting the high school facilities. The key was to convince Sacred Heart families who sent their daughters to the school to send their sons also.

Sister Patricia was pro-active in engaging her present families and in enlisting volunteers to serve on an enrollment committee. Though the annual Tea in 1971 used the theme "Bridge over Troubled Waters," by 1975, enrollment in the two grade schools had risen to 329. It would continue to climb, attracting families not only from Saint Charles, but from west Saint Louis County.

THE BROTHERS OF MARY AND M.A.C.

Yet another congregation, the Brothers of Mary, found itself launching a new adventure in the post-conciliar years. The Brothers

---

70 Jane Cannon. *Legacy of Love and Learning: A History of the Academy of the Sacred Heart in St. Charles, Missouri, from its Founding in 1818, Written for its Bicentennial Celebration in 2018*. St. Charles: Academy of the Sacred Heart. 2017. P. 129.

had a long history in the Archdiocese of Saint Louis. They were invited by Saints Peter and Paul Pastor Franz Goller to establish a boys' high school in his parish in 1898. In 1910 they opened Chaminade College Prep in rural Kirkwood. It had both a day and boarding element. In 1925 the Brothers took control of William McBride High School on North Kingshighway, just a few blocks north of the gutted Christian Brothers College, which was destroyed by fire in 1916. In 1933 they assumed administration of Saint Mary's High School on South Grand Boulevard. The school had been established two years earlier as Southside Catholic, run by the Christian Brothers. The Brothers wanted to concentrate their efforts on the one high school they owned, CBC in Clayton, and so happily gave the school to the Brothers of Mary.

One more high school came under the administration of the Brothers of Mary, Vianney High School. Cardinal Joseph Ritter wanted a Catholic boys' high school for south Saint Louis County. In the fall of 1960 the school was opened with 304 students on the grounds of what had been Maryhurst Novitiate grounds. That year, the novitiate was relocated to Glencoe, Missouri, across the valley from La Salle Institute, the novitiate for the Christian Brothers.

In 1949, the Brothers of Mary purchased an estate in far West County, Woodcliff. On it stood a stately summer house surrounded by 130 acres, resting along the banks of the Meramec River. They renamed it Marycliff and intended it to house the Provincial Headquarters as well as The Institute for Marianist Studies, a second novitiate for members as a sort of sabbatical after years of apostolic work.

The estate and summer house were built by James Yeatman, president of Merchants' Bank and co-founder of Washington University. Wealthy Saint Louisans retreated to the woods and cool Meramec River during hot summer months. Later, the property was sold to the Brewers' Association and was used for the same purpose.

After the Marianists purchased the property, Brother Eugene Myerpeter, C. M. had a vision of including a retreat center on the property. He traveled far and wide, visiting retreat centers around the country, gathering ideas and best practices. He hired Maurice Carroll as the architect.

The Maurice Carroll firm had been around for decades. The early works were rather traditional. The Church of the Assumption in Topeka, Kansas, was built in 1924 in the Renaissance Revival style. Earlier, Saint Vincent de Paul in Kansas City, 1921, earned a gold medal from the American Institute of Architects. Even during the Great Depression, Maurice Carroll was busy. Joining another architect, he designed the Infirmary Building at the Missouri State Hospital Number 3 in Nevada, Missouri. Its style was stark and listed as an example of "the modern movement." In 1938, he designed the Knute Rockne Memorial Building at Notre Dame University and in 1939 was the architect for the Father Francis Hayden High School in Topeka.

While most of the early work was done in Kansas or western Missouri, he was commissioned to design the new Immaculate Conception Church in New Madrid, Missouri. Due to the history of the area, it was constructed to be earthquake-proof.

By the time Brother Myerpeter engaged Maurice Carroll, the taste in architecture had turned distinctly modern. Immaculate Heart of Mary, built in 1964 in south Saint Louis, was such an example, as was Saint Catherine of Siena in Pagedale. The building for the Marianist Apostolic Center was to be another example of pushing the modern envelope.

The building was angular, a two-story with a refectory in the lower level, encompassing 32,000 square feet. Lines were horizontal with lots of glass and aluminum trim. The chapel was stark and square with modernistic stained-glass windows. Originally designed to accommodate forty retreatants, each person had his own bedroom with bath. Brother Myerpeter designed that specifically to cut down on late-night corridor traffic. At the end of each residence floor, a suite was set aside for staff members, giving them a clear line of sight on each floor.

The building was dedicated on October 1, 1967 and cost upwards of $1,000,000. This was an extraordinary commitment on the part of the Marianists to encourage the retreat movement among young Catholics. Marianist schools, McBride and Vianney, provided the first among the retreatants, but these were soon joined by other schools like Incarnate Word, a girls' high school.

In the early 1970s, the staff consisted of five brothers and two priests. By 1979 five brothers were joined by two priests, a religious, Sister Chris Hucik, a Marianist Daughter of Mary Immaculate, and a laywoman, Mrs. Margaret Brandt. With time, as many as fifty-six retreats a year were scheduled. Besides youth retreats, adult retreats were added as well as retreats for women, and Advent and Holy Week retreats. For several years, the priests of the Archdiocese of

Saint Louis held retreats in June at MAC, especially for those priests involved in Catholic education, as they were not free to make retreats during the school year.

The stark simplicity of the Marianist Apostolic Center took a dramatic turn when fifty-five-year-old Brother Mel Meyer, S. M. arrived to add his artistic touch. Brother Mel worked out of a studio on the grounds of Vianney High School. Over his lifetime, he created over 8,000 works of art in a distinctive style which Saint Louisans instantly recognized. Whether it be in a church, a hospital, a school, or a doctor's office, the reaction was always the same. "Oh, that's a Brother Mel!" He began work in the center's chapel in 1983 and lent modern statuary to the grounds of the retreat center.

Today MAC is called Marianist Retreat and Conference Center. It still hosts youth as well as adult retreats. Various denominations use the facility as well as Contemplative Outreach groups. It is no longer staffed by Marianist priests and brothers, but it remains true to its mission, "With Mary, to engage in the spiritual and educational development of all God's people."[71] Over the past fifty years, it is estimated that the retreat center has served over 100,000 guests.

Saint Paul wrote to his protégé, Saint Timothy, "I have fought the good fight, I have finished the race, I have kept the faith" (II Timothy 4:7). So many men and women of religious congregations could say the same thing after what appeared to be a period of flux, loss of confidence, an age when everything seemed to be turned upside down in their Church and in America. Despite the zeitgeist of relativism and instability, despite the free-fall of religious vocations in most congregations, despite dissension and disobedience, there were many who took to heart the call of their Savior to leave all and to follow him. Their efforts would be joined by enlivened laity who fought the good fight in the pro-life movement, in direct service to the poor and disadvantaged, in evangelization, in saving communities, and for some Catholic men in an invitation to clerical service as permanent deacons.

---

71 Mission Statement. "A Retreat Ministry is Born." Marianist Retreat and Conference Center. http://mretreat.org/wp-content/uploads/2017/08/mrcc-history.pdf

St. Agnes Home residents and two postulants gather around the piano in the common area for some musical entertainment. Photographer Richard Finke, 1974. From the Archdiocese of St. Louis Archives and Records.

The St. Louis Priory church building in Creve Coeur is shared by the English Benedictines of the St. Louis Abbey and St. Anselm Parish. Photographer Richard Finke, 1988. From the Archdiocese of St. Louis Archives and Records.

Father Luke Rigby, Prior of the Benedictines at the St. Louis Priory, took the oath of U.S. citizenship on April 4, 1975. Photographer Richard Finke. From the Archdiocese of St. Louis Archives and Records.

Sister Mary Paschal of the Society of Our Mother of Peace went door-to-door in St. Augustine Parish in north St. Louis to proclaim the Gospel message. She was in the Visitation Park neighborhood with Sisters Mary Grace and Mary Monica, right. Members of the Society of Our Mother of Peace live in contemplative solitude but stress evangelization, material simplicity, and evangelical poverty. Photographer Teak Phillips, 2016. Courtesy of St. Louis Review.

ABOVE: Cardinal Carberry discusses the publications with a Daughter of St. Paul at the dedication ceremony of the St. Paul Catholic Book and Film Center located at 1001 Pine Street. At the dedication in 1974, Carberry called the book store "a great source, a powerhouse from which the Word of God will go out." Photographer Richard Finke. From the Archdiocese of St. Louis Archives and Records.

Christian Brothers High School cadets march with flags and arms in 1974. Photographer Richard Finke. From the Archdiocese of St. Louis Archives and Records.

Bishop George J. Gottwald celebrated Mass at the blessing and dedication of the Marian Apostolic Center in Glencoe, Missouri on October 1, 1967. From the Archdiocese of St. Louis Archives and Records.

Brother Mel Meyer, S.M., shows off the Marianist Art Center on the grounds of Maryhurst Preparatory School in Kirkwood, later to become St. John Vianney High School. Brother Mel estimated that he made over 10,000 pieces of work during his career as an artist. Photographer Richard Finke, 1969. From the Archdiocese of St. Louis Archives and Records.

Chapter Three

I HAVE FOUGHT THE GOOD FIGHT

THE SOUNDS OF MUSIC: LITURGICAL MUSIC AFTER THE COUNCIL

In August 1964 at the Liturgical Week Conference, 20,000 Catholics were given a new experience in celebrating the Mass. Much of it was in English. The celebrant, Monsignor Martin Hellriegel, stood at the far side of the altar, facing the congregation, and congregational singing included the Lutheran hymn, "A Mighty Fortress is Our God," as well as a Negro spiritual, "God is Love," by Father Clarence Rivers.

Father Rivers was a convert and priest of the Archdiocese of Cincinnati. He brought with him a deep love of Negro spirituals and, as an assistant pastor, was encouraged by his pastor to tap into his musical talents. In 1963, Father Rivers had already published and recorded *Father Rivers Leads His Congregation in An American Mass Program.* Many of his songs were scripture-based and employed a call-and-response format, bringing out the role of cantors.

Father Rivers served on the Liturgical Conference board for many years, was director of the National Office for Black Catholics, and was honored by the National Conference of Catholic Bishops when they dedicated the hymnal *Lead Me, Guide Me* to him.

Another composer of contemporary liturgical music was Ray Repp, a Saint Louis seminarian influenced by Msgr. Hellriegel. It was from Hellriegel that he realized that the Catholic liturgical movement had been going on for twenty years. His love of folk music, his talent in playing the guitar, and his enthusiasm to compose liturgical music led Ray Repp to publish *Mass for Young Catholics* in 1965. Eventually, he left the seminary and became a volunteer for the Catholic Extension Society based in Chicago. With time, he branched out to include secular music, much of it tinged with sentiments of the political left.

Many Saint Louis Catholics who embraced the new liturgy turned to a group of five Jesuit scholastics who called themselves The St. Louis Jesuits. They began composing as early as 1965 and performed in the basement of Fusz Memorial Hall on the campus of Saint Louis University. By 1974, they had composed fifty-eight liturgical songs which were published by North American Liturgical Resources. Their second publication, *Earthen Vessels*, sold over a million copies. They had become a sensation in liturgical music. *Earthen Vessels* was also used in the soundtrack for the 1995 film *Dead Man Walking* starring Susan Sarandon and Sean Penn.

One member ended his studies as a Jesuit scholastic and drifted in and out of the group until 1984. Another left the priesthood in the 1980's but held the position of Composer-in-Residence at the University of San Francisco. Another, Father John Foley, returned to Saint Louis University where he founded the Stroble Center for Liturgy. Father Robert Dunford was responsible for the creation of the hymnals *Glory and Praise* and *Gather*, both widely used in parishes throughout the United States. The group had received Grammy nominations on five different occasions.

The Saint Louis Jesuits group had a further influence on liturgical as well as contemporary music. An undergrad, Jim Ford, often sat in on practice sessions in the Fusz Hall basement. This inspired him to form his own group, Followers of the Way. He was joined by Peggie Telscher, lead vocalist, and Dan Boucher. Their music, using biblical and spiritual themes, was a synthesis of the liturgical music of the Saint Louis Jesuits and the Christian Life Communities, active in the Saint Louis Catholic community.

Christian Life Communities were the post-Vatican version of the once-massive Sodalities of Our Lady movement. When Father Daniel Lord, S. J. became the national director of the Sodalities, based in Saint Louis, there were more than 80,000 sodalities world-wide. His extraordinary influence in print and film caused the membership to explode to over two million members, mainly teenagers. Father Lord edited the popular magazine *The Queen's Work* and wrote more than ninety books, three hundred pamphlets, plays, and songs, including *For Christ the King*.

Lord's involvement with Hollywood began in 1927 as a technical consultant to Cecil B. DeMille as he produced the silent film *King of Kings*. He helped create the Production Code, a way to help censor some of the excesses finding their way into movies. In 1938, as anti-Semitism raged in Nazi Germany, similar sentiments were being heard in America, especially questioning the role of Jews in Hollywood. Father Lord reacted with a pamphlet entitled "Dare We Hate the Jews," in which he attacked anti-Semitism as a violation of Christian principles and encouraged others to do the same.

Father Lord resigned as editor of *The Queen's Work* in 1948. Seven years later, the priest died of lung cancer at Saint John Mercy Hospital in Saint Louis.

The Christian Life Communities movement was established in 1967, though it traced its origins to the years after the suppression of the Society of Jesus. The CLC continued to have close ties to the Jesuits and steeped its members in Ignatian spirituality. After the Second Vatican Council, some sodalities disappeared while others turned their attention to the corporal works of mercy.

The Followers of the Way formed in 1972. Unlike the Saint Louis Jesuits, whose music was mainly for liturgy, The Followers "explored biblical and spiritual themes in contemporary music settings."[72] The use of acoustical guitar has led their songs to be categorized as "Jesus Music" or "Jesus Rock." They recorded their first album in 1973, *Followers of the Way*. Later, Jim Ford had the opportunity to present a copy to Pope Paul VI. In 1995, they created a second album, *Blessed Weakness*, and were joined in this effort by Father John Foley. Both albums were sponsored by the National Federation of Christian Life Communities.

THE ARCHDIOCESAN PRO-LIFE COMMITTEE

On September 25, 1972 Monsignor Fenton J. Runge sent a letter of invitation to area medical doctors to celebrate Respect Life Week, October 1 to 8, and to attend a meeting at Marillac College Auditorium. Monsignor Runge was moderator of the Catholic Physicians Guild. The doctors were to be addressed by Cardinal Joseph Carberry and a doctor, a legislator, a lawyer, and a theologian. *Roe v. Wade* and *Doe v. Bolton* were still being argued before the Supreme Court, but several states were taking it upon themselves to loosen the abortion laws. It was time to rally pro-life support.

The day the fateful decisions were made, January 22, 1973, the Missouri Catholic Conference, led by Jefferson City Bishop Michael F. McAuliffe, issued a powerful statement.

"We are outraged at this decision which contradicts what was until recently the consistent legal and medical tradition of this nation. The Supreme Court, by stressing the woman's right to privacy, ignores the unborn baby's rights and the other issues in the debate on abortion."

The bishop went on to question what would stop the elimination

---

72 Interview with Jim Ford, April 12, 2019, Marianist Retreat and Conference Center.

of "the mentally retarded, the elderly or economically unproductive" now. He pointed out the irony that this same Court ruled the death penalty unconstitutional.

Decoupling the abortion issue from religion, McAuliffe wrote, "This is a moral issue, a legal issue, a social issue. Our response is not dictated by theological teaching removed from the world of human anguish. We know it is shared by lawyers, doctors and clergymen. We are sure that the decision offends the sensibilities of many citizens of all faiths and those of no formal religious affiliation."[73]

Cardinal Carberry was quick to move. On March 14, 1973, he called a meeting at Saint Joseph Academy to create an Archdiocesan Pro-Life Committee. In his address, the Cardinal asked four questions: What are the most effective means to educate Catholics and society at large that the fetus is a human being and deserves to live? How can we influence legislation to protect pro-life people from being forced to cooperate with abortions? How can we help to introduce a constitutional amendment which would protect the sanctity of human life? How can we influence our state legislature, as it must revise Missouri's laws on abortion, to still give as much protection to the unborn as possible?[74]

Soon after that meeting, the Archdiocesan Pro-Life Committee began sending out notices. One such letter spoke of a slide show and cassette developed by Dr. John C. and Mrs. Willke, co-authors of the *Handbook on Abortion*. The book sold 1.5 million copies. The Pro-Life Committee announcement said that the Willkes' slide show and cassette were available at Catholic Supply and could be signed out free of charge. The Committee added, "We commend Catholic Supply Company for this service."

The first annual report of the Archdiocesan Pro-Life Committee, by Rev. Edward J. O'Donnell, was impressive.

He began by explaining that right after the March 14th meeting at Saint Joseph Academy, he hired Mrs. Mary Carbry as secretary, who was assisted by two volunteers. Very rapidly, Father O'Donnell organized pro-life committees in all but ten parishes in the Archdiocese. Some pastors were not involved, while many were enthusiastic sup-

---

73 Missouri Catholic Conference Statement. 22 January 1973. Saint Louis Archdiocesan Archives. RG III. C8.1.
74 Formation of the Archdiocesan Pro-Life Committee. Saint Louis Archdiocesan Archives. 14 March 1973. RG III. C8.1.

porters. A layman headed each parish committee which put together phone trees so that information could be disseminated very quickly. Father O'Donnell added, "Many of these are people that have not been particularly active in parish or archdiocesan activities before and we are unearthing a whole new group of Catholic lay leaders, especially among young parents."[75]

The priest outlined other activities of the committee. In September 1973, a twenty-nine-page pamphlet was sent to all pastors and parish chairmen called "The Parish Handbook." It was filled with programming ideas. Homily helps and Prayers of the Faithful were regularly sent to parishes.

Four thousand eight hundred pro-life bracelets were purchased for $13,000 and sold over the year netting a profit of around $1,000. The Knights of Columbus got on board and donated 95,000 bumper stickers. The committee gave out 20,000 copies of the Willke's brochure, "Life or Death," as well as seven hundred and fifty copies of *Handbook on Abortion*.

The committee compiled a list of federal and state legislators and their contact information, to lobby for pro-life causes. Father O'Donnell cited a *Post-Dispatch* article of May 19 which said the ACLU was carefully watching the committee's work.

The committee cooperated with a variety of other entities: The Catholic Youth Council, Missouri Nurses for Life, Missouri Doctors for Life, Birthright, AWARE (a clinic teaching morally acceptable methods of birth control). The other three Missouri dioceses were included.

Missouri Clergy for Life got off to a rough start, as there was great dissension in the Lutheran Church Missouri Synod over events happening at Concordia Seminary. By October, the Synod was firmly in the hands of Dr. Jacob Preus, who hosted a meeting of Missouri Clergy for Life at the headquarters of the Lutheran Church Missouri Synod on North Broadway. Attending were clergy from the Catholic Church, as well as Baptist, both black and white, Reformed Presbyterian, Greek Orthodox, and the Salvation Army.

The school office under Father John Leibrecht provided curriculum and extra-curricular activities for the schools, including a message from Dr. and Mrs. Willke to ten thousand children. Confraternity of Christian Doctrine classes for Catholic public-school children were

---

75 Rev. Edward J. O'Donnell. "First Annual Report. Archdiocesan Pro-Life Committee." April 1973. Saint Louis Archdiocesan Archives. RG III. C8.1.

included. Sister Francis Marie Sellmeyer, SSND organized women religious in parishes to begin a "Crusade of Prayer."

A billboard was donated at the Vandeventer exit on Highway 40. Pro-life material was made available for public libraries. And a speaker bureau was set up by Monsignor Joseph Baker and Mrs. Mary Francis Horgan.

But most impressive were two massive rallies. The first was held at the Old Court House on October 22. Thirty-thousand pro-lifers gathered to hear Missouri Senators Thomas Eagleton, a Democrat, and John Danforth, a Republican, give speeches along with Cardinal Carberry. It was the largest pro-life rally in America. While Missouri Citizens for Life organized the event, the Archdiocesan Pro-Life Committee brought out the troops.

On the first anniversary of *Roe v. Wade*, the New Cathedral was packed for Mass, and then celebrants marched to the abortion clinic just blocks away on Euclid Avenue. This inaugurated a peaceful daily picket in front of the clinic, organized by Missouri Citizens for Life.

The report concluded with praising several lay people who spearheaded all these efforts. They included co-chairs Mary Frances Horgan and Eugene Walsh, treasurer George Sweeny, Ellen Carter and innumerable Knights of Columbus as well as the many parish coordinators.

Father O'Donnell attached to the six-page report a financial statement. Revenues until March 31, 1974 were $37,933.13, which included the $20,000 grant from the Archdiocese. Expenses were $35,654.05. A mere $4,590 were salary expenses, showing the incredible participation by volunteers.

MEDIA: CATHOLIC SUPPLY, VINCENTIAN PRESS, LIGOURI PRESS

Another area of lay activity enriching the Catholic environment of the Midwest was the establishment of Catholic bookstores and retail outlets for religious supplies. Vincentian Press, located next to Saint Vincent de Paul Church in the Soulard neighborhood, opened its doors in 1923. While it carried some religious literature, Vincentian Press was mainly a supplier of vestments, sacred vessels, rosaries, and other religious items. It had a small staff of one Vincentian priest and a few volunteers or employees.

On a larger scale was Catholic Supply, founded in September 1960. It was the inspiration of Bishop Charles Helmsing and Monsignor Harry Byrne. Bishop Helmsing was the founding bishop of Springfield-Cape Girardeau Diocese in southern Missouri. Ordained in 1933, Helmsing took a keen interest in spreading the faith, instructing converts and promoting the Legion of Mary. He was later named bishop of Kansas City-Saint Joseph diocese.

Bishop Helmsing suggested to his brother, Clem Helmsing, that he join in partnership with a friend and fellow parishioner at Saints John and James Parish in Ferguson, William Byrne, and set up a Catholic retail and bookstore. It would be called Catholic Supply. Byrne had already established such a store in Pine Lawn, in partnership with Roger Doyle, called Byrne Doyle Religious Goods. William Byrne was the brother of Monsignor Harry Byrne who had been involved in youth work most of his priesthood. After ordination, he served as an assistant pastor for four years and then was appointed chaplain to the Saint Joseph Home for Boys. After serving there for five years, he was appointed the director of Father Dunne's Newsboys Home, where he served for twenty-five years.

The store was established in the western part of the city of Saint Louis. Later, branches were opened in Florissant, from 1974 to 2008, in Manchester, where a tragic murder took place in 2018, and in O'Fallon in 2008. William Byrne remained active in providing Catholic goods, founding O'Byrne Religious Goods store in his old age. He died at 98 years of age.

The current mission statement of Catholic Supply speaks of the spirit of William Byrne and Charles Helmsing: "Our mission is to provide the finest quality goods and services to bring people closer to Christ. We are a resource center that provides for the spiritual needs of the individual and the parish, and our goal is to support and assist the church in building the kingdom of God."[76]

To the south of Saint Louis, in Jefferson County, the Redemptorists established Ligouri Press in October 1947. They had a long history in the vicinity, opening Saint Clement Seminary in Desoto in 1900. Their main work at Ligouri was to publish the *Ligourian*, a magazine. Soon, other editing and publishing followed. In 1948 they got their own post office to aid in distribution of religious materials. From their monastery, many Redemptorists went out to preach missions in nearby parishes. Besides books and the magazine, the publishing house also produces parish bulletins.

---

76 Daniel C. Stutte, email interview January 31, 2019.

FATHER TURRIDU AND THE BATTLE FOR THE EDWARD STREET BRIDGE

A laconic observation was made about the construction of interstate highways in Saint Louis. "Land clearance for urban renewal through the central city opened up another southern route and I-44, an east-west expressway parallel to the Daniel Boone, opened in 1972." Later, in the same book, the impact of this highway on a close-knit neighborhood was hinted at briefly. "Residents of 'the Hill' (just west of Tower Grove Park) won an extra overpass when I-44 threatened to bisect the neighborhood."[77] The story of the battle for the Edwards Street overpass is a tale worth telling, the story of an ethnic community, a Catholic parish, and an indefatigable priest who faced down the federal government.

The Hill, with its restaurants, bakeries, delicatessens, and residents, many of whom still speak Italian, is unique to Saint Louis, and is indeed extraordinary for any city in America. It is held together by the parish of Saint Ambrose, the creation of Father Cesare Spigardi. The Hill was first occupied by Lombards, northern Italians working in the clay mines south of Manchester Boulevard. Those who had religious sentiment attended Monsignor Frederick Holweck's Saint Aloysius Gonzaga Parish, as Holweck was fluent in Italian as well as several other languages. In 1903, Father Spigardi founded Saint Ambrose with the blessing of Archbishop John Glennon. He and his assistant, Father Luciano Carotti, split their time between the Lombards on the Hill and the Sicilians downtown in Little Italy. Eventually, Little Italy disappeared under heavy industrial development. Its Sicilians gravitated to the Hill, outnumbered two to one by the Lombards.

A robust Italian culture was preserved on the Hill. Luigi Carnovale founded two Italian newspapers. One, *Il Pensiero*, is still printed weekly. When the construction of Highway 44 threatened to split the neighborhood in two, forces mobilized to save the community. These were not babes in the woods. Three times already the Hill had been in crisis. Each time, the community united to defend itself.

In August 1965, neighbors learned of a plan to build a drive-in theater on the Hill. They were incensed to find that their alderman, Anthony Mascazzini, favored the development.

---

77 Colin Gordon. *Mapping Decline: St. Louis and the Fate of the American City*. Philadelphia: University of Pennsylvania Press. 2008. Pp. 161, 206.

A group calling itself the Improvement Association of the Hill challenged the alderman and newly elected mayor, A. J. Cervantes. The Improvement Association worked closely with radio, television, and newspapers to get their message out. In the end, the drive-in plan was dropped.

A second challenge came as I-44 was being proposed. Plans included a ramp onto Macklind Avenue, eliminating much of Virgo Park, which had just been renamed Berra Park, after the beloved Hill politician, Louis "Midge" Berra. This would impact the 6,000 people who used the park and would eliminate ten houses. The Improvement Association rallied opposition and stormed the state capital in Jefferson City. The ramp idea was dropped.

The third challenge came from a firm which operated in the area, breaking ordinances and polluting ground water on the Hill. National Lead poured up to 40,000 gallons of polluted water into mines underneath the houses of Hill residents. After meetings with city officials, National Lead was ordered to cease operations, though no permits were issued, and no punishments meted out.[78]

These three challenges to the welfare of the people on the Hill prepared them for the fight of their lives. They were now organized, had leadership, and had three victories under their belt.

Going back to the mid-1950s, there had been talk of an interstate highway cutting through the Italian neighborhood. It was all just talk, until 1965. Then representatives of the highway department began visiting homes and making offers. The Improvement Association sprang into action.

Realizing that they were powerless to stop the construction of the highway, the Improvement Association joined with Saint Ambrose Parish to do what was possible to ameliorate problems. Meeting at the parish hall and guided by the assistant pastor, Father Sal E. Polizzi, they translated for the elderly who spoke no English. They helped negotiate for the sale of the targeted houses. They sought to find alternative houses on the Hill for the displaced residents.

On September 10, 1971, Tom Turin, a firefighter and resident on the north side of Pattison Avenue, met with fellow resident, Paul Gianella, a city worker. They called a meeting with the state representative Eugene Mazzuca and residents living on the north side. When

---

78 Reverend Sal. E. Polizzi. "The Edward Street Overpass: A Lesson in Political Expediency." Research Paper. Saint Louis University. 1972. P. 5.

Father Polizzi was informed, he offered Saint Ambrose as a venue and further invited Alderman Giuffrida and City Treasurer Paul Berra. Together, they planned a visit to Jefferson City to meet with the Missouri Highway Department on September 24th.

Busloads of locals joined, and local newspapers were invited to send reporters. Several Hill residents were prepared to give testimony, which they did seemingly to no effect. Paul Berra argued that a pedestrian walkway at Marconi was impractical, too steep for the elderly. He pointed out that four hundred residents would be isolated north of I-44 and that the neighborhood would die on the vine, probably turning industrial. Father Polizzi argued that 90% of Hill residents were Italian and 95% were Catholic. He pleaded, "These people all shop in the area. It is one of the few areas left in the city where the local neighborhood grocery stores exist." He pointed out that over 125,000 people attended the annual "Hill Day" celebration the previous year. He added, "The idea today is identity ... trying to get people back to a community. We do not want to abandon these 400 people north of the interstate. Those people have lived there, their fathers and mothers, their grandfathers and grandmothers have lived there, and they want to continue to live there."[79]

A local Jefferson City newspaper carried the headlines, "State Turns Deaf Ear to Residents' Plea for Edwards Overpass."[80]

But the Hill would not give up. Another meeting was held on October 3, 1971. Three hundred people attended. Fred Weber, whose firm was in charge of the construction of the highway, was impressed and promised to help. Quietly, he reassigned his workers to other projects, and the I-44 construction crawled to a halt. This gave the Improvement Association time to petition Governor Warren E. Hearnes. He said to Father Polizzi, "Father, I wish to give you a lesson in political science; never go to the second person in charge first; you go to the top man first." Though he sympathized with the Association and was a personal friend of Paul Berra, he pointed out that he could not now overturn the decision of a commission which he himself had appointed.

The struggle between the Improvement Association and the Missouri State Highway Commission turned ugly. When Commis-

---

79 Reverend Sal. E. Polizzi. "The Edward Street Overpass: A Lesson in Political Expediency." P. 12
80 Ibid. P. 11.

sioner Robert Hunter dug in his heals, rejecting an Edwards Street overpass, one resident, Mrs. Rose H. Puricelli wrote him, "Your inconsistent reports regarding the feasibility and cost status for the Edwards Street Overpass in St. Louis is most assuredly devoid of public accountability. Your actions in this matter discredit you as a person and do a great disservice to the words represented on our state seal."[81] To emphasize the point, Mrs. Puricelli included the state motto, *Salus Populi Suprema Lex Esto*, The Health of the People Is the Supreme Law.

Paul Berra went further. At an October 18, 1971 meeting, he called Hunter "a damned liar." He contacted Missouri's U. S. senators Stuart Symington and Thomas Eagleton as well as Representative Lenore K. Sullivan. That was the political route. Father Polizzi decided to use the ethnic route. He knew that Richard Nixon had appointed John Volpe, head of the Department of Transportation, partially to court the Italian American vote. How to get the ear of John Volpe?

Father Polizzi contacted Joe Garagiola, former Saint Louis Cardinal baseball player, television and radio personality, and boy from the Hill. Garagiola promised to contact friends in high places in New York City and to place a call to Senator John Pastore of Rhode Island. Father Polizzi called his sister, Sister Marcella Polizzi, for advice. She made some calls and found out that John Volpe had a friend who lived on the Hill, Thomas Gioia, a respected lawyer

The priest then contacted Louis Calcaterra, director of the Calcaterra Funeral Homes in both Saint Louis and in Detroit. This resulted in letters to Volpe from the Italian American Chamber of Commerce of Michigan, The American-Italian Club of Michigan, the president of the Columbus Day Celebration committee, the Congress of American Italians, and Boys Town of Italy, Inc. A plan was hatched to meet with John Volpe personally in Washington, D. C.

Thomas Gioia penned a letter to Deputy Federal Highway Administrator Ralph Bartelsmeyer arguing that without the Edwards Street overpass, some 180 families north of I-44 would have inadequate fire protection. He copied John Volpe.

Here was a new line of attack, public safety. It was pointed out that when trains blocked Manchester Boulevard at Macklind, fire engines could not get to that neighborhood. Father Polizzi was quoted by the

---

81 Ibid. P. 23.

Post-Dispatch saying, "They're going to have to put me under with a bulldozer before I give up on the fight for the overpass."[82]

Things began to change. Bartelsmeyer, the Federal Highway administrator, replied to Thomas Gioia that the Office of Engineering would be working with the field office in Missouri. The Hill delegation was invited to make its case in the nation's capital. Six members were selected, including Paul Berra and Father Polizzi.

They met with Senator Eagleton and his friend Senator Mike Mansfield of Montana, Senate Majority Leader, over breakfast. Then a visit was made to the office of Congresswoman Lenore Sullivan. Following that, they met with Elizabeth Keelman, director of the Urban Institute at the Secretary of Transportation office. Five testimonies were given. Father Polizzi described the history of the Hill. Al Giuffrida pleaded that three-quarters of the residents on the north side of I-44 were related by marriage or blood to people on the south side and that these bonds went back three and four generations.

Gene Mazzuca spoke about the economic loss to the Hill businesses if the north side were cut off. Tom Turin cited the isolation of the north side if the Edwards Street overpass was not built. And Paul Berra spoke about the ethnic pride which is engendered by Hill 2000. He even offered the Transportation Department $50,000 toward the project.

The nearly two-hour long meeting ended well, with one commissioner complimenting the team. A second meeting was held in Jefferson City. This time, the commission reversed its previous stance. The Edwards Street Overpass would be built. That night, Saint Ambrose rang its bells to celebrate the victory. Later, John Volpe was in Saint Louis for a Republican fund-raiser. Father Polizzi made sure he was present and conversed with the transportation secretary in Italian. The secretary assured the priest that everything would be done to protect the Hill.

The Italian community, rallying around Saint Ambrose parish under the leadership of Father Sal Polizzi, had thwarted the federal and state governments in their quest to split the Hill in two. Years later, a novel by Dan Conway would be based on the exploits of Monsignor Sal Polizzi. With the title of the priest's nickname, it was called *Father Turridu: The Savior of the City*. Not too far from the truth!

---

82 Reverend Sal. E. Polizzi. "The Edward Street Overpass: A Lesson in Political Expediency." P. 27

THE PERMANENT DIACONATE

On November 21, 1964 the fathers of the Second Vatican Council approved the Dogmatic Constitution on the Church, *Lumen Gentium*. Number 29 contained a bombshell which would change the face of many dioceses around the world. It called for the restoration of the permanent diaconate. In a September vote on those paragraphs, the fathers voted 2,055 in favor while 94 opposed.

The document outlined the scope of the deacon's work within the Church. "It pertains to the office of a deacon, in so far as it may be assigned to him by the competent authority, to administer Baptism solemnly, to be custodian and distributer of the Eucharist, in the name of the Church, to assist and to bless marriages, to bring Viaticum to the dying, to read the sacred scripture to the faithful, to instruct and exhort the people, to preside over the worship and the prayer of the faithful, to administer sacramentals, and to officiate at funeral and burial services."[83]

The particulars regarding the restoration of the permanent diaconate had to wait until June 18, 1967, when Pope Paul VI published *Sacram Diaconatus Ordinem*, authorizing the episcopal conferences to organize a diaconate program and to seek approval from Rome. The rules concerned age for ordination, training and formation, obtaining the wife's consent, adhering to a celibate life if the wife should die or if he was celibate at the time of ordination, and various forms of ministry a deacon could be expected to follow.

Despite the initial opposition from some powerful voices, such as Cardinal Francis Spellman of New York, the American bishops moved swiftly in this task and presented a plan to the Vatican on May 2, 1968. The Vatican responded as swiftly by approving the plan just three months later.

By 1971 the United States Catholic Conference published "Permanent Diaconate in the U. S.: Guidelines on Their Formation and Ministry."

The Archdiocese of Saint Louis moved more cautiously. The little USCC pamphlet gave no clear directive on how to establish a formation program. The only functioning model was that of the seminary system, but that could not be used. While seminarians studying for the priesthood could utilize all their time to the project, most deacon candidates had jobs

---

83 "Lumen Gentium," 29. Austin Flannery, O.P. ed. *Vatican Council II*. Volume 1. New York: Costello Publishing Company. 1998. P. 387.

and families. They were older also. The average age of the new candidates was between forty-five and fifty-five years old.[84]

On September 6, 1973, auxiliary Bishop McNicholas wrote Father Clarence Deddens, in the name of Cardinal Carberry, to join a small Ad Hoc committee for the establishment of the permanent diaconate in the Archdiocese of Saint Louis.

Deddens responded four days later with a letter laying out his objections to the project. First, he feared that a permanent diaconate would draw men away from priesthood. "Why," he asked, "be a priest when you can be a deacon and still get married?" His second objection had to do with the liturgy. Already the use of lay ministers for Holy Communion "left our people with a mentality that Holy Communion is not sacred." He asked, "How much 'future shock' can Catholics stand?" He read the NCCB document and found paragraphs that "leaves one with a shaky attitude about the whole thing."[85]

Regardless of his objections, Father Deddens served as secretary on the committee. It was chaired by Bishop McNicholas and included Father John Shocklee, heavily engaged in the inner-city work, and Father Xavier Albert, the only black priest in the archdiocese. These were chosen specifically to attract black candidates to the permanent diaconate.

Other members included Fathers Bernard Huhn from the Priests' Council, Robert Coerver, C.M., adding expertise in academics and formation, Donald Brinkman from the vocation office, and three other priests.

To stir up interest in the permanent diaconate, articles began appearing in the *Saint Louis Review*. On January 11, 1974, a headline read "Diaconate Plans Here Require More Interest." Bishop McNicholas observed, "So far, lack of interest from potential lay candidates." Plans were set for the Spring Priests' Conference to introduce the program to the priests, in hopes that they would encourage some of their parishioners to consider the diaconate.

In a March 29th article entitled, "Wives and Children of the Permanent Diaconate Find Drawbacks Only Temporary," one wife spoke of a broken hip and how her deacon husband showed great care and attention to her. She quipped, "He knows after I'm gone, he can't marry again!"

---

84 La Rue H. Velott. *The Order of Deacon: Past and Present*. Columbus: National Association of Diaconate Directors. 2008. P. 111.

85 Inter Office Communication. September 10, 1973. Father Deddens to Cardinal Carberry and Bishop McNicholas. RG III E 13.4. Saint Louis Archdiocesan Archives.

Other articles appeared in 1974. On August 16, the *Review* ran an article, "Applicants Being Sought for Permanent Diaconate Training," and followed up with another article, "Permanent Diaconate in U. S. Almost Equals World Total." The article pointed out that sixty-five U. S. dioceses had permanent deacons, and another eleven were formulating plans.

It took Saint Louis a full year to implement a program. It was determined that classes would take place through the Paul VI Pontifical Institute, and the costs would be split evenly among the candidate, his parish, and the Archdiocese. The same would be true to pay for weekend retreats.

Cardinal Carberry appointed Bishop George J. Gottwald as chairman of the Archdiocesan Committee on the Permanent Diaconate on October 7 and named Father John Gaydos as secretary, though Father Deddens continued to have a very active role despite the Cardinal's observation that he had too much to do already. Bishop McNicholas continued to have a strong influence on the development also.

Father Deddens formed Paul VI classes running each Wednesday night from 7:30 to 9:00 from early November to late December. It was called "RE 190 Orientation to the Permanent Diaconate." Sixteen candidates attended. Father Deddens told Bishop McNicholas the class was "heavily populated by charismatics." Several belonged to a prayer group run by Father Robert Hermann. Deddens added, "I am, therefore, confident that the academic credentials of our candidates will be far and above others around the country." He added that the candidates were expected to attend daily Mass, make frequent confessions, and have a spiritual director.

The man who had once questioned the restoration of the diaconate now enthusiastically laid out the program. "The most characteristic theme of the St. Louis Program as I see it, is that Permanent Deacons are not being ordained as helpers in the liturgical ministry of the Parish; rather, they are being ordained to the ministry of charity, i. e. as visitors to hospitals, visitors to the imprisoned, Saint Vincent de Paul workers, drug counsellors, religion teachers, Legion of Mary organizers, etc."[86]

On January 29, 1977 Cardinal Carberry ordained twelve permanent deacons at the New Cathedral. They had finished two years of training and, after ordination, would experience one full year of orientation. The next year on February 3, fourteen of the original seven-

---

86 Inter Office Communication. August 22, 1975. Father Deddens to Cardinal Carberry and Bishop McNicholas. RG III E 13.4. Archdiocese of Saint Louis Archives.

teen candidates were ordained, along with a Jesuit Brother. Deacon Daniel S. Austin of Most Blessed Sacrament Parish was the first African American to be ordained in Saint Louis.

A major feature article appeared in the *Saint Louis Review* on September 9, 1983. Entitled "Restored Diaconate Making New Impact in Ordained Ministry," it was authored by staff writer, Teresa Coyle. She noted that there were sixty-five ordained deacons in the archdiocese and another fifty-five in formation. These were not "liturgical flowerpots, glorified altar boys or mini-priests." "They are ordained ministers working and living in the lay world."

The article showed how deacons begin their day attending daily Mass in their parishes and then going off to work. Coyle featured three deacons to make her point. Deacon Peter Gounis of Sacred Heart Parish in Florissant began his day with Mass, then went off to his flower shop. Deacon Lawrence McVey of Our Lady of Providence went to his place of business as a print shop salesman. Deacon Jack Riley was retired at age seventy-one which allowed him to spend much of his day doing apostolic projects for our Lady of Loretto Parish in Spanish Lake.

The article stressed the need for balance. The family came first, then the career, then the diaconate. But Deacon Gounis observed, "To a certain extent, they're all number one together, but by the same token, you do have to draw the line somewhere and know your limitations." It was noted also that wives of deacons tended to be engaged in parish activities.

The director of the permanent diaconate at the time was Father John M. Costello. He compared the permanent deacons favorably when set against the priest-worker program in postwar France. There priests went into factories and mines and fields to work side-by-side with laity. It did not work; they were not accepted. Father Costello observed, "We're finding more and more that the real value of the deacon is in the work setting." They were in the work setting before they were ordained and were seen as equals, with a little something special added.

Father Costello replaced Father John Gaydos as director of the permanent diaconate, though maintaining his position as associate pastor of Saint Blaise. The status of director was enhanced as he got an office on the campus of Cardinal Glennon College. His successor in

1987 was the first deacon to run the program, J. Gerard Quinn, who also served on the Tribunal.

CHARISMATIC RENEWAL IN SAINT LOUIS

When Father Clarence Deddens reported to Bishop McNicholas that the first class of candidates for the permanent diaconate was "heavily populated by charismatics" and that many belonged to a prayer group started by Father Robert Hermann, he was acknowledging one of the most significant developments in the post-conciliar Church, the Charismatic Renewal movement. Not only did this movement enliven the spiritual lives of countless Catholics, but their fervor found an outlet in many other expressions of faith, having a ripple effect down to today.

Key to the movement was a Dominican, Father Francis MacNutt. He taught homiletics at Aquinas Institute of Theology, was editor of *Homiletics and Pastoral Review*, and was president of the Christian Preaching Conference as well as the Thomas Merton Foundation. He had been profoundly touched by the writings of Merton while in college. MacNutt became interested in the Pentecostal communities, especially their healing ministries.

Father MacNutt brought together a prayer group which grew rapidly and was moved to Visitation Academy in Town and Country in 1968. The Visitation Nuns, semi-cloistered and staffing the Academy since 1844, were very supportive.

That same year, five women made a retreat at the Cenacle in Creve Coeur and formed a prayer group afterwards. Two years later, they joined the Visitation Academy group.

Archbishop John Joseph Carberry took an interest in the movement and encouraged a parish-based approach rather than the formation of covenant communities. Life in the Spirit Seminars were scheduled throughout the Archdiocese. Each seminar included talks, scripture study, prayer and singing, and small group discussions. After the seminars, the participants would set up prayer groups in their parishes. At one point, such groups could be found in one hundred and forty parishes, though the number stabilized at something over seventy.

The groups found encouragement in Father MacNutt's 1974 book, *Healing,* as well as his periodical *The Spirit and the Bride.* His 1977 book, *The Power to Heal,* sold over 220,000 copies.

In this book, MacNutt tells the remarkable story of Roell Ann Schmidt, a three-year-old girl being treated at Children's Hospital for a form of cancer which was 95% fatal. The Schmidts were members of Saint Roch Parish and joined a Wednesday evening prayer group but did not stop there. David and Barbara Schmidt appealed for prayers to the Jesuits at Saint Louis University, to the Benedictine Nuns, and even to Grace Methodist, just a block west on Waterman from Saint Roch.

Then, they came in contact with Father MacNutt at Merton House. Every Thursday afternoon, the Schmidts came for prayer with him or Sister Mary Margaret McKenzie, a Visitation nun. The prayer sessions lasted around a half-hour and ended with the recitation of the Lord's Prayer. At one point, the prayers evolved into speaking in tongues, which at first confused David and Barbara. Later, they became quite comfortable with the format.

The medical therapy was gruesome. Roell lost most of her hair. She lost any interest in eating. Her blood count dropped, and she caught viral infections. It did not look good. But the Schmidts soldiered on.

Every Wednesday, they attended the Saint Roch prayer group. Every Thursday, they took Roell to Merton House. They attended a "Life in the Spirit" Seminar at Saint Francis Xavier Parish, and were both baptized in the Spirit, recommitting themselves to the Lord.

On June 22, 1976, the doctors finally felt confident enough to perform surgery to remove the tumor which had been determined to be 100 percent malignant and spreading. They discovered it had become a calcified mass. Lab tests three days later showed no living cancer cells. Instead, healthy nerve tissue cells were growing in their place. All the doctors could say was that this development was extremely uncommon.

David Schmidt was cautious in attributing this happy turn of events to a miracle. "We don't have medical evidence that a miracle occurred. But neither do we have evidence that the therapies effect the cell differentiation, the cure. Who knows? Maybe someday they'll discover how this differentiation occurs."

He continued, "All I know for sure is that God cured our daughter. Whether it was through the efforts of the team at Children's Hospital or whether the malignant cells just disappeared, is a moot question."

Msgr. Robert Peet, pastor at Saint Roch, celebrated a Mass of Thanksgiving on August 23, attended by so many who had prayed for

Roell through her ordeal. Her father made one last observation. "I've prayed for healing, and I've prayed in thanks – and, believe me, it's much nicer to give thanks!"[87]

In 1975, Father MacNutt met Judith Sewell while giving talks in Jerusalem. They stayed in touch, eventually falling in love. Francis MacNutt sought a dispensation from his vows and married her in 1980 in a ceremony conducted by Bishop John Snyder of Saint Augustine, Florida. Thereafter, the couple continued to be active in the Christian healing ministries.

Shepherding the charismatic renewal fell to Monsignor Bernard Sanheinrich, leading the Metropolitan Area Service Team. This office was responsible for choosing speakers at the Regional Charismatic Conferences. Besides continuing *The Spirit and the Bride* periodical, MAST joined efforts with Rev. Larry Rice at the New Life Evangelistic Center to set up a Christian television station. Father Frank Krebs, besides editing the periodical, often celebrated Mass on the station and spoke on several radio stations.

The Regional Charismatic Conferences were powerful vehicles to help the movement grow. They had been held near Milwaukee, Notre Dame University, and Minneapolis before the International Conference was held in Rome in May 1975.

In 1977 the Midwest held its own conference in Kansas City. It was held in Arrowhead Stadium each night, attended by more than 50,000 people. It was an extraordinary experience. Catholic charismatics made up nearly half of the assembly, followed by Pentecostals, Lutherans, Episcopalians, and even some Messianic Jews. Each group had break-out sessions in various locations throughout Kansas City.

One attending was Father Raniero Cantalamessa, a Capuchin friar, who received a baptism in the Holy Spirit there. He later became a preacher in the Papal Household for Popes John Paul II, Benedict XVI, and Francis. Several Saint Louisans also attended the Kansas City conference and were inspired to stage a similar conference at Kiel Auditorium.

The first night featured a talk on the history of the Pentecostal movement from its founding in Topeka, Kansas in 1901. That was followed by a talk on the Catholic developments starting at Duquesne University, Pittsburgh in 1967. The keynote speaker that night was

---

87 Francis MacNutt. *The Power to Heal*. Notre Dame: Ave Maria Press. 1977. P. 87.

Kevin Ranaghan who spoke of the three streams, classical Pentecostals, mainline Protestant Pentecostals, and charismatic Catholics, as coming together as a "mighty river thundering over this Arrowhead Stadium waterfall."[88] The crowds went wild.

The second night featured five speakers, two of whom, Father MacNutt and Ralph Martin, were Catholic. The keynote speaker, Larry Christianson, called upon the assembly to find a path to unity.

The third night featured three dignitaries, Cardinal Joseph Suenens of Belgium, Bishop J. O. Patterson of the Memphis-based Church of God in Christ and Thomas Zimmerman of the American Assemblies of God. One of the speakers that evening was Maria Von Trapp. The keynote speaker was non-denominational Rev. Bob Mumford. In the middle of his talk, he called for a "Holy Ghost break." The stadium stood silent until he erupted, "Glory to God; Jesus is Lord." Fifty thousand voices joined in.

The last night included Father Michael Scanlan, president of Franciscan University of Steubenville, a school he turned back from near extinction by dedicating the campus to Christ and encouraging the charismatic movement there.

The Jefferson City newspaper, *Daily Capital News*, reported, "Participants are spontaneous, demonstrative believers, who stress the gifts – the charisms – of the holy spirit for healing, prophecy, evangelical zeal and speaking in unknown, God-inspired tongues."[89]

Cardinal Carberry gave permission for the first Annual Midwest Regional Charismatic Renewal Conference to be held October 12 to 14, 1979. Speakers included Father Francis Martin, who also had attended the Kansas City conference. At the time, he was a member of Mother of God charismatic community in Washington, D. C. He would later be a professor of scripture at Catholic University of America, Franciscan University of Steubenville, and founder of The Word Proclaimed Institute. Over five thousand people attended this conference.

Over time, several parish prayer groups merged, and leaders began to appear. The Central City Cluster was made up of Saint Mark's, Nativity, Saint Philip Neri, and Saint Adelbert. There, Father Marty Manion, Msgr. Robert Hermann, and several others stood out. Msgr. Hermann helped set up a prayer group at Saint Ann's in Normandy, while Deacon

---

88 Vinson Synan. *An Eyewitness Remembers the Century of the Holy Spirit.* Grand Rapids: Chosen. 2010. P. 91.
89 "Religious Groups Gather." *Daily Capital News.* Jefferson City. July 21, 1977.

Ken Potsman from the first class of ordained permanent deacons and his wife, Barb, founded a group at Saint Christopher's.

When Father Ed Griesedieck became pastor of Saint Rose in North Saint Louis, he invited two Precious Blood sisters to come to lead a Life in the Spirit seminar. After that, he too became very active in the renewal movement.

While there were many changes in venue and in personnel over the years, the Charismatic Renewal, with its office in the Archdiocesan curia to give it stability, would continue to be a blessing to the Catholic Church in Saint Louis.

During Respect Life Week in 1972, Cardinal Carberry talked as part of a panel of speakers at a Respect Life seminar at Marillac College on October 6. Photographer Richard Finke. From the Archdiocese of St. Louis Archives and Records.

On May 24, 1973, around 100 people joined the picket line outside Missouri's first abortion clinic at Euclid and West Pine Avenues in St Louis. The protest was sponsored by the Missouri Citizens for Life. The clinic opened a few days after the federal court ruled that Missouri's anti-abortion law was invalid. Photographer Richard Finke. From the Archdiocese of St. Louis Archives and Records.

On October 21, 1973, over 30,000 people gathered in front of the Old Courthouse in downtown St. Louis during a statewide rally to protest abortion and to support a human life amendment to the U.S. Constitution. Photographer Richard Finke. From the Archdiocese of St. Louis Archives and Records.

During the St. Louis pro-life rally in October 1973, Missouri Attorney General Senator John C. Danforth, Republican, spoke to the crowds against the *Roe v. Wade* abortion ruling by the U.S. Supreme Court in January of that year. Both sides of the political aisle were represented at the rally. Photographer Richard Finke. From the Archdiocese of St. Louis Archives and Records.

Both sides of the political aisle were represented at the pro-life rally in downtown St. Louis on October 21, 1973. United States Senator Thomas F. Eagleton, Democrat from Missouri, spoke with reporters at the St. Louis rally to urge the passing of a human life amendment to protect the sanctity of life. Photographer Richard Finke. From the Archdiocese of St. Louis Archives and Records.

Cardinal Carberry and Dr. Jacob Preuss, president of the Lutheran Church-Missouri Synod, were among the 18 founding members of Clergy for Life, an interfaith organization to protect unborn life. Here, they announce the establishment of the group at a press conference in 1973. Photographer Richard Finke. From the Archdiocese of St. Louis Archives and Records.

Msgr. Vincent Bommarito, pastor of St. Ambrose Parish, offered a blessing prior to the start of the 25th annual Giro della Montagna, a stage of the Gateway Cup bicycle race, in front of the parish church, Sept. 5, 2010. Photographer Teak Phillips. Courtesy of the St. Louis Review.

Paul M. Berra was a city and state official for almost 40 years, and lived in the Hill Neighborhood his entire life. Photograph circa 1972. From the Archdiocese of St. Louis Archives and Records.

On January 29, 1977, the first group of permanent deacons was ordained at the Cathedral Basilica. Pictured are, left to right, [first row] Rev. Robert F. Coerver, Bishop John Wurm, Cardinal John Carberry, Bishop Joseph McNicholas, Rev. John Gaydos, Rev. Clarence Deddens; [second row] Jerome Toohey, Maurice Yahl, Kenneth Potzman, Brother Lawrence Christensen; [third row] John A. Cummings, Francis Naumann, Daniel Austin, Daniel Hefele, Andrew Niemeyer, Harold Longmeyer; [fourth row] Norman Jansen, Sylvester Deeken, Herbert Gettemeier, and Joseph Otzenberger. Photograph courtesy of the Office of the Permanent Diaconate.

Around 4,000 people attended the third annual St. Louis Regional Catholic Charismatic Conference held at the Cervantes Convention Center in October 1981. Participants included priests, religious, Catholics, and non-Catholics from eighteen different states. Photographer Richard Finke. From the Archdiocese of St. Louis Archives and Records.

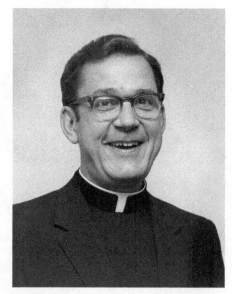

Msgr. Bernard Sandheinrich was appointed Director of the Charismatic Renewal office in 1975. Photographer Richard Finke. From the Archdiocese of St. Louis Archives and Records.

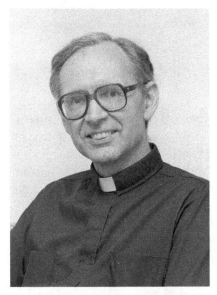

Auxiliary Bishop Robert J. Hermann was heavily involved with the charismatic renewal movement in the archdiocese. This photo was taken in 1985 while he was pastor of St. Andrew Parish in Lemay. Photographer Richard Finke, 1985. From the Archdiocese of St. Louis Archives and Records.

Deacon Kenneth Potzmann ministers to a woman at St. John's Mercy Hospital in 2002. Deacon Potzmann and his wife Barb founded a charismatic renewal prayer group at St. Christopher Parish. Photographer Mark Kempf. From the Archdiocese of St. Louis Archives and Records.

William B. Byrne (right) retired as owner and president of Catholic Supply of St. Louis, Inc. in 1983. Dan Stutte (left) began working for Byrne in 1964 as a maintenance man. In 1983, he and his wife Mary bought the business from Byrne and have run the company ever since. Photographer Richard Finke. From the Archdiocese of St. Louis Archives and Records.

Chapter Four

THE HERMENUTICS OF RUPTURE

On November 7, 1972 President Richard M. Nixon won a remarkable landslide for re-election, taking forty-nine of the fifty states, 60.7 percent of the popular vote. Yet twenty-one months later, he became the first president in American history to resign. The nation was shocked by months of congressional hearings into what became known as the Watergate affair.

Around 2:00 AM, June 17, 1972 James McCord, chief security officer for the Committee to Re-Elect the President, and four Cuban Americans were arrested while planting listening devices in the phones of the Democratic National Committee, housed in the Watergate complex. The police found an address book with the name and telephone number of Howard Hunt, a former CIA operative now working for President Nixon's security unit, nicknamed the Plumbers.

Worse, McCord had been recruited for the burglary by G. Gordon Liddy, a former FBI agent now acting as a lawyer for CREEP, the Committee to Re-elect the President.

The secret behind the Watergate break-in began to unravel when the burglars went to trial in early January 1973. During the grand jury investigation, both Jeb Stuart Magruder, deputy at CREEP, and his boss, John Mitchell, former attorney general and now head of CREEP, perjured themselves.

On February 7, 1973, the United States Senate voted unanimously to create a select committee to investigate the Watergate affair. It was led by South Carolina Senator Sam Ervin. At the same time, James McCord wrote a confidential letter to Judge John Sirica, asking to meet with him in chambers after sentencing. Sirica turned to a law clerk and exclaimed, "This is going to break this case wide open."[90]

Indeed, it did. As the Ervin committee continued its work, it became obvious that the corruption reached into the highest levels of the executive government, that President Nixon had become aware of the connection of the break-in to the CREEP, and that his closest ad-

---

90 Tim Weiner. *One Man against the World: The Tragedy of Richard Nixon.* New York: Henry Holt and Company. 2015. P. 240.

visers were involved. There was evidence that Nixon tried to use the CIA to get the FBI to drop its investigation of the Watergate break-in.

A special prosecutor, Archibald Cox, was appointed to investigate the president. Meanwhile, the Ervin committee was doing its work. First called to witness was the head administrator of CREEP, Robert C. Odle, Jr. He had hired McCord as security chief but dismissed him the moment he heard about the break-in. Then the arresting officers were interviewed. After that, James McCord.

McCord implicated Jack Caulfield, aid to John Ehrlichman, assistant to the president for Domestic Affairs. McCord told of a meeting with Caulfield in which he was promised executive clemency if he remained silent. On May 22, Caulfield was called before the committee.

Under oath, Caulfield confirmed everything that McCord had told the committee. Then, he added something else. He had attended a drug conference in San Clemente when he got a phone call from Howard Dean, legal counsel to President Nixon. Dean asked Caulfield to intercede with James McCord, which he had done. Now the trail led directly to the oval office.

Then on June 6, President Nixon was told that Archibald Cox, the special prosecutor, was aware that there were secret tapes of oval office conversations, and he wanted them. That became public knowledge when Alexander Butterfield, deputy assistant to the president during the first term, was asked directly by two Watergate staff investigators.

The noose tightened as Bob Haldeman, then John Ehrlichman, and finally John Mitchell were called before the Watergate committee. In an extraordinary exchange between Mitchell and lawyer Herman Talmadge, when asked if the former attorney general had placed re-election over his duties of office, Mitchell replied, "In my mind, the re-election of Richard Nixon, compared to what was available on the other side, was so important that I just put it in that context."[91]

In desperation, Nixon fired Elliot Richardson, the current attorney general, then William Ruckelshaus, the deputy attorney general, when they refused to fire Archibald Cox and shut down the special prosecutor's office. Cox was fired by the next in line, Robert Bork. But the whole event of October 20, 1972 was a PR disaster for the president and became known as the Saturday Night Massacre.

---

91 Tim Weiner. *One Man against the World: The Tragedy of Richard Nixon.* P. 282.

Impeachment was in the air, and 1974 did not go well for Richard Milhous Nixon. The House Judiciary committee convened and began gathering evidence against the president, specifically regarding the abuse of power and obstruction of justice. Nixon tried to keep the tapes out of the hands of the new prosecutor, Leon Jaworski, but was unanimously overruled by the Supreme Court. Nixon went on an international tour to try to take the media's attention off Watergate.

On July 27, 1974, the House impeachment committee voted 27 to 11 on the first article of impeachment. That was followed by a second vote, 28 to 10 and a third 27 to 11.

After the tapes were turned over, it took merely nine days to discover the June 23, 1973 recording in which Nixon told Haldeman to get the FBI to call off the investigation. Here was the cover-up which everyone had suspected. On August 9th, Nixon became the first president in American history to resign, before a full House impeachment vote could be taken.

Nixon was succeeded by Gerald R. Ford, the only unelected president in American history. He had taken the place of Spiro T. Agnew, who had resigned in disgrace just a year earlier.

Ford's presidency did not last even nine hundred days. It began badly when he gave a full pardon to Richard Nixon, angering many Americans. Congress cut off funding for the war in Vietnam, and South Vietnam fell to the communist North under Ford's watch. He appointed Nelson Rockefeller as his vice-president, which outraged conservative Republicans. The economy tanked as inflation rose and employment declined. Ford's WIN program, Whip Inflation Now, utterly failed. The press and comedians made fun of a few gaffs and stumbles to give the impression that President Ford was a fool. He almost lost the Republican nomination to California Governor Ronald Reagan.

Even so, Ford did remarkably well in the 1976 election. He took twenty-seven states to Jimmy Carter's twenty-three, lost the popular vote by just over two percent, but lost the Electoral College, 297 to 240.

These were years of foment in the Church also as she grappled with the meaning of the Second Vatican Council, with many people more inspired by its "spirit" than by its documents. Setting the course into the future proved difficult, as Pope Paul VI did not exert decisive leadership.

As early as 1964, the Dutch journal *Concilium* gave voice to progressive theologians including Hans Küng, Karl Rahner, Yves Congar, and Edward Schillebeeckx. Others included Henri de Lubac, Joseph Ratzinger, and Hans Urs von Balthasar, although these latter left in 1970 and by 1972 formed their own think tank and publication, *Communio.*

At the heart of the theological debate was the hermeneutics of rupture, that is, the belief that Vatican II was a decisive turn away from the past and toward a new adventure into uncharted waters. That was the position of *Concilium. Communio* came to see Vatican II as a natural outgrowth of ecclesial development and so constructed a hermeneutics of continuity. The next decades would be a contest between the two outlooks, all events interpreted though these two lenses.

This so alarmed the pope that in a sermon at Saint Peter's marking the tenth anniversary as Roman pontiff, he remarked that "through some crack in the temple of God, the smoke of Satan has entered."[92]

Earlier, in 1971, theologian Henri de Lubac wrote, "Today we are witnesses of an endeavor that wants to dissolve the Church into the world... The tide of immanentism is growing irresistibly."[93]

In 1975 writing in *Communio,* Joseph Ratzinger observed, "Something of the Kennedy era pervaded the Council, something of the naïve optimism of the concept of the great society. It was precisely the break in historical consciousness, the self-tormenting rejection of the past, that produced the concept of a zero hour in which everything would begin again and all those things that had formerly been done badly would now be done well."[94]

Things were not going well. In Italy, there was a push to repeal the divorce law. Though the Church fought a campaign to retain the law, the repeal easily passed the Parliament, only to go down in defeat in the general referendum. Nonetheless, forty-one percent of the vote favored easy divorce.

In December 1974, Pope Paul VI invited the International Theological Commission to come to Rome to discuss "The Origins of the Christian Moral Conscience." It would raise again the issues behind *Humanae Vitae* as well as consider new challenges in bioethics.

There had been considerable turn-over among the ITC's member-

---

92 Peter Hebblethwaite. *Paul VI: The First Modern Pope.* New York: Paulist Press. 1993. P. 595.
93 Massimo Faggioli. *Vatican II: The Battle for Meaning.* New York: Paulist Press. 2012. P. 71.
94 Ibid. P. 73.

ship, and the ITC had a difficult relationship with the Congregation for the Doctrine of the Faith. One of its most prominent members, Karl Rahner, resigned quipping, "I felt I did not need to go to Rome for that. I could do it just as well with my colleagues in Germany...I can eat ice cream in Germany too, excellent though the ice cream in Rome may be."[95]

The ugliness turned personal at one point when Cardinal Giovanni Benelli, considered a reformer within the Curia, came out to the Vatican car park to discover the tires on his automobile slashed.

Meanwhile, heads were rolling in the Vatican. The pope combined the Congregation for the Discipline of the Sacraments and the Congregation for Divine Worship and gave the new post to Australian Cardinal James Knox. Paul abruptly dismissed Archbishop Annibale Bugnini, the chief architect of the liturgical changes after Vatican II, and sent him off to be Apostolic Delegate in Tehran, Iran.

The pope also reached out to Archbishop Marcel Lefebvre who had caused a schism in the Church after the Council. In 1970, Lefebvre formed the Society of St. Pius X, SSPX, after rejecting many of the Council documents, particularly *Dignitatis Humanae*, the "Declaration on Religious Liberty." This was a hermeneutics of rupture, with a twist. Followers of Lefebvre saw the Council as illegitimate, a break with the traditions of the Church.

Archbishop Lefebvre met with Pope Paul VI on September 11, 1976 at Castelgandolfo. It did not go well. The only witness was Cardinal Benelli, who later reported that Lefebvre offered nothing by way of concessions, and the Pope received him coldly, refusing to embrace him when he came forward.

There was a wide range from disappointment to forceful dissent in the years following the Council. Many were saddened at the loss of their beloved Latin Mass, with its sense of transcendence and solemnity. They quietly accepted what was coming their way and tried to make the best of the Novus Ordo, the new vernacular Mass. Others, like Lefebvre, went further and organized into open rebellion. The SSPX seminary in Ecône, Switzerland was growing by leaps and bounds, the earliest seminarians coming from the Pontifical French Seminary in Rome. These students told Lefebvre that they were being persecuted for adhering to traditional teachings and prayers. At

---

95 Peter Hebblethwaite. *Paul VI: The First Modern Pope*. P. 633.

the extreme stood the sedevacantists, who argued that the Throne of Peter was vacant, as Paul VI had ceased to be a legitimate pope when he promulgated the decrees of Vatican II.

If Pope Paul VI had to fend off attacks from the right flank, Cardinal Carberry was fending off the left. His headaches came from a break-away group of Montfort missionaries. Cardinal Ritter had invited the Montfort Fathers to the Archdiocese in 1962. They bought property owned by the Sisters of Mercy in Saint Mary, Missouri and called it Marian Cliff. In 1966, they established Montfort House on the campus of Saint Louis University and enrolled their seminarians in the School of Divinity. Their director was Father Patrick Berkley, author of *Reconstructing Religious Life*. The seminarians engaged in inner-city apostolic work as well as their academic studies.

The Montforts purchased three inner-city properties, setting up the Triple City Mission. The largest was on North 14th Street. In November 1966, five seminarians formed a band to play "Christian Folk Songs." The band included three guitars, a banjo, and a bass. The seminarians achieved notoriety when they produced a record with twelve original songs.

Things deteriorated rapidly in 1967. A new provincial wanted to emphasize academics over social work and ran into opposition from Father Berkley. The two sides squabbled throughout the year.

On April 14, 1968, the Montfort seminarians appeared on national television on the Ed Sullivan Show. They were now a force to be reckoned with. When the provincial and his council continued to press for greater academic studies, thirteen Montfort seminarians, including the five singers, left the community and set up their own house, calling it Contemporary Mission. It was located on North 13th Street, and the group was joined by the former director of Montfort House, Father Patrick Berkley. That same year, five other seminarians withdrew from the community, leaving just twenty-six in formation.

This caught the attention of the superior general of the Montforts. He demanded that each seminarian renew his vows individually. Instead, on August 15, the breakaway seminarians allowed their annual vows to lapse. Father Berkley announced that he was seeking secularization, that is, withdrawing from the Montforts and seeking to become a diocesan priest.

All was at an impasse until May 11, 1971. Five of the breakaway seminarians traveled to Holy Apostles Seminary in Cromwell, Connecticut and convinced Bishop Peter K. Sarpong of Kumosi, Ghana to ordain them. They had paid for his travel expenses and lodging and promised to send stipends to his diocese when they showed they were not interested in serving in Ghana.

The five returned to Saint Louis and announced they would celebrate their first Mass on June 13 in Saint Francis Xavier "College" Church on the lower level. When interviewed, Father John O'Reilly said he had permission from the university priests, but only if Cardinal Carberry allowed it. If that did not happen, he threatened that the priests "will probably have Mass in the open in one of the parks or rent a hall."

In the standoff between the newly-ordained priests and the cardinal, the priests blinked. Around two hundred attended the Mass, but the five sat in the front pew and did not attempt to concelebrate. The Mass was celebrated by Father Robert A. Johnston, S. J., chairman of the speech department, with Father Patrick Berkley concelebrating.

Father O'Reilly went to the press to complain. "The rest is part of his (Carberry's) little inquisition. He is trying to white-wash the real issues. The real issue is that he has no interest in the inner-city. He has done nothing for blacks."

That is a strange observation, considering Cardinal Carberry's support of the Human Rights Office, his encouragement of inner-city parishes, attempts to provide Catholic education to some of the most depressed neighborhoods, his support for Father Placid's inner-city evangelization, and his encouragement of black candidates for the permanent diaconate.

Cardinal Carberry himself went to the media. I have "made no attempt to defend myself against the accusations which the priests in question made against me in the media. I have prayed for them, and I have asked for light and guidance in facing up to the responsibility which is mine in the very serious matter."

The new superior general of the Montforts got involved and wrote Father Berkley on June 25, 1971. He pointed out that Berkley had been called back to community several times but had failed to come. He set a deadline of July 31, or "we shall have no choice but to institute proceedings that would terminate in your official definitive severance from the congregation."[96]

---

96 Marcel Gendrot, SMM to Rev. Patrick Berkley. June 25, 1971. Rome. RG 06 Box 7, Folder 23. Archdiocese of Saint Louis Archives.

The day after attending Mass in the lower church level, one priest, Father John F. Coyle, flew to New York City to celebrate his first Mass in Flushing with his parents present. An article with a photograph appeared in the *New York Times*. Later, others would celebrate Masses in Hartford, Boston, and Davenport, Iowa.

Later in July, a bombshell hit. Over a news service a headline read, "Forgeries Charged in Contemporary Mission Controversy."

Father John O'Reilly reacted to attempts by Cardinal Carberry to get to the truth of the matter. He called the cardinal's questions "ridiculous," and added, "Those questions are none of his business. We weren't ordained for his diocese; we were ordained for Kumasi. This is just one example of his vindictiveness because what he really is opposed to is change – change in seminary training, change in the way priests should work with people. He is opposed to us."

But the accusation of forgeries which were used to convince Bishop Sarpong to ordain the five seminarians piled up. Father George Klubertanz, S. J., director of the divinity school at Saint Louis University, said none of the seminarians had completed more than two years of studies. Father Peter J. McCramm, SSM, pastor of a local parish, said his letter of recommendation was a forgery. Father Edward F. Jordan, secretary to the bishop of Austin, Texas, said his letter was a forgery, and so did Probert L. Hasenstab, assistant dean of SLU divinity school.

To address these charges, the Contemporary Mission, particularly Father O'Reilly, appeared twice on Channel 5, KSDTV with Julius Hunter. The first appearance, June 6, 1971, included four members of the group, and topics ranged from the reasons why they left the Montforts to their opinions on Church affairs and the Jesus Movement. They criticized the archdiocese for denouncing "Jesus Christ Superstar," a rock opera very popular at the time. They said the opera represented young people finding a way to express their religious beliefs.

They spoke of the way they produced contemporary music as being "Beatle-approach," "Bob Dylan-approach." They complained that the seminary was "a structure that can destroy you" and felt they were victims of "a backlash that comes from organized religion."[97]

On July 17, 1971, Father John T. O'Reilly returned for a second interview and to conduct a question-and-answer session with viewers.

---

97 Contemporary Mission Students Interview with Julius Hunter. Channel 5 News, KSDTV. June 6, 1971. Cassette History/ 142022. Saint Louis Archdiocesan Archives.

Julius Hunter asked him if he considered himself a revolutionary or a rebel. Father O'Reilly replied that he was a revolutionary in as much as he was trying to bring about good change, to help the Church "be up with the times."

When asked about support he was receiving from ACTION, the Action Committee to Improve Opportunities for Negroes, a radical group which picketed Archdiocesan facilities often and even disrupted Masses, O'Reilly replied that Contemporary Mission and ACTION had similar goals.

When asked if there was any question of the validity of their ordinations, O'Reilly quoted Cardinal Carberry in recognizing the validity of ordination, but added, "we've been having a few problems with him lately."

He addressed the question of forgeries, particularly a transcript from Saint Louis University, by blaming the issue on the *Saint Louis Globe-Democrat* which, he said, was out to get them.

As to not being permitted to celebrate Mass in Saint Louis, O'Reilly called it, "so vindictive, not warranted in any way," and "vicious and cruel for no good reason." Regardless, he pointed out that the newly-ordained priests obeyed and did not celebrate Mass in Saint Louis.

During the question-and-answer period, Father O'Reilly received several affirmations from callers. One asked what Saint Louisans could do to help. He replied that writing letters of support to the chancery was welcomed, but he feared that these letters caused the latest recriminations to fall upon him and his group.

One caller cut to the root of the issue and asked if Father O'Reilly understood the notion of incardination, the formal ties a priest makes to a superior or bishop in order to serve in a diocese. Clearly, the Contemporary Mission priests had not been incardinated into the Archdiocese of Saint Louis, but O'Reilly side-stepped the question, saying that they were incardinated into the Diocese of Kumosi, Ghana. That meant they were just as legal as anyone else, he added.

A final tough question was also addressed by deflection. Father O'Reilly was asked about a house in Lake Saint Louis which the Mission had purchased. Was it a retreat house for the priests or was it a place for youth from the inner city to come? He said the basis for this charge was again the *Globe-Democrat* which tried to make a big deal out of nothing. While he admitted that inner-city kids had come to the house, it was "not large amounts of inner-city children." He then vented his anger against "real estate men" who were making it an issue, and promised the property would be sold shortly.[98]

The Contemporary Mission forged on. On August 21, the group performed "The Jesus Revolution," a rock opera at Southern Illinois University, Edwardsville.

On October 27, Bishop Sarpong spoke out publicly. A headline read, "Misled, Bishop Says." Father Berkley responded by claiming that Cardinal Carberry was behind this. After all, both he and Bishop Sarpong knew each other, serving together on the Sacred Congregation for the Evangelization of the Peoples.

On February 18, 1972, in an "Inter Office Communication" memo, Bishop McNicholas suggested to Cardinal Carberry that he follow the advice of Cardinal Wright and take the matter to Cardinal Krol. He should point out that the five priests, validly ordained but not licitly ordained, are suspended ipso facto by Canon Law 2374 and should not be given faculties in any U. S. diocese. This Carberry did ten days later.

Eventually, the five moved to the East, performing a rock opera concert in New York City on November 17. It was entitled "Virgin" and was written by Father John O'Reilly. Attendance was dismal; just forty came.

Later, in 1978, Cardinal Carberry received a letter from Kenneth A. Graham, adjudicator for the State of Connecticut. He was inquiring about the connection between Contemporary Mission and the Archdiocese of Saint Louis. It seems they were claiming tax-exempt status while selling mail-order bath-oils. They had purchased a large home on a two-acre property.

The Cardinal replied on May 19, 1978, "They remained in Saint Louis for a period of time. But eventually left and took up residence in the State of Connecticut in the Diocese of Bridgeport. To my knowledge they have never returned to Saint Louis. They never had authorization to exercise their Priesthood in the Archdiocese of Saint Louis, and are not listed, nor were ever listed in the Catholic Directory under the Archdiocese of Saint Louis."[99]

The Contemporary Mission outreach was not the only experiment by Catholics in impoverished neighborhoods. In 1970 Brother I. Phil-

---

98 Contemporary Mission Students Interview with Julius Hunter. Channel 5 News, KSDTV. July 17, 1971. Cassette History/ 142023. Saint Louis Archdiocesan Archives.
99 Cardinal Carberry to Kenneth A. Graham. May 19, 1978. RG 06 Box 8, Folder 4. Archdiocese of Saint Louis Archives.

ip Matthews, former visitor of the Christian Brothers' Midwest province, floated the idea of a commune as an alternative to traditional religious life. He was appalled at the decline in vocations and declared, "Either we must return to our cloistered life or provide a situation that will encompass this new development in our community."[100]It would be based on the model of Israeli kibbutzim.

When Brother Philip was ignored by the District Council in October 1970 meeting, he published a letter to the editor in the *National Catholic Reporter* touting his idea. He argued that several young brothers were open to the idea of living in a Christian commune, and some former brothers were considering it, too. It might also attract single teachers, working at small salaries, with a way to conserve money.

The Christian Brothers had serious questions and objections to Brother Philip's commune idea. Would the members be considered part of the Saint Louis District? Would the commune be open to married couples or even families?

Brother Philip wore down his opposition, and finally, at the March 1971 District Council meeting, he got approval to set up an exploratory committee. A recruiting letter was sent to each member of the District, but the provincial, Brother John Joseph Johnston, added, "Membership on the committee does not necessarily imply a desire to become actively involved in such a commune."[101]

The committee met in the spring of 1972. It met only once. Showing the fragility of the project, eventually every member of the committee, except Brother Philip, left the congregation.

There were failed attempts to found communes in Omaha and Kansas City. It took until August 1973 to form one in Saint Louis. It consisted of one Christian Brother, who had previously been a critic of the project, a husband and wife with four pre-teen children, a religious sister on a leave of absence, a female graduate student, and a young woman beginning a teaching career at a North Saint Louis school. Without formal recognition from the Christian Brothers, despite its title Lasallian Society, it quietly died, and no attempt was made to revive it.

The June 13, 1971 Mass celebrating the ordination of the five Contemporary Mission priests was not the first time that the "low-

---

100 Michael J. Witt. *I. Phil: The Journey of a Twentieth Century Religious*. Winona: Saint Mary's Press. 1987. P. 167.
101 Ibid. P. 171.

er church," at Saint Francis Xavier made the news. On September 6, 1969, the pastor, Father Louis Hanlon, S. J. was replaced by Father J. Derrig. Father Hanlon had banned services in the lower church for "managerial, theological, liturgical and financial reasons." He feared that a parish within a parish was forming, as Father Patrick J. McAnany, S. J. was drawing as many as a thousand in the congregation, singing tunes like "Born Free" and "The Times They Are A Changing." It was not uncommon to have five and six concelebrants at the lower church Masses. Meanwhile, the congregation in the upper church declined, as did collection revenues.

Press reaction was loud. The *Saint Louis Post-Dispatch* headlines read, "Priest Who Banned Mod Mass Replaced." The *Globe-Democrat* rang out, "Guitar Mass OK'd at College Church." Cardinal Carberry urged the new pastor to find ways to bring together the two communities into a single parish again. But certain norms were to be observed.

Holy Communion was to be received only on the tongue. Both species could be received only by authorized celebrants. Readings were to be taken only from scripture. It had become common practice to take readings from secular sources. Most popular was the writing of Kahlil Gibran who toyed with the Bahá'i Faith, particularly in his book *The Prophet*. The Kiss of Peace was to be a simple greeting. A collection was to be taken up for the support of the parish at large, and pastoral letters from the Archbishop were to read at Mass. As often as not, the regulations were honored in the breach.

Back in Rome, Pope Paul triggered another explosion in the Church when the Congregation for the Doctrine of the Faith published *Personae Humanae*, which condemned sexual relations between people of the same sex as "disordered according to the objective moral order."[102] It did not condemn homosexuality, but rather the homosexual act. Regardless, it drew criticism from Father Robert Nugent, a Salvatorian priest, founder of New Ways Ministry. He was in the forefront of engaging with gay and lesbian Catholics, encouraging them to assert their place in the Church.

Nugent was encouraged by a 1973 decision of the American Medical Association which removed homosexuality from its list of mental and emotional disorders. *Personae Humanae* stood in stark contradiction to that statement.

---

102 *Personae Humanae*. Austin Flannery. *More Post-conciliar Documents*. P. 491.

The controversy had wide ramifications. In Boston, a group calling itself the North American Man Boy Love Association advocated homosexual relations between adult men and boys. The founders included a priest of the Archdiocese of Boston. A year earlier, in 1977, police made a raid on the Revere neighborhood, discovering an interrelated group of men who were buying sex with teenage boys. The raid and its findings were publicized in the media, but both the police and the press came under withering attack from gay rights advocates.

Dade County, Florida loosened its restrictions on homosexual behavior the same year as the Revere raid. A popular figure, Anita Bryant, former Miss Oklahoma, popular singer and spokesperson for the Florida Citrus Commission, became alarmed and organized the Save Our Children campaign. She took her efforts to television, appearing on the evangelical program *700 Club*. She saw a direct link between homosexuality and child abuse. Her efforts made her a darling of conservative Protestants and Catholics. They also made her the target of militant gays.

When Bryant's Save Our Children won a county referendum to tighten restrictions on homosexuality, 69 to 31, the homosexual community reacted by declaring, "Miami is our Selma!" equating their movement with the civil rights movement of the 1960's. Bryant won the Dade County referendum. Other referenda in Minnesota, Oregon, Kansas, and Washington State were losses. The referendum in California, forbidding the teaching of homosexuality in public schools, lost by a million votes.

The media turned against Anita Bryant, painting her followers as fanatics. There were massive pro-gay demonstrations in San Francisco, New Orleans, Chicago, New York, and Los Angeles. A nation-wide boycott of orange juice caused the Florida Citrus Commission to drop Bryant as their spokesperson. Her singing engagements were cancelled. Under enormous pressure, her marriage fell apart. All this pointed to an important lesson for those who would take public stands on controversial issues. "While it could be dangerous for a public figure to speak in favor of homosexual rights, it was positively lethal to oppose them."[103]

Organizing for political and social action was ubiquitous. A campaign was underway in the Episcopal Church to ordain women, and

---

103 David Fromm. *How We Got Here: The 70s*. New York: Basic Books. 2000 P. 207.

in 1974, eleven women were ordained in Philadelphia. Other liberal mainstream Protestant Churches followed suit.

Activists were on center stage in Detroit at the 1976 Call to Action conference. There were demands for radical changes in ecclesiastical structure, including the role of bishops and priests. The state of the nation and of the world was roundly criticized. Cardinal John Dearden of Detroit voiced support for the conference even as Archbishop Joseph Bernardin, president of the National Conference of Catholic Bishops, tried to control it by sending issues to a committee.

This was not a grass-roots movement of laity. Rather these were professional activists who had trained in seminars throughout the country before coming to Detroit. It was telling that most were white and middle-class. But for all their preparation, the three-day conference devolved into chaos. Cardinal John Krol of Philadelphia was shouted down in one committee which voted to ordain women. Even liberal Catholics became disillusioned by the happenings. Father Andrew Greeley called it "A ragtag assembly of kooks, crazies, flakes, militants, lesbians, homosexuals, ex-priests, incompetents, castrating witches, would-be messiahs, sickies and other assorted malcontents."[104]

Locally, more serious efforts were taken in the Archdiocese to address the political and social crises of the time. Parts of the city of Saint Louis were blighted. The population was declining, and the north part was becoming poorer and blacker. Mayor Alphonso Cervantes had definite plans to stem the tide. Cardinal John Joseph Carberry took a different tack.

Cervantes purchased the Spanish Pavilion from the New York World's Fair, dismantled it and reconstructed it downtown. The project cost six million dollars, and although the business community was skeptical, most went along with the mayor. To the pavilion was added a replica of the *Santa Maria*, the flagship of Christopher Columbus. The hope was to improve museums, convention centers, and other venues to attract tourists. Two months after it arrived, the *Santa Maria* broke free of its moorings during a violent storm and was smashed beyond repair on the pillars of a Mississippi bridge. The twenty-four thousand square-foot pavilion, dubbed the Cervantes

---

104 Trans. Steven Rendall and Albert Wimmer. Michael Zöller. *Washington and Rome: Catholicism in American Culture.* Notre Dame: University of Notre Dame Press. 1999. P. 203.

Center, failed to reinvigorate the neighborhood. More money, federal, state, and local, poured into projects which had little effect.

Meanwhile, Cardinal Carberry centered his efforts on education. In an October 1969 meeting with Catholic teachers, he brought up three important topics. He recognized that the resources available for Catholic education were limited and would have to be used wisely. He was concerned about the content of the curriculum, particularly religion classes. He speculated out loud, "Are any of our Catholic schools infected with any of the heresies that have achieved so wide a popular acceptance in our day?"[105]

Carberry's third concern was that of education for inner city children. As city parishes closed and Catholic parochial schools disappeared, would Catholic education be denied to these needy children?

For the present, the Archdiocese showed a solid commitment to the north side. Twenty-one parishes sponsored parochial schools. There were also two parish high schools, Saint Alphonsus "The Rock Church," and Saint Mark's, as well as a junior high, Providence, located at Saint Leo's. One hundred and thirty-three sisters taught in those schools, along with seventy lay teachers.

Five years later, the attrition was beginning to show. Just fifteen parishes continued schools, and only Saint Mark continued a high school, with six sisters teaching 170 students. By 1979 the vast majority of the student body was black and non-Catholic.

Some parishes consolidated into one central school. One example was Bishop Healy School located on the grounds of Most Blessed Sacrament on North Kingshighway. The school was sponsored by Blessed Sacrament, Visitation-Holy Ghost, and a new combined parish called BREM, Saints Barbara, Rose of Lima, Edward, and Mark. Two Christian Brothers had replaced the seven sisters who had served there through 1975. The lay faculty rose from nine to twelve. The student body stood at 311, with only around ten percent coming from the sponsoring parishes. The school, like most on the north side, was heavily subsidized by the Archdiocese.

In 1976 Cardinal Carberry tried to find an alternative funding for these schools. He began a program called "Fairness in Education." It would sponsor Amendment 7 which, if passed, would enable the

105 Monsignor Nicholas A. Schneider. *Changing Times: The Life of John Joseph Carberry, Cardinal Archbishop of Saint Louis, Pro-Life Pioneer, Mary's Troubadour*. Saint Louis: Independent Publishing Corporation. 2008. P. 101.

state legislature to provide funding for the handicapped, transportation for non-public pupils, and textbooks for the secular subjects in the curriculum. He noted that these services were already declared constitutional in several U. S. Supreme Court cases.

While attending the Eucharistic Congress in Philadelphia, Carberry got word that the August 3rd vote did not go well. Amendment 7 was handily defeated. Saint Louis and Kansas City voters were for the amendment, but they were overwhelmed by the negative rural vote. Catholic education, the one ray of hope to desperate children stuck in poverty, would continue to dwindle as resources were spread thinner and thinner.

If the Catholic Church was experiencing a hermeneutics of rupture with the decline in religious vocations, the closing of schools, dissent by leading theologians, and unauthorized adaptations in sacred liturgy, a hermeneutics of rupture in the secular realm came with the election results of 1976.

Out was the old order of *Realpolitik*, represented by Richard Nixon and Henry Kissinger and, to a lesser extent, Gerald Ford. The new president was Jimmy Carter, former governor of Georgia. He made known his intent to change the way America operated when he spoke before the graduating class of Notre Dame University in 1977. "We can no longer separate issues of war and peace from the new global question of justice, equality and human rights... We have reaffirmed America's commitment to human rights as a fundamental tenet of our foreign policy... We want the world to know that our nation stands for more than financial prosperity."

Carter also signaled a change within the Democratic Party, as he was among the more conservative candidates, along with Henry "Scoop" Jackson of Washington State. His nomination was a clear, though temporary, repudiation of the hard left which had served up George McGovern, and a massive defeat, in 1972. Being a proud Southern Baptist, Carter appealed to evangelicals, especially in the South. His background as a peanut farmer gave him an appeal as a rural, honest American, the polar opposite of the Imperial Presidency of Richard Nixon.

Regardless, Carter's party was anything but conservative. The party platform for 1976, for those who cared to read it, was more Mc-Govern than Carter. It defended abortion rights, called for the heavy restriction of handguns, criticized South African apartheid and emphasized human rights, while ignoring Soviet expansion. One pro-life candidate, Ellen McCormack, a New Yorker, was rebuffed at the convention, receiving only twenty-two votes.

Abortion rights was not a settled issue in either party at the time. Kristen Day, executive director of Democrats for Life of America, pointed out that even in 1978, one hundred of the two hundred ninety-two Democrats serving in the House of Representatives were pro-life.[106]

These pro-life Democrats joined most Republicans in 1976 to pass the Hyde amendment, named for its sponsor, Republican Henry Hyde of Illinois. The amendment to a Medicaid funding bill restricted federal funding of abortions. When asked about the Hyde amendment and the fact that it prevented abortions for the poor but not for those who could pay for it, Carter simply replied, "Well, as you know, there are many things in life that are not fair, that wealthy people can afford and poor people can't."[107]

This was not the ringing endorsement of the pro-life cause which many had expected out of Carter. Indeed, his presidency would disappoint many who had voted for him.

Besides abortion, another issue in the forefront during the Carter administration was the Equal Rights Amendment. The idea of a constitutional amendment assuming women's equal rights to men in all things, including divorce, property rights, employment, etc. dated back to a proposal by the Women's Party in 1923. It was passed in the House of Representatives in 1971 and the Senate in March 1972. It was immediately endorsed by President Nixon and sent to the states for ratification. Within a year, twenty-two states were on board, and eight others joined the next year. The ERA needed only eight more states, but then something happened.

The anti-ERA movement found a leader, Phyllis Schlafly. The mother of six, a devout Catholic, sporting a bouffant hairdo, dressing smartly, Schlafly proved to be a brilliant organizer and dynamic speaker. Her STOP ERA organization went to work on sympathetic states, her home state of Illinois, Oklahoma, Missouri, Arizona, Utah, and Nevada. She got Tennessee to rescind its vote, and Kentucky, Nebraska, and Idaho did likewise.

---

106 Ramesh Ponnuru. *The Party of Death*. Washington, D.C.: Regnery Publishing. 2006. P. 217.

107 Thomas Bornstelmann. *The 1970's: A New Global History from Civil Rights to Economic Inequality*. Princeton: Princeton University Press. 2012. 159.

Phyllis Schlafly tapped into evangelicals, Baptists, Mormons, and conservative Catholics. The ERA was causing a fissure in the New Deal coalition of Democrats and Catholics. While the Catholic hierarchy stood squarely with New Deal legislation and with civil rights advances, American bishops were concerned about the ramifications of the ERA. With *Roe v. Wade*, and now the ERA, Catholics found themselves for the first time in alliance with evangelical Protestants.

There were concerns that the Equal Rights Amendment would lead to unisex restrooms. Senator Sam Ervin of North Carolina worried that the ERA would open women to the military draft.

Phyllis Schlafly was not new to politics. She had defended the candidacy of Barry Goldwater in 1964 by writing *A Choice Not an Echo*, a book that would become a classic among conservatives.

She was also active in the Republican National Convention of 1976, chairing a subcommittee for the Platform Committee. It was an uphill fight to get pro-life wording on the national platform. The Chair of the Republican National Committee, Mary Louise Smith, was pro-abortion. The First Lady, Betty Ford, declared the same thing in a CBS 60 Minutes interview in August 1975. She even hinted that couples engaging in pre-marital sex might be less likely to divorce.

Schlafly steered her subcommittee to include a plank which would "protest the Supreme Court's intrusion into the family structure" and promised to work toward a constitutional amendment "to restore protection of the right to life for unborn children."[108] The plank passed thirteen-to-one and went on to win the approval of the Platform Committee and then the National Convention, making it the official position of the Republican Party.

Gerald Ford won the nomination in a hotly contested vote. Ronald Reagan, governor of California and darling of the conservatives, lost by a mere 117 votes out of 2,257 votes cast.

Phyllis Schlafly next found herself embroiled in a further feminist debate during the 1977 Houston National Women's Conference. This gathering grew out of the 1975 International Women's Year organized by the United Nations. This same year, Pope Paul VI declared a Holy Year dedicated to reconciliation and "the civilization of love."

Chief among the issues discussed in Houston was the need to get an extension for the ERA. Time would run out in 1979, and the

---

108 Phyllis Schlafly. *How the Republican Party Became Pro-Life*. Dunrobin Publishing. 2016. P. 9.

amendment would die otherwise. Schlafly and some twenty percent of the delegates were there to stop the effort. The atmosphere was openly hostile. These women were confronted by lesbians and signs were flourishing which read "Jesus was a homosexual" and "A woman needs a man like a fish needs a bicycle."[109]

When Betty Friedan, author of *The Feminist Mystique*, visited the Vatican, she refused to wear a mantilla or any head covering. She gave the pope an equality cross, the biological female sign, and later recalled, "The Pope said, again, that the Church had always upheld the dignity of women... He took my hand in both of his, as if he really meant his concern for women. He seemed much more human, somehow, than I had expected, with a warm and caring expression."[110]

In November 1978, President Carter signed legislation to extend the end date for the ERA. It helped him only a little with women voters. Many pro-choice women had been angered by his tepid acceptance of a Supreme Court ruling upholding the Hyde amendment.

It seemed as if no one was happy during the Carter years. Movies like *All the President's Men* sowed more seeds of distrust for the government. A popular film on the period was the 1976 film, *Network*. It depicted a news commentator, Howard Beale, who was fired. On his last program on the air, he went into a rant that stirred the nation, and he became a hit sensation, crying out, "I'm as mad as hell and I'm not going to take this anymore."

That one sentence spoke volumes about the mood of America.

Jobs were fleeing American cities. Chicago, Boston, Pittsburgh, and Philadelphia lost a third of their manufacturing jobs in just ten years. Saint Louis lost a net of 3,000 jobs during this time, but 165,000 good-paying manufacturing jobs were replaced by lower-waged services jobs.[111] The U. S. poverty rate in 1980, 12.4 percent, was the same as it had been in 1965. The War on Poverty was a bust.

When an electric blackout took place on the night of July 13, 1977, New York City erupted into a scene of chaos and mayhem. As much as the Ford administration failed in its Whip Inflation Now campaign, the Carter administration was even worse. By August 1978 inflation was running at thirteen percent, even while the unemployment rate

109 Philip Jenkins. *Decade of Nightmares: The End of the Sixties and the Making of Eighties America.* Oxford: Oxford University Press. 2006. P. 111.
110 Peter Hebblethwaite. *Paul VI: The First Modern Pope.* P. 639.
111 Colin Gordon. *Mapping Decline.* P. 17.

rose. The trade deficit with Japan, fueled by auto sales, went from $1.7 billion in 1975 to $11.6 billion in 1978.

On October 24, the president delivered a nationwide address on the economy. It was low-key and challenged critics who said, "that we have lost our ability to act as a nation rather than as a collection of special interests." But in denying that criticism, he gave credence to it.

In 1978, Title IX of the 1972 Education Act took effect, changing high school and college athletics, making sports available to girls and women. Until that time only seven percent of high school girls participated in sports, mainly cheerleading. By 1978, that number was as high as thirty-two percent and growing.

Whole groups of people felt under siege by their own government. As families sought ways to avoid court-ordered bussing, many enrolled in Christian schools, which, while usually white, offered a curriculum that was bible-based and grounded in traditional moral values. Many felt they had lost control of public schools, now in the hands of secular humanists. By 1975, enrollment in these Christian schools increased by 200%. The Carter administration saw these new schools as attempts at re-segregation.

In 1978 Internal Revenue Service commissioner, Jerome Kurtz, maneuvered to remove the tax- exempt status of these Christian schools. It ruled that any private school which did not enroll at least five percent minorities would be scrutinized. Evangelical Christians, normally a non-political entity, sprang into action. Over 125,000 letters arrived on Kurtz's desk, prompting him to ask for Secret Service security.

Also in 1978, the IRS revoked the tax-exempt status of Greenville, South Carolina Bob Jones University because its student conduct code forbad interracial dating. Five years later, the ruling was upheld by the Supreme Court.

The IRS move was a major political blunder. Reverend Jerry Falwell galvanized opposition into a movement he called the Moral Majority. He sought to reach out to conservative Catholics and orthodox Jews.

In 1979 the Southern Baptist Convention elected conservative pastor Adrian Rogers of Memphis as president. His engagement in civic affairs in the name of public morality showed clear signs that the largest Protestant body in America was shifting rightward and becoming politically active.

In the 70s two developments spelled change in the near future.

One was a landmark Supreme Court case while the other was a tax referendum.

In 1973, thirty-two-year-old Allan Paul Bakke applied for admission to the University of California Medical School Davis. He was rejected though his academic work and interviews were stellar. Sixteen percent of the places had been reserved for minority students, all of whom scored lower than Bakke. He filed suit that the university had used its affirmative action program to deny him equal protection under the law.

When the case reached the Supreme Court, it split the court asunder. Four justices saw no problem with the UC-Davis regulations, as they made up for past discrimination. Four others saw the regulations as violating the "color-blind" standard. The deciding vote went to Justice Lewis Powell, Jr. His ruling split hairs. He believed that academic institutions could use race and ethnicity as a factor in creating a diverse student body, but that it should be only one of several criteria.

Bakke was later admitted to the university, graduated, and was hired by the Mayo Clinic in Rochester, Minnesota as an anesthesiologist. But his case changed the way Americans thought of race and diversity. In a puzzling observation, Justice Harry Blackmun, speaking for the minority, wrote, "To get beyond racism, we must first take account of race. And in order to treat some persons equally, we must treat them differently."[112] The old notion of America being a melting pot gave way to images of a stew, where each element retained its uniqueness while creating of the whole something new.

The other change-maker in the late 1970s was a seventy-five-year-old Los Angeles businessman, Howard Jarvis.

Americans were being pressed financially as inflation raged out of control and wages stagnated. Through the late 1960s and all of the 1970s, social security payroll tax increased 800%. In California, new property taxes propelled the middle class into a tax protest. Governor Jerry Brown got over 200,000 letters denouncing the new tax, but he refused to budge.

Anti-tax groups gathered one-and-a-quarter million signatures to put Proposition 13 on the ballot. In June 1978 the proposition passed by a two-to-one margin, rolling back property taxes by 57%

---

112 Andrew Hartman. *A War for the Soul of America: A History of the Culture Wars.* Chicago: University of Chicago Press. 2015. P. 105.

and capping future increases to no more than 2% a year. Eighteen other states followed suit, squeezing the budgets of cities and states. On the federal level, Congress slashed capital gains taxes from 49% to 28% despite President Carter's objections.

The final years of the Carter administration were not pleasant. On March 28, 1979, word came that there was a partial melt-down at a nuclear power plant, Three Mile Island, near Harrisburg, Pennsylvania. While no one was injured, the accident was nerve-racking, as it took place only ten days after the release of the film *China Syndrome*, the story of a melt-down at a nuclear power plant!

At the same time, word came that Communist insurgents called the Sandinista National Liberation Front were challenging the dictator of Nicaragua. By July, they had succeeded, and Communist insurgents made gains in El Salvador and Guatemala. Carter looked weak and indecisive even as many resented his gifting of the Panama Canal to Panama in 1977.

Closer to home, in Greensboro, North Carolina a peaceful anti-racism demonstration turned deadly when Neo-Nazis and Ku Klux Klan members attacked, killing five and injuring eleven. Indeed, KKK membership tripled during the 1970s.

In the spring of 1979, President Carter was fishing on a lake near his hometown of Plains, Georgia. Out of the blue, a swamp rabbit began swimming toward his boat. Carter used his oar to turn back the rodent, but word got out and even his press secretary, Jody Powell, told the story, making light of the incident. Some denied the story, but the *Washington Post* printed the article along with photographs of the president slapping the waters around his boat to fend off the rabbit.

The incident went viral. A *Washington Post* headline screamed out, "President Attacked by Rabbit." Recounting the 1975 suspense film, *Jaws*, the incident was dubbed "Paws," making the Carter administration look all the more incompetent.

A low point in the Carter presidency came on July 15, 1979, in what was called "the malaise speech." Though the president never used that word, malaise was the tone of his address. Carter sought to assure the American people during a prolonged energy crisis but added "a crisis ... strikes at the very heart and soul and spirit of our national will. We can see this crisis in the growing doubt about the meaning of our own lives and in the loss of unity of purpose for our

Nation. The erosion of our confidence in the future is threatening to destroy the social and the political fabric of America."[113]

To fulfil a campaign promise, President Carter called for a national conference on the family. Three conferences would be held in different locations. The title was White House Conference on Families. The fact that families was plural was a concession to those who wanted to discuss non-traditional arrangements, setting off a storm among evangelicals, conservative Catholics, and orthodox Jews.

The first conference was held in Baltimore in June. President Carter attended and tried to sooth the warring sides. In the end, the traditionalists boycotted the gathering, allowing the radical side to endorse the ERA and abortion rights. Columnist James J. Kilpatrick observed that the conference was "stacked, packed, and rigged to produce these prepared affirmations. Fiasco No. 2 and Fiasco No. 3 will follow identical scripts."[114]

At the Minneapolis conference, the traditionalists did not bolt. Instead they hammered out resolutions which endorsed the ERA and approved of abortion but defined the family as excluding homosexual relations. While this was better than the Baltimore experience, it left many feeling empty, searching for a new home.

One final event sealed Carter's fate as a one-term president. On November 4, 1979, an Iranian mob attacked the U. S. embassy in Tehran and took sixty-six Americans hostage. It was the same day that the exiled Shah of Iran, Reza Pahlavi, arrived in New York for cancer treatment.

After over five months of captivity, and with the nightly news counting each day, President Carter authorized a secret rescue of the hostages. Dubbed *Operation Eagle Claw*, it was flawed from the beginning. To be politically sensitive, each branch of the military was represented. But as they had not worked together before, and followed different protocols, any slip-up could be disastrous. And that is what happened.

On the night of April 24, 1980 eight helicopters landed in a remote area called Desert One. Three of the vehicles were malfunctioning by that point. Then a sandstorm came up. As there would not be enough room for the rescuers and the released hostages, it was decided to

---

113 Philip Jenkins. *Decade of Nightmares*. P. 156
114 Bruce J. Schulman. *The Seventies: The Great Shift in American Culture, Society, and Politics*. Da Capo Press. 2001. P. 188.

abort the mission. Preparing to withdraw, one helicopter slammed into a transport plane, setting the fuel on fire and killing eight servicemen. The next day, the Iranian government showed pictures of the charred wreckage, and Ayatollah Khomeini announced that the mission had been thwarted by "the angels of Allah."

The year 1980 was an election year, and nothing seemed to go Carter's way. Former Watergate special prosecutor, Leon Jaworski, formed a committee called Democrats for Reagan. Just months earlier he had called Ronald Reagan an extremist. When asked about the incongruity of forming a committee to support Reagan, Jaworski quipped, "I would rather have a competent extremist than an incompetent moderate."[115]

The hermeneutics of rupture which was on display during the 1970s would give way to a hermeneutics of continuity, as Americans and Catholics grew weary of their ever-changing nation and their ever-changing Church.

---

115 David Frum. *How We Got Here: The 70's*. P. 344.

CBS filmed the Montfort Fathers for an episode of Look Up and Live, which aired on KMOX-TV in 1967. Here, they stand outside one of the Triple City Mission houses at 3507 N. Market Street. The three clergy, left to right, are Br. Bob Cassidy, Br. Joe Coviello, and Br. John O'Reilly. The CBS equipment crew, from left to right, are assistant cameraman Bob Mingalone, cameraman Bob Clemens, and soundman Larry Gianneschi. Photographer Richard Finke. From the Archdiocese of St. Louis Archives.

Singing Montfort Brothers pose with their 1966 vinyl release of "There'll Come a Day." In front, left to right, are Joe Valentine, Paul Baker, and Jack Coyne. Don Middendorf and John O'Reilly stand in back. Photographer Richard Finke. From the Archdiocese of St. Louis Archives.

Through its Parish Social Ministry program, Catholic Charities worked with the
BREM Catholic Social Ministry program, a coordinated effort by Sts. Barbara,
Rose, Edward, and Mark parishes. Pictured here are members of the project's
executive committee, from left to right: Loretta Miller, Julius Fuse, Joseph Stegall,
and Father Richard Creason. Photograph circa 1980. From the Archdiocese of
St. Louis Archives.

Science class at Bishop Healy School in 1973. Photographer Richard Finke. From
the Archdiocese of St. Louis Archives.

The teaching Sisters of Divine Providence stand with students at Mount Providence Boarding School in 1983. Photographer Richard Finke. From the Archdiocese of St. Louis Archives.

Chapter Five

THE HERMENEUTICS OF CONTINUITY

On March 16, 1978, the head of the Christian Democratic Party in Italy and a friend of Pope Paul VI, Aldo Moro, was kidnapped. His five personal bodyguards were brutally murdered in the abduction. Two days later the Red Brigade, an Italian terrorist organization, took responsibility for the action and threatened to hold a mock trial.

Paul prayed for his release. The Italian government refused to negotiate with the terrorists. Paul wrote an open letter to the terrorists, asking for Moro's release. The government again refused to negotiate, to release captured Red Brigade members in an exchange, but gave a green light to Vatican efforts to seek to ransom Moro.

On May 9th the body of Moro was discovered in the trunk of a car, his body full of bullet wounds. Pope Paul was heart-broken and retired to his chapel in silence. Thereafter, Paul's health deteriorated. He had repaired to Castelgandolfo. On August 6th, he could not get out of bed to celebrate the feast of the Transfiguration..

From his bed, the pope attended the evening Mass, as a door was opened between his bedroom and the chapel. He received communion. Later that night, as life was slipping from him, Pope Paul VI began repeating over and over the first words of the Lord's Prayer. At nine-thirty that ceased, and Cardinal Villot began reciting the prayers for the dying. Paul's eyes opened slightly, and he turned to the cardinal to whisper, "Grazie," and then dozed off again, dying at 9:41 that night.

Cardinal Joseph Carberry hurried to Rome for the funeral of one pope and the election of another. It was his second trip in 1978. He had been there in June to make a report during his "ad limina" visit, a once every five-year trek to the Holy See.

More than 75,000 attended the outdoor funeral Mass. Cardinal Carberry joined the other 103 Cardinals in concelebrating the liturgy. Over 100 delegations came from the corners of the earth, twice as many as attended the funeral of Pope John XXIII, no doubt as a tribute to the man who traveled so much during his pontificate.

The funeral was not without its political aspects. Over 7,000 police, sharpshooters, and plainclothes men provided security. Overhead, helicopters hovered searching for signs of terrorists. An organization

called Civilta Cristiana placed signs around Saint Peter's Square calling for the cardinals to elect a doctrinaire pope. In contrast, the Italian Communist Party headquarters flew its flag at half-staff to honor
the pope who had opened dialogue with the Left.

Soon after the funeral, the cardinals assembled in the Sistine
Chapel to begin deliberation in conclave. Carberry joined eight other
Americans. Cardinal John Wright, a Bostonian serving as Prefect for
the Congregation for Clergy, was unable to attend, having undergone
surgery. Three other Americans were over eighty, ineligible to vote.
Of the 111 voting cardinals, 102 were experiencing a conclave for the
first time.

Cardinal Carberry received a particular honor at this conclave. He
was selected, along with Hoffner of Cologne and Guerri of Rome, to
oversee the physical arrangements in the Sistine Chapel as well as
the modest apartments for the cardinals.

On Saturday, August 26, after a concelebrated Mass and a light
breakfast, the cardinals assembled in the Sistine Chapel. Each received a few ballots which came in two parts. The upper part of the
ballot had printed on it, "Eligo in summam pontificem," I choose as
supreme pontiff... The lower part was blank, allowing for a name to
be written in.

After the first ballot was filled in, the cardinals proceeded in strict
rank to place their ballot on a plate and then to drop it in a large
chalice. One scrutineer opened the cards, and he passed them to the
second scrutineer who then passed the cards to the third scrutineer
who read the name out loud. A tally was kept.

On the first ballot, Cardinal Giuseppe Siri received more votes
than anyone else. He was the Archbishop of Genoa, a traditionalist
voice at the Second Vatican Council. Next to him was Cardinal Albino
Luciani, the Patriarch of Venice. Seven other cardinals had received
votes. The whole process took only one hour.

The conclave prepared for a second vote in the afternoon. The
third scrutineer kept calling out Luciani who eventually scored ninety
of the one hundred and eleven votes. Cardinal Carberry had stashed
away ten chocolate bars to see him through the ordeal of electing a
pope. The conclave was over so fast that he only had time to eat two
of them!

Cardinal Villot approached Cardinal Luciani and asked him if he
accepted the election. He did. Then Villot asked by what name he
should be called. Luciani replied "John Paul."

As the new pope was led off to be fitted for a white cassock, there was confusion in Saint Peter's Square. Smoke began to billow out of the stack, at first white, then black, then mixed. Someone shouted out "Grigio!" gray, and everyone laughed.

Finally at 7:15 that evening, the doors swung open, and a cross-bearer appeared. Behind him was Cardinal Pericle Felici who announced the election of Luciani. One observer, Father Andrew Greeley, speculated, "Luciani has more pastoral experience than any other of the leading candidates. He may have persuaded the non-Italian cardinals that he will make major changes in the way the papacy is run... He will probably not be an impressive pope; he does not seem to be the kind who will restore the impact of papal leadership in religion and morality around the world."[116]

Cardinal Carberry returned to Saint Louis, only to be brought back to Rome just one month later. Pope John Paul had a bad heart, but there were wild speculations. Some say the pope was depressed after his election. Some say the curia had not cooperated with him and kept him at arm's length. There was a rumor that he had offered Venice to a bishop who refused him. Some saw a sinister plot and assassination.

As the cardinals gathered for a second conclave within five weeks of the first, health was on everyone's mind. One American wag quipped, "Anyone who wants the job had better buy himself a sunlamp."[117] Besides good health, it was considered essential that the next pope had to speak Italian, whether he was Italian or not. Chicago's National Opinion Research Center, led by Father Andrew Greeley, used its computer model to find the candidate who most closely mirrored John Paul I and determined that it was the archbishop of Naples, Corrado Ursi. The prediction amused the Italians as they travelled to Rome.

A better assessment came from the analysis by the Spanish journal *Blanco y Negro*. They broke the College of Cardinals into four camps. The largest, forty-two of them, were called the "Moderate" *Montiniani*. These wanted to maintain the reforms of Pope Paul VI. John L. Allen, Jr. called these the moderate Salt of the Earth party. These were mainly European and Latin American integralists, that is, those who wanted to order politics and society according to the light of Catho-

---

116 Andrew M. Greeley. *The Making of the Popes 1978.* Kansas City: Andrews and McMeel, Inc. 1979. P. 157.
117 Ibid. P. 187.

lic teachings. In the United States, these integralists fought for family values, opposed abortion, and wanted a voucher system in which tax dollars would follow the child rather than a school district, even if that child went to a private or parochial school. Certainly, Cardinal Carberry fit into this party and represented the sentiment of most of his Archdiocese.

"Reform" *Montiniani* were concerned with social systems which bred injustice and inequality. For them, human rights were paramount, and they sought alliances with secular and non-Catholic bodies to bring about change. For these cardinals, the poverty of the Third World was an essential focus. One author counted twenty-seven cardinals in this camp.[118]

Allen called this wing The Reform Party, as it also looked inward to the reforms of the Second Vatican Council to emphasize collegiality, reform of the Roman Curia, diversity, and experimentation. Allen identified Austrian Cardinal Franz König as the chief spokesman for this wing, but at ninety-six he could not vote in the conclave. Others in this camp would later include German Cardinals Karl Lehmann (made a cardinal in 2001) and Walter Kasper (2001), Italian Carlo Maria Martini (1983), Belgian Godfried Danneels (1983), and American Roger Mahony (1991). Many of these were members of the so-called Saint Galen Group which met regularly in Switzerland to plot out progressive changes in the Church.

A third group identified by *Blanco y Negro* was some fourteen cardinals from the Third World. The journal called them "radical evangelicals," and while they agreed with some of the "Reform" *Montiniani*, they kept their distance on other issues.

The fourth party identified was made up of conservatives, twenty-eight of them. *Blanco y Negro* identified them as members of the Curia, a few Latin Americans, and interestingly, Karol Wojtyła of Krakow. These critiqued the modern trends of secularism and relativism, pointing to the Netherlands as the western country most progressive, with legalized abortion, euthanasia, and weak laws regarding drug abuse and prostitution. Allen called these the Border Patrol cardinals. Their chief concern was for doctrinal clarity and restoring the sacredness of the liturgy. The chief spokesman for the conservatives was the once-liberal Cardinal Joseph Ratzinger.

---

118 Francis A. Burkle-Young. *Passing the Keys: Modern Cardinals, Conclaves, and the Election of the Next Pope.* Lanham: Madison Books. 1999. P. 269.

Even so, the most prominent among the conservatives was Cardinal Guiseppi Siri, Cardinal-Archbishop of Genoa. He had been a traditionalist voice at the Council and had lost to Luciani in the previous conclave by only a few votes. He was seen as the chief rival to Cardinal Giovanni Benelli, recently named Archbishop of Florence, the man to whom most of the Italian progressives were rallying.

Before going into conclave, Cardinal Siri gave a taped interview in which he shot himself in the foot. Not only did he hint that he would reverse most of the post-Council changes if elected pope, but bit at the interviewer, commenting, "I do not understand how you could ask such a stupid question. If you really want an answer, you will have to sit down and be quiet for three hours."[119]

In the first vote, Siri scored only twenty-three votes, just one ahead of Benelli. The rest of the progressive *Montiniani* split among three other candidates.

Karol Wojtyła got five votes. This caught the attention of Cardinals König of Vienna and John Joseph Krol of Philadelphia. By the third vote, Wojtyła scored a distant second behind Benelli, 65 to 24. Before the seventh vote, the cardinal from Krakow was visited by the Polish primate, Cardinal Wyzynski, and Cardinal König. They convinced him that he would probably be named pope in the next round or two of votes.

Wojtyła suggested he would take the title "Stanislaus" to which König responded, "You will be called John Paul II!" The response was, "Let us see what happens in the afternoon."[120] On the eighth ballot, Wojtyła scored 97 to Benelli's 14. The Catholic Church had not had a non-Italian pope since the Dutchman Pope Adrian VI was elected in 1522.

The announcement of the new pope caused quite a stir in Saint Peter's Square. At first, the crowd was silent, trying to understand what had just happened. One woman turned to someone standing next to her and asked who the pope was. The other responded "Di Polonia," but she thought he said, "Di Bologna." He had to correct her "No, Signora, di Polonia. Un Polacco."

John Paul II immediately won over the throng. He spoke Italian, adding "I do not know whether I can explain myself well in your – no, our – Italian language. If I make a mistake you will correct me."[121]

---

119 Francis A. Burkle-Young. *Passing the Keys*. P. 276.
120 Ibid. P. 285.
121 Ibid. P. 287.

The early days of the reign of Pope John Paul II heralded considerable change for the leadership of the Catholic Church. John Paul had been a bishop for twenty years and Archbishop of Krakow, often under difficult circumstances, for fourteen years. He had no use for curial handlers and made that known when he rejected several models for a coat-of-arms for his papacy. He caused eyebrows to be raised when he designed his own, a large M beneath a cross with the motto, "Totus Tuus," totally yours, referring to the Blessed Virgin Mary.

With an ever-watchful eye to his homeland, the Pope found out that the state-controlled Polish TV would cover three hours of his inaugural Mass. It was assumed that the Mass would be shorter than that, giving a communist spokesman time to make a commentary on the event. John Paul spoiled the strategy by staging the Mass to be exactly three hours long. The last image Polish viewers saw was the Polish pope giving a papal blessing to the thousands gathered in Saint Peter's Square!

Less than five months into his papacy, John Paul II had to fill the most important post of secretary of state. Cardinal Jean Villot, seventy-three years old, died of bronchial pneumonia. His replacement came as something of a surprise: Archbishop Agostino Casaroli, the architect of Pope Paul's *Ostpolitik*, a détente with the communist governments in Eastern Europe. He had been roundly criticized by then-Cardinal Wojtyła. Since the secretariat of state was always led by a cardinal, John Paul called for a consistory on June 30, 1979 and raised fourteen prelates to the honor.

The appointment of Casaroli as secretary of state did not calm the anxieties of the Soviet Politburo. Yuri Andropov, chief of the KGB, commissioned a study to assess the danger a Polish pope might cause to the Warsaw Pact. Poland was essential to the military alliance. It was the link between Russia and East Germany. Andropov became convinced that the election of Wojtyła was the work of a German and American plot hatched by Jimmy Carter's national security adviser, Zbigniew Brzeziński.

John Paul's papacy could destabilize more countries than Poland. Deeply Catholic Lithuania could be swayed by this pope who spoke Lithuanian. The Greek Catholic Church in western Ukraine was another flashpoint in the Warsaw Pact.

Before events developed in Eastern Europe, John Paul II took center stage at the General Assembly of CELAM, the influential Latin American bishops' conference. It was set in the beautiful city of Puebla de Los Angeles, an hour's drive southeast of Mexico City.

The visit was fraught with danger. Previously, the pope announced that he wished to celebrate Christmas in Bethlehem but was persuaded to stay in Rome instead. While Mexico was an intensely Catholic country, the government was not. Throughout the twentieth century, the Church had been ignored and even persecuted. President José López Portillo was persuaded by his mother and sisters to allow the pope to come, though he would be treated as a private citizen, requiring a visa.

On January 26, 1979, Pope John Paul II landed in Mexico City. President Portillo decided at the last minute to greet him at the airport in an unofficial capacity. The pope first knelt and kissed the tarmac, a gesture he repeated over and over on papal visits. More than a million people came to cheer him on, joined by hundreds of cassock-clad priests and habited nuns, defying a government ban on wearing religious garb in public.

The pope visited the shrine of Our Lady of Guadalupe and celebrated Mass with 300,000 Mexicans. He paid a visit to President Portillo's mother and sisters and blessed their little chapel at the presidential palace. On January 28, he addressed the CELAM assembly and denounced what was called "liberation theology," so popular among radical elements of the Latin American Church.

While the documents of the Second Vatican Council called for freedom and peace and respect for human dignity, these radicals called for base communities to struggle against rightist governments and, if necessary, even the hierarchy. Some called for armed resistance.

John Paul began by applauding the assembled bishops and cardinals. They came to Puebla "not as a symposium of experts, not as a parliament of politicians, not as a congress of scientists or technologists, but as ...pastors of the Church." Their chief role was as shepherds of souls, spreading "the Truth concerning Jesus Christ."[122]

He then went on to describe Marxism as incompatible with Christianity, for Marxism was basically wrong about the human person. The address was well-received.

The next day, John Paul celebrated Mass for a half-million Indians who had come from Oaxaca and Chiapas. His homily spoke of human rights and human dignity. He said he wanted to be their voice and

---

122 George Weigel. *Witness to Hope: The Biography of Pope John Paul II*. New York: HarperCollins. 2001. P. 284.

added, "The depressed rural world, the worker who with his sweat waters also his affliction, cannot wait any longer for full and effective recognition of his dignity, which is not inferior to that of any other social sector. He has a right to be respected and not to be deprived, with maneuvers which are sometimes tantamount to real spoliation, of little that he has... He has the right to real help – which is not charity or crumbs of justice – in order that he may have access to the development that his dignity as a man and as a son of God deserves."[123]

The Mexico visit was an overwhelming success.

His sentiments expressed in Mexico were developed more completely in the Pope's first encyclical *Redemptor Hominis,* the Redeemer of Mankind. This was truly a statement worthy of the Second Vatican Council.

Gaudium et Spes, the Pastoral Constitution on the Church in the Modern World, to which Wojtyła had made major contributions, began, "The joy and hope, the grief and anguish of the men of our time, especially of those who are poor or afflicted in any way, are the joy and hope, the grief and anguish of the followers of Christ as well." *Redemptor Hominis* ratified that solidarity between mankind and the Church. The Incarnation tells us about God, but it also tells us important things about humankind. It shows a special dignity bestowed by the Creator and the Redeemer. And chief among the human rights which flow from that dignity is religious freedom.

This leitmotiv would be played out in full force in the pope's first visit to Poland. The trip was publicized as a pilgrimage to celebrate the nine hundredth anniversary of the martyrdom of Saint Stanislaus, bishop of Krakow.

On June 2, 1979, the pope landed in Warsaw and kissed the ground before being greeted by President Henryk Jabłoński and Cardinal Wyszyński. His motorcade traveled to downtown Warsaw amid crowds in the hundreds of thousands. Going first to the Cathedral of Saint John, he reminded the masses of the failed 1944 Warsaw Uprising where the Polish Home Army fought hand-to-hand against the German occupiers. Perhaps it was a subtle reminder also that the Soviet Red Army had sat outside of Warsaw until the slaughter was complete before attacking the Wehrmacht. Sometimes gestures need no words to make a statement.

---

123 Ibid. P.286.

While the Polish Pope thanked the communist government for letting him visit his fatherland, he pressed the theme of human dignity and the proper role of the state to protect that dignity.

The next day, the pope flew by helicopter to the site of Poland's first martyr, Saint Adalbert in Gniezno. More than a million Poles attended the outdoor Mass there.

On June 4th to the 6th, Pope John Paul visited the shrine of Our Lady of Częstochowa, the Black Madonna. Again, the crowd numbered a million. Later he met with the Polish hierarchy at Jasna Góra monastery and emphasized the need to remain united to preserve the Catholic Church in a communist country.

The next stop was his beloved Krakow. He arrived on the evening of June 6th. As he was driven in an open car into the city, the place went wild. Night after night, crowds of young people serenaded the pope under the window of his bedroom. They begged him for a speech. Instead, he joked with them. "It's bad enough being the Pope in Rome. It would be far worse being the Pope in Krakow, spending all the time standing at this window with no time to sleep and no time to think." Then he added, "You are asking for a word or two, so here they are – Good night!"[124]

On June 7 John Paul visited the death camp of Auschwitz-Birkenau. He walked on foot to Block 11, Cell 18, the site of Maximilian Kolbe's death. He was accompanied by West German Cardinal Hermann Volk and embraced Franzciszek Gajowniczek, the man whose life was spared when Kolbe took his place.

John Paul attended the Polish Episcopal Synod in Wawel Cathedral in Krakow. As his Polish trip was coming to an end, he was driven back to his residence but was clearly emotional, covering his face with his hands, crying.

The Polish government refused to give John Paul permission to visit Nowa Huta, the scene of a severe struggle while Wojtyła was archbishop of Krakow. So, as his helicopter flew over the church, he leaned out and dropped flowers onto the Ark Church.

On his last day in Poland, Pope John Paul II celebrated an outdoor Mass in Krakow for an estimated two to three million people, the largest assembly in Polish history. In all, thirteen million Poles, one out of every three of his countrymen, had seen the Polish pope in per-

---

124 George Weigel. *Witness to Hope.* P. 313.

son. Those nine days had changed Poland forever. It was something the Polish Communist party and the Soviet Politburo would have to grapple with, but in the end, they would come up short.

The Polish visit would catch the attention of the new American president.

Later in June, the pope named Archbishop Pio Laghi as apostolic delegate to the United States. He replaced Archbishop Jean Jadot, whose six-year tenure in that office resulted in a considerable disruption of the Church in America. Laghi was given the instruction to renew the sacredness of the celebration of sacraments, to promote religious education, to oversee the appointment of doctrinal bishops, and to review religious life in monasteries, convents, and seminaries.[125]

After a pilgrimage to Brazil, John Paul turned his attention to West Germany. Here was the very fault-line of the post-conciliar Church. Theologians, once allies and confreres, were now at odds over the reforms. Mass attendance was in free-fall. German society, except in pockets in Bavaria or in the Mosel Valley, had become thoroughly secularized. What could this Polish pope say to these Germans?

As with the Polish bishops, John Paul encouraged the Germans to seek unity, to defend marriage, and to foster a proper appreciation for human sexuality. Though many pundits had predicted a papal disaster in West Germany, John Paul's visit was a success.

A first-hand witness to the German trip was Cardinal Carberry, selected by the U. S. bishops to represent them on the trip. Leaving the meeting of the NCCB, Carberry flew to Frankfurt to join the pope. Not speaking German, he was given an interpreter and struggled to keep up with the pope's schedule.

John Paul made fifty-two addresses during his four-day visit to seven German cities. Carberry found himself frustrated by the schedule, as the pope traveled by helicopter, but his entourage traveled by bus. The weather was miserable, and the Saint Louis cardinal wore several sweaters at once, all under a heavy raincoat.

Cardinal Carberry had met Karol Wojtyła in September 1969 when he visited Saint Louis. They met again after the conclave which elected him pope, as each of the cardinals gave the new pope their obedience. Now they met again, three times during the German trip. The first was at the bishops' dinner at Fulda, then passing each other

---

125 George Weigel. *Witness to Hope.* P.379.

at an outdoor Mass in Munich in which 300,000 attended, and finally at the departure from Frankfurt am Main airport.

In an interview with Antoni Gronowicz, John Paul was asked about his familiarity with American prelates. He replied, "Certainly, I think I met them all. There was Joseph Francis Dearden from Detroit with his droopy chin, and in St. Louis, John J. Cardinal Carberry. He and I were nominated to the Cardinals College at the same time."[126]

Cardinal Carberry had been available for the German visit because his resignation had been accepted by the Vatican the previous July when he turned seventy-five.

His last years had been active. In April 1978, the Missionaries of Charity arrived in Saint Louis, accompanied by their foundress, Mother Teresa of Calcutta. A local Chapter of her International Association of Co-Workers of Mother Teresa had already been in the city a year.

Another initiative came with the renovation of the shrine of Saint Joseph on Biddle Street. While several other downtown historic churches had been demolished, a lay group calling themselves the Shrine of Saint Joseph Friends put up a vigorous defense for the building. They were aided by a seventy-nine-year-old archdiocesan priest, Father Edward Filipiak, who refused retirement and moved into the dilapidated rectory in 1979. The archdiocese retained ownership of the buildings, but the Friends began to make repairs, forming a 501(c)(3) non-profit organization.

Father Filipiak lived a simple life, never owned a car, and was happy to try to save this historic church at which a Vatican-certified miracle had occurred. Often, his Sunday Mass was attended by only ten or twelve people. He was undeterred and once said he would die for that church.

On September 30, 1979, the priest did not come down to say Sunday Mass. The parish secretary went to find him, only to discover that he had been murdered. His hands and feet were tied with electrical cords, and a pillow had been placed over his mouth to keep him from screaming. Though he had been beaten, with his face bruised and ribs broken, it was the pillow which caused his death, as he had suffocated.

Police were tipped off that loot stolen from the rectory was being sold in the Cochran housing complex. Three sixteen-year-old

---

126 Antoni Gronowicz. *God's Broker: The Life of Pope John Paul II as Told in His Own Words*. Richardson & Snyder. 1984. P. 315.

youths were arrested and tried. It seems that they had broken into the church to steal altar wine but went on a rampage when the priest, on crutches, discovered them.

The boys were tried as adults, and each was given a life sentence with a chance for parole. Three days into prison life, one of the boys committed suicide. The other two learned a trade while in prison and were released after serving fifteen years. The ringleader, Andrew Daugherty, founded his own construction company, turned religious, married, and on April 28, 2012, he was shot to death as he stood in the doorway of his mother's home. His murderer was never caught.

Father Filipiak's death brought notoriety to the Shrine of Saint Joseph. Businesses began donating to its restoration. Unions sent members to work on the building gratis. In the end, the shrine was completely restored to its glory, and a plaque honoring Father Filipiak was posted. It read, "He always said he would die for this church, and he did."

Even in retirement, Cardinal Carberry remained active. He preached at the funeral Mass for Father Filipiak. In January 1980, he sent out a pastoral letter regarding *Roe v. Wade* to be read at all Masses and spoke for the Archdiocesan Pro-Life Committee at an event at Our Lady of Sorrows. His successor, John L. May, native Chicagoan and bishop of Mobile, was installed on March 25, 1980.

Archbishop May allowed Cardinal Carberry to remain in the archbishop's residence in West County. The new archbishop took up residence in Cardinal Glennon's home on Lindell near the cathedral. The cardinal was given an office at the Round House, the chancery, along with a secretary. He did not intend to be forgotten.

When the National Conference of Catholic Bishops sent out a survey regarding holy days of obligation, Carberry did not receive one. He promptly wrote the General Secretary to get a copy. Besides representing the American bishops during the papal visit to West Germany, he wrote the General Secretary of the NCCB supporting a movement to consecrate the world to the Immaculate Heart of Mary.

In 1982 Carberry spoke out vigorously against using the name "American Church" when referring to the Catholic Church in America. He used the November meeting of the Administrative Committee to express his views and, in October, sent the bishops of the NCCB a letter outlining his objections. Later, Carberry sent copies of his letter to Pope John Paul II and to the Benedictine Cardinal Mayer, secretary for the Sacred Congregation for Religious and Secular Institutes. The cardinal replied expressing agreement with Cardinal Carberry.

Cardinal Carberry continued to be an active member of the Sacred Congregation for the Evangelization of Peoples until he turned eighty and received word from the secretary of state that he needed to resign that post also.

Meanwhile, Pope John Paul II kept up his own vigorous schedule. He had felt that the way *Humanae Vitae* had been presented did not serve the message well. He wanted to approach human sexuality in a strong and positive way. Previously, John Paul had written about this in a rather difficult book, *Love and Responsibility*. His prose was philosophically dense, so he began to use his Wednesday general audiences to present a theology of the body. Eventually, he spoke on the topic at 129 audiences, and these talks inspired a whole new approach to human sexuality which caught on with theologians, and pastors, and laity.

At the same time, the pope censured Father Hans Küng, professor of theology at the University of Tübingen. Often edgy in his theology, Küng now was questioning the very idea of infallibility and caught the attention of the Congregation for the Doctrine of the Faith. Instead of excommunicating Küng, Pope John Paul said he was no longer a professor of Catholic theology. Küng continued to teach at Tübingen, but his international influence began to wane.

Far more serious than dealing with a dissident German theologian, John Paul was in a monumental struggle with the Soviet Union. The June pilgrimage to Poland had caused alarm in the Politburo. During the visit, the Soviets put pressure on Stanisłas Kania, head of the Communist party's administrative department and chief liaison to the Church in Poland, to get the pope to temper his remarks. It had some effect. By the time John Paul arrived at Częstochowa, his emphasis was clearly spiritual and no longer overtly political.

Regardless, the KGB developed a plan to thwart Vatican initiatives in Eastern Europe. This included better use of media in the Soviet bloc countries as well as finding allies in the west among anti-Wojtyła Catholics and peace movement advocates. Propaganda efforts would attempt to show that the Polish pope was harmful to the Catholic Church, and the Soviet Academy of Sciences would counter Catholic intelligentsia with better arguments regarding scientific atheism.

While John Paul was unaware of this KGB plan, he was launching his own initiatives. In March 1980, he hosted the Synod of Greek Catholic bishops, addressing the importance of Ukrainian religious freedom and arranging the transition of Church leadership to a younger prelate.

One month later, he turned his attention to the Church in Hungary, trying to energize the episcopacy there.

These efforts supported work already done: a visit to Ireland in September 1979, a major address to the United Nations, and a visit to the United States as part of the same trip. He visited Patriarch Dimitrios I in Turkey and visited Africa and France in 1980, along with his visit to West Germany.

In the summer of 1980, Roman and Muscovite eyes became fixed on Poland. The 1979 papal visit had stirred deep currents in Poland. This became obvious when groups calling themselves Workers Defense Committees began to show themselves. These committees were made up of laborers and intellectuals encouraged by Catholic bishops, and they emphasized human rights inspired by their Polish pope.

All along the Baltic coast, major cities began to experience general strikes. On one day, more than 180 factories were idled. Vacationing at Castelgandolfo, Pope John Paul received reports on the activities from his secretary, Father Stanisłas Dziwisz, and watched news reports on television. The workers were calling for an independent labor union and gathered under the leadership of an unemployed electrician, Lech Wałęsa. They had closed down the Lenin Shipyard in Gdańsk.

On August 20, the bishop of Gdańsk presented Wałęsa and other union leaders with medals from the pope. The Soviets put pressure on the Polish Communists to declare martial law and to squash the trade unions before events became irreversible. First Secretary Edward Gierek appealed to elderly Cardinal Stephan Wyszyński who spoke to the nation on national television, calling for compromise and calm. Lech Wałęsa ignored him. The Cardinal was openly criticized by some Polish bishops. Even the pope was dismayed.

Only on August 31 was the crisis averted. The government agreed to recognize an independent union, a first in Communist history. But this upset Communist governments in East Germany, Hungary, Czechoslovakia, and Russia. This might set a precedent which would be replicated in other Communist countries. The Poles ignored them.

They could do no less. Solidarity, the labor union, had ten million members. The Polish Communist party had only two and a half million members, and by now, seven hundred thousand of these were also members of Solidarity.

On December 16, three large crosses were erected in the Lenin Shipyard in memory of workers who had been slain ten years earlier. Even the president of the Polish Republic attended the ceremonies. A telegram from the pope was read, thanking God that the crisis had been ended without bloodshed.

Also watching these events with great interest was Zbigniew Brzeziński, national security adviser to President Jimmy Carter. He had struck up a friendship with Wojtyła in 1976 and was in constant correspondence with him. Though Carter had lost the 1980 election, Brzeziński remained engaged in the developments in Poland. He gave a phone call to the pope to warn him that the Soviets were considering "Warsaw Pact maneuvers" like the ones that crushed Hungary in 1956 and Czechoslovakia in 1968. Both Carter and president-elect Ronald Reagan sent strongly worded warnings to Moscow not to intervene.

Ronald Reagan was very comfortable around working-class people and Catholics. His father was Catholic, his mother Protestant. Though his vice-president, George Herbert Walker Bush, was a blue-blood, Reagan gathered around him many advisers who were devout Catholics. Bill Casey, his 1980 campaign manager and transition team member, became director of the Central Intelligence Agency and assumed the role Brzeziński had had during the Carter administration, that of a liaison between the White House and the Vatican. He was a daily communicant.

Another daily communicant was General Vernon Walters, Reagan's ambassador-at-large until 1985, when he was named U. S. Ambassador to the United Nations. Secretary of State Alexander Haig had a brother, Father Francis Haig, a Jesuit who served as a university president. Richard Allen, a Notre Dame graduate, served the president as a national security adviser. Judge William Clark had been executive secretary to Reagan when he was governor of California. He served as national security adviser and encouraged Reagan to be tough on the Soviet Union, believing it was fragile, and he thought that with the help of the Catholic Church, it could be brought down.

Casey and Clark often dropped by the residence of Archbishop Pio Laghi, the papal nuncio to the United States, for coffee and conversation. Allen, Casey, and Reagan met frequently with Cardinal John Krol of Philadelphia, a close associate of Pope John Paul II. During the Second Vatican Council, the two developed a deep friendship, conversing in Polish.

Reagan ratcheted up the policies begun under Carter. He encouraged the AFL-CIO to filter money to Solidarity, and Social Democratic parties in Western Europe did the same. Radio Free Europe and Voice of America kept Eastern Europeans up-to-date about events developing in Poland.

An early sign of future cooperation between the White House and the Vatican came when President Reagan reaffirmed the Mexico City Policy, in which U. S. foreign aid would be suspended to any country which used the funding for abortions. That caught the attention of John Paul II.

On March 27, 1981 millions of Polish workers staged a four-hour general strike. On March 30, Reagan spoke to a building trades workers' meeting and commented, "Their courage reminds us not only of the precious liberty that is ours to nourish and protect, but of the spirit in each of us, everywhere. The Polish workers stand as sentinels on behalf of universal human principles and they remind us that on this good Earth, the people will always prevail."[127]

Leaving the building, President Reagan was shot in the chest by John Hinckley Jr. The bullet came within an inch of his heart and aorta. The Pope, hearing of the assassination attempt, stopped what he was doing and prayed for the president's recovery. The doctors attending President Reagan said his survival was nothing short of a miracle.

That same day, Polish farmers demanded and received recognition from the government to establish Rural Solidarity. Leonid Brezhnev was furious with the Polish government, whom he sarcastically called "our fraternal comrades." But the general secretary had his hands tied. He was bogged down in the invasion of Afghanistan. The social and economic conditions of the Soviet Union were deteriorating under its command economy. While Reagan was recovering in the hospital, Prime Minister Margaret Thatcher rallied Western leaders to warn the Soviets not to intervene in Poland. A rumor floated around the Vatican that the Pope would fly to Poland and stand in

---

127 Carl Bernstein and Marco Politi. *His Holiness: John Paul II and the Hidden History of Our Times.* New York: Doubleday. 1996. P. 275.

front of Soviet tanks to rally the Polish people. While there was no validity to the rumor, it kept the Soviets thinking.

General Wojciech Jaruzelski, prime minister of the Communist government, was summoned to Russia in a secret meeting. It went on for six hours, as two members of the Soviet politburo harangued him. He was in a terrible position. His party was the weakest of the Eastern Bloc countries and yet had to deal with the strongest Church in Eastern Europe.

Jaruzelski returned to Poland only to learn that Russian soldiers who spoke Polish had been garrisoned near the border.

On May 13, death nearly visited Pope John Paul II. After the Wednesday audience, the Pope was driven in an open-air car around Saint Peter's Square. A shot rang out, and Mehmet Ali Agca was tackled by a nun standing next to him. Others disarmed and held him for the police. He had fired a second shot which wounded two American visitors.

The pope was rushed to Gemelli Clinic, an eight-minute drive. Arrangements were made that all the elevators would be on the ground floor to receive him. As in the case of Ronald Reagan, the bullet came within an inch of a vital artery. The attempted assassination occurred on the feast of Our Lady of Fatima, and the Pope, on the first anniversary of the shooting, went to Fatima to present the bullet to her image.

Was the attempted assassination a KGB plot or the actions of an Islamic extremist? While CIA director William Casey thought it was the former and tried to prove it, it remains an unsolved mystery. Agca showed no signs of Islamic fanaticism, and it would have been counter-productive for the Soviets to have killed this Polish pope. Though he stirred up nationalist feelings in Poland, he also used his influence to favor the moderates in Solidarity and to temper the hotheads who wanted an out-and-out confrontation with the government.

Meanwhile, America was recovering from its 1970s wounds even as President Reagan was recovering from his assassination attempt.

During his debates with President Carter in the 1980 campaign, Reagan asked the nation, "Are you better off than you were four years ago? Is it easier for you to go and buy things in the stores than it was four years ago? Is there more or less unemployment in the country than there was four years ago? Is America as respected throughout the world as it was? Do you feel that our security is as safe? That we're as strong as we were four years ago?" Later he added, in a bit of Reagan humor, "Recession is when your neighbor loses his job. Depression is when you lose yours, and recovery is when Jimmy Carter loses his."[128]

Reaganomics was a combination of tax cuts, defense spending increases, and deregulation. Its philosophical underpinning was that government was too big, and individual freedom would unleash the creative spirits of the nation. He passed the Economic Recovery Tax Act of 1981 with the help of conservative southern Democrats nicknamed the boll weevils.

Even as some of America's most important industries, steel and automobiles, were collapsing, others were coming into their own. In defense and aerospace, in financial services and information, in computers and fiber-optic technology, ground-breaking advances created new jobs and new opportunities. The inflation rate, which ran as high as 13% in Carter's last year plummeted to 4% by 1982. The Reagan presidency was a grand experiment in free market capitalism.

People began talking about the Austrian school of economics and began reading Friedrich Hayek again. Hayek had fled Austria but became disillusioned with his new home, Great Britain, which was socializing at a rapid pace. Hayek called for limited government and maximum freedom of economic activity for the individual. He saw considerable notoriety during the last decades of his life. Margaret Thatcher applied his principles when she became Prime Minister of Great Britain. That was 1974, the same year Hayek won the Nobel Prize for economics. Three years later Milton Friedman won it also.

Friedman taught economics at the University of Chicago. He became an adviser to both Reagan and Thatcher, encouraging free enterprise. He was a monetarist, paying close attention to the money supply, arguing that inflation came when too much money chased after too few goods. His book *Capitalism and Freedom* sold a half million copies. The Chicago school, which shared many of the characteristics of the Austrian school, led to the creation of "supply-side economics," popularized by Arthur Laffer of the Massachusetts Institute of Technology. The idea was that lowering tax rates would spur the economy and thus create new wealth, which when taxed, would offset the loss of tax revenues due to the cut in taxes. All this was music to Reagan's ears.

---

128 Philip Jenkins. *Decade of Nightmares: The End of the Sixties and the Making of Eighties America.* Oxford: Oxford University Press. 2006. P. 173.

It might have worked if it had not been for the massive increase in defense spending. Instead, the deficit soared, and income inequality became more apparent.

Ronald Reagan brought an agenda of limited government and lower taxes, rebuilding the military, personal responsibility, and respect for life and family values. The 1980 Republican convention which nominated him had a strong pro-life platform which did not come about by accident. When the subcommittee responsible for writing the pro-life statement ended its work around 6 PM, Phyllis Schlafly realized that pro-abortion figures in the Republican Party would get to work trying to persuade members of the committee to change their vote when the committee resumed the next morning.

She contacted a wealthy Texan, Jimmy Lyons, and persuaded him to invite the whole committee to the Detroit Athletic Club for dinner. There they partied until midnight, thwarting efforts from pro-choice Senator John Tower to make phone calls to the members.

Schlafly and other pro-life Republicans were so successful that co-chairman Mary Dent Crisp, a pro-choicer, bolted from the Party to join John Anderson's third-party bid for the presidency.

The 1980 election saw many pro-life Democrats support a Republican candidate. Family values also brought many more. Carter's White House Conference on Families had set off alarm bells. Evangelicals opened Christian schools, only to see them besieged by federal agencies like the IRS. There was a stirring on the Right as evangelicals abandoned the Democratic Party and made alliances with pro-life Catholics who also found a home for the first time in the Republican Party.

There was a sea-change underway in the late 1970's, a reaction to *Roe v. Wade*, militant gay rights advocates, and radical feminists. This became evident in the Southern Baptist Convention between 1976 and 1979. In 1976 the convention was safely in the hands of "moderates" who were doctrinally conservative, but who kept away from political and cultural issues.

In 1979 the SBC elected Adrian Rogers as executive officer. Rogers was pastor of a Memphis mega-church. He held deeply conservative convictions. He believed in full engagement in social and political affairs. He steered the platform to condemn abortion, homosexuality, pornography, and even human evolution. The SBC specifically withdrew support from the Equal Rights Amendment and criticized Carter's White House Conference on Families.

In June 1980 Tim LaHaye, author of the *Left Behind* series, wrote, "Is Jimmy Carter a Christian who is naïve about humanism and respects humanists more fully than he does Christians? Or is he a humanist who masqueraded as a Christian to get elected and then showed his contempt for the 60 million 'born again' by excluding them from his government?"[129]

As evangelicals turned to the Republican Party, they brought with them powerful tools of influence. Many had large television and radio ministries which reached millions of viewers and listeners. Viewership was estimated at twenty million. Others had publishing houses for books and journals. Some had universities and bible schools. Many led mega-churches like Adrian Rogers with a congregation of eleven thousand members.

But the arrival of the evangelicals meant that the Republican Party became beholden to them. As pro-choice Republicans found out in the case of Phyllis Schlafly, they would be a minority within their own party.

At his inauguration, Ronald Reagan signaled to the Religious Right that his administration would not be indifferent to religion. The bible he used, the King James Version, was opened to 2 Chronicles 7:14. That verse had not been used in an inauguration since Dwight D. Eisenhower. It assured the people of God that if they "pray and seek my face and turn from their wicked ways; then will I forgive their sins and will heal their land." During the campaign, Reagan had spoken of America as a city on a hill. His biblical references were reassuring, as were some of his early appointments. C. Everett Koop, an abortion foe, became the surgeon general. James Watt, an evangelical, was named Secretary of the Interior. Other lower positions went to evangelicals in the Department of Health and Human Services and in the Department of Education.

In this new *Kulturkampf*, schools would be a key battleground. A 1983 article in the *Humanist* exclaimed, "The classroom must and will become an arena of conflict between the old and the new – between the rotting corpse of Christianity, together with all its adjacent

---

129 Daniel K. Williams. *God's Own Party: The Making of the Christian Right*. Oxford: Oxford University Press. 2012. P. 158.

evils and misery, and the new faith of humanism."[130]

Many Christians did not believe they were part of a rotting corpse, and such rhetoric energized millions. In Saint Louis, Mae Duggan, a little dynamo of action, wife of the *Globe-Democrat* Editor-in-Chief Martin Duggan, had founded Citizens for Educational Freedom in 1959. While the organization was best known for advocating vouchers which would follow the child, rather than tax dollars going to public school districts, other goals included recognizing that the family had primary responsibility for raising the children, and that minority children should get a chance to attend schools which supported their family's cultural and religious values.

Ronald Reagan admired the work of Mae Duggan and the CEF and nominated his Secretary of Education Terrel Bell based on the same principles. Speaking to a 1982 "family forum," Bell said, "Education is a family matter. The parent is the foremost teacher, the home is the most influential classroom, and the school should exist to support the home."[131]

Some families took Bell's words to their logical conclusion and pulled their children out of school entirely. By 1985, over a quarter of a million households homeschooled their children. The numbers would have been much higher, but homeschooling required permission by local school boards, and conservative families were refused at a higher rate than other families.

Though devout Catholics like Mae Duggan and Phyllis Schlafly were not inclined to read Vatican documents, their lives were very much in keeping with the vision of Pope John Paul II.

Having met with 232 bishops and 60 lay "auditors" from October 1 to 30, in 1978, the Pope wrote the apostolic exhortation *Christifideles Laici*, Christ's Faithful Lay People. He used the passage in Matthew's gospel, 20: 3-4, when the owner of a vineyard finds men idle in the marketplace and tells them, "You too go into the vineyard." The Second Vatican Council, and now *Christifideles Laici*, called on the laity to take an active role in their secular lives to live out the gospel and their baptismal vows.

He wrote, "A new state of affairs today both in the Church and in social, economic, political and cultural life, calls with a particular ur-

130 Andrew Hartman. *A War for the Soul of America.* Chicago: University of Chicago Press. 2016. P. 202.
131 Ibid. P. 205.

gency for the action of the lay faithful. If lack of commitment is always unacceptable, the present time renders it even more so. *It is not permissible for anyone to remain idle."*[132]

This theme was echoed repeatedly by the pope. Celebrating the thousandth anniversary of the baptism of Prince Vladimir and Princess Olga of Kievan Rus', John Paul issued *Euntes in Mundum Universum*, Going Out into the Whole World. When the pope was not permitted to join in the celebrations in Moscow, he succeeded by this exhortation to make the anniversary not a Russian affair, but an event for the whole Christian world.

With his sixth encyclical, *Redemptoris Mater*, Mother of the Redeemer, the Pope showed the primacy of the Marian Church over the Petrine Church, showing that the clerical Church was to serve the universal Church, the Church of the laity, rather than the other way around. The encyclical hinted at a kind of papal feminism which was made specific the next year in *Mulieris Dignitatem*, a letter regarding the dignity of women.

Attention returned to Poland when, on August 16, miners in Upper Silesia struck, and sympathy strikes popped up all over the country. The government had to rely on Lech Wałęsa to bring an end to the strikes. Three months earlier, the Hungarian Communist party turned to a reformer, eventually announcing that opposition parties would be permitted. In Czechoslovakia, the communist party made changes, trying to maintain its iron grip on the nation.

On February 6, 1989, the communist party entered talks with Solidarity in what was called the Polish Roundtable. Elections for parliament would take place in June. The vote would be free, and Solidarity could field a range of candidates. This was a major concession by the communists, but they got an agreement from Solidarity that if they won the election, they would reelect General Jaruzelski as president.

Solidarity won every open seat in the lower house and ninety-nine of the one hundred seats in the Senate. True to its promise, Solidarity voted Jaruzelski back into office, but cleverly by only one vote. When the president was unable to name his choice for prime minister, he turned to Solidarity's Tadeusz Mazowiecki. For the first time, a Warsaw Pact government was led by a non-communist.

As unthinkable as this Polish development was, another unthink-

---

132 *Christifideles Laici*. Paragraph 3.

able event happened in Rome on December 1, 1989. A black limousine made its way to the Cortile San Damaso. When it stopped, Mikhail Gorbachev, the president of the Soviet Union emerged along with his wife, Raisa. They were greeted by the prefect of the pontifical household and Swiss Guards. The two were met by Pope John Paul II.

Gorbachev and the pope withdrew to the papal library while Raisa was given a private tour of the Sistine Chapel. The audience went on for an hour-and-a-half, with John Paul emphasizing that the Cold War should not be seen as a win/lose proposition, but rather a chance for a European coming together, "from the Urals to the Atlantic."

When Raisa joined them, her husband said, "Raisa Maximovna, I have the honor to introduce the highest moral authority on earth... and he's Slavic, like us!"[133]

The two gave statements to the press, and a promise was made to open diplomatic relations between the Vatican and the Soviet Union. But this meeting of the pope and the president of the Soviet Union was about more than diplomacy. It meant the defeat of the strongest force for scientific atheism and a turning point in which freedom of conscience would spread to the rest of Eastern Europe.

Not bad work for a man who had been on the throne of Saint Peter just over ten years! The story of how this happened is bound up in the lives of two key players, Pope John Paul II and President Ronald Reagan, as well as other essential participants in these world-changing events, Mikhail Gorbachev, Polish General Wojciech Jaruzelski, Prime Minister Margaret Thatcher, Chancellor Helmut Kohl, and an unemployed electrician named Lech Walesa.

The new archbishop of Saint Louis, John Lawrence May, would not be a side-lined spectator in all these events. While leading his archdiocese, he would engage particularly the two principals of this story, the pope and the president of the United States.

---

133 George Weigel. *Witness to Hope: The Biography of Pope John Paul II*. P. 602.

In 1969, then-Cardinal Karol Wojtyla, Archbishop of Krakow, Poland, toured the United States and Canada to thank Catholics for their assistance to the Polish people in the wake of World War II. Wojtyla of course became Pope John Paul II in 1978, and was canonized in 2014. Here, Fr. John J. Lang, associate pastor at the Old Cathedral, guides Cardinal Wojtyla around St. Louis. Photographer Richard Finke. From the Archdiocese of St. Louis Archives.

This young woman stood outside the Cathedral Basilica, where over 2,000 young people went to watch Pope John Paul II live in Los Angeles on September 15, 1987. Photographer Richard Finke. From the Archdiocese of St. Louis Archives.

From the packed pews of the Cathedral Basilica, over 2,000 young people watched the Pope speak live from Los Angeles. Called the "Papal Space Bridge," the teleconferenced event was displayed on a 20-foot long screen on the altar of the Cathedral. Despite the jubilant atmosphere, one priest remarked that a pin could have been heard to drop in the huge church while the Pope spoke. Photographer Richard Finke, 1987. From the Archdiocese of St. Louis Archives.

During her visit in 1982, Mother Teresa of Calcutta stands with the Missionaries of Charity at the Cathedral Basilica during her visit to St. Louis on June 8, 1982. More than 3,500 people crowded into the Cathedral to see Mother Teresa talk about abortion, which she called "The greatest destroyer of peace." St. Teresa of Calcutta was canonized in 2016. Photographer Richard Finke. From the Archdiocese of St. Louis Archives.

In 1988, Msgr. Salvatore Polizzi chauffeured Mother Teresa during her visit. This photograph was taken outside St. Teresa parish, where Mother Teresa attended Mass and spoke. When asked about his experience, Msgr. Polizzi said, "To think that I had a Saint in my car, and shook hands with her – what an honor!" Photograph from the personal collection of Msgr. Salvatore Polizzi.

The Missionaries of Charity participated in the Rosary March in North County that was held in conjunction with the 20th anniversary of the St. Louis Division of the World Apostolate of Fatima, or the Blue Army, 1995. Photographer Richard Finke. From the Archdiocese of St. Louis Archives.

The Friends of the Shrine of St. Joseph set up a fundraiser for restoration efforts in 1983 in the church piazza. Photographer Richard Finke. From the Archdiocese of St. Louis Archives.

Father Edward Stanislaus Filipiak grew up in the Polish parish of St. Casimir in North St. Louis City. He was ordained at Kenrick Seminary by Archbishop John J. Glennon on June 10, 1923. From the Archdiocese of St. Louis Archives.

On Sept. 29, 1979, Father Edward S. Filipiak was murdered in his bedroom at the Shrine of St. Joseph. His mission in life was to preserve the church in a deteriorating and unsafe neighborhood. The room where he died has been kept as it was when he left it. His cassock, crutches, manual typewriter and adding machine are in their original positions. Photographer Lisa Johnston, 2014. Courtesy of St. Louis Review.

Chapter Six

QUID PUTAS? JOHN L. MAY'S EARLY YEARS

On March 25, 1980, the Archdiocese of Saint Louis received its sixth archbishop, John Lawrence May, bishop of Mobile, Alabama, and a native Chicagoan.

Saint Louis had given several bishops to Chicago. James Oliver Van de Velde, S. J. had been a professor at Saint Louis University before serving as Chicago's second bishop, 1849 to 1853. He was followed by Anthony O'Regan, rector of the theological seminary in Carondolet, 1854 to 1858. Next, James Duggan who had served as interim seminary rector in Saint Louis, became bishop of Chicago from 1859 to 1880. He was succeeded by Saint Louisan, Patrick A. Feehan, who became the first archbishop of Chicago, 1880 to 1902.

The last Saint Louisan to serve as archbishop of Chicago was the former secretary and chancellor for Cardinal John Joseph Glennon, Cardinal John Cody, 1965 to 1982. When May was made a bishop in June 1967, Cardinal Cody was his main consecrator. He served as auxiliary bishop under Cody just two years before being made bishop of Mobile. During that time, Bishop May served as pastor of Christ the King Parish.

Bishop May served as bishop of Mobile for ten years. These were years of growth and development. Ten new parishes were created, and twelve new churches were consecrated. He opened two schools as well as parish centers. May showed his interest in the elderly by creating a low-income home for them, Cathedral apartments. Providence Hospital received an intensive care unit. He established an Office of Youth Ministries, a Pastoral Council, and a Board of Education.

While many of these apostolates already existed in Saint Louis, May brought some Mobile ideas with him, including a retirement program for lay employees as well as health insurance. His enthusiasm for the pro-life cause and for the permanent diaconate would build on the foundations which had been laid under Cardinal Carberry.

May's style of episcopal leadership can be summed up in an internal memo he regularly sent to his priests. The May 20, 1988 memo headlined, "Quid Putas?" asked what they thought about the first draft of "Partners in the Mystery of Redemption." It was the upcoming pastoral letter of the U. S. bishops on the role of women in the Church and in society.[134]

John Lawrence May served as archbishop of Saint Louis throughout the 1980s. He resigned on December 9, 1992, battling brain cancer. During that decade, two key figures dominated his Church and his nation, Pope John Paul II and President Ronald Reagan.

The pope had only been on the Throne of Peter fifteen months when he named May to head the Church in Saint Louis. But those months had been packed with activity. Besides visits to Italian shrines and parishes, John Paul intervened to prevent a war between Argentina and Chile. He had made a historic visit to Mexico and reset the debate regarding liberation theology. He had promulgated his first encyclical, *Redemptor Hominis*. He had made a pilgrimage to Poland which would set in motion extraordinary changes behind the Iron Curtain. He would visit Ireland, the first pope to do so, and the United States.

The path to prominence for Ronald Reagan, "a rendezvous with destiny," as he was fond of saying, was even more extraordinary. As a teenager growing up in Dixon, Illinois, Dutch Reagan was a lifeguard on the Rock River, where he saved seventy-seven lives. He graduated from little Eureka College, did a stint as a radio sports announcer, and moved to California in search of fame and fortune in the movie industry. Between 1937 and 1964, Reagan appeared in, or starred in fifty-three films.

Ronald Reagan got involved in politics as president of the Screen Actors Guild in 1946, having served in World War II stateside, due to his poor eyesight. In this position he learned two valuable lessons. One was the art of negotiation taught to him the hard way, dealing with the movie moguls of Hollywood. The other was an acute distaste for communists.

The movie industry was infiltrated by communists. Screenwriter John Howard Lawson summed up their position when he wrote, "As a writer do not try to write an entire Communist picture, try to get five minutes of Communist doctrine, five minutes of the party line in every script that you write... It is your duty to further the class struggle by your performance."[135]

---

134 Notanda. Volume IX #3. May 20, 1988. "Quid Putas?" RG I H 6 "Notanda Blue Notes." Archives of the Archdiocese of Saint Louis.

135 John Howard Lawson, *Film in the Battle of Ideas*, 1953, as cited in Paul Kengor, *The Crusader: Ronald Reagan and the Fall of Communism*. New York: Regan. 2006. P. 15.

When Reagan tried to thwart the influence of the communists, he was physically threatened, and it was implied that acid would be thrown on his face to ruin his acting career. In October 1947, he testified before the House Un-American Activities Committee, along with other actors and producers.

Reagan took his anti-communist activities further by founding the Crusade for Freedom, encouraging other members of the Screen Actors Guild to join General Lucius Clay in seeking ways to liberate Eastern European countries from the grip of the Soviet Union. This became a passion for Reagan, even after he left Hollywood and became a spokesman for the General Electric Corporation and host of the television weekly, *GE Theater*.

On one broadcast, February 3, 1957, after a Hungarian rebellion had been crushed by Soviet tanks, Reagan ended the program with the words, "Ladies and gentlemen, about 160,000 Hungarian refugees have reached safety in Austria. More are expected to come. These people need food, clothing, medicine, and shelter. You can help."[136]

As Ronald Reagan entered the 1960s, his anti-communism was joined with a revulsion against big government and the creation of what he called a "dependency class." It was a major re-thinking of his previous admiration of Franklin Delano Roosevelt and the New Deal. In the end, he left the Democratic Party and became a Republican. Previously, his wife, actress Jane Wyman, left him, citing his obsession with politics. In 1952, he married Nancy Davis.

While Reagan produced and narrated a documentary entitled "Truth about Communism" in 1963, it was a speech he gave supporting Barry Goldwater's 1964 candidacy for president of the United States which got people's attention. Called "Time for Choosing," it was a powerful half-hour argument against communism, creeping socialism, and big government. It emphasized the importance of individual liberty and self-reliance. It soon became known as "The Speech," one of the few bright spots in the Goldwater campaign. The GOP lost the Electoral College, 486 to 52.

It was later revealed that Goldwater's opponent, President Lyndon Baines Johnson, had used the CIA to plant a spy in the Goldwater campaign to smuggle out speeches so that a group housed in the West Wing of the White House called the "Anti-campaign" could send

---

136 Paul Kengor, *The Crusader.* P. 24.

out operatives before and after Goldwater spoke to drown his message. What was more disturbing was an FBI wiretap of the Goldwater campaign.[137]

When Ronald Reagan returned to California, he had won a following. Supporters wanted him to run for governor, though he had never sought political office before and would be facing a seasoned politician, Governor Pat Brown. In November 1966 Reagan beat Brown by a million votes, 400,000 of them coming from crossover Democrats. He won reelection in 1970, having taken California out of the red and creating a surplus.

Reagan watched in silent disgust as national politics collapsed due to the protracted war in Vietnam, the Watergate scandal, and the lackluster presidency of Gerald Ford. He felt America was on the wrong track, squashing individual initiatives at home and compromising with communists abroad. He was vehemently against the détente policies of Richard Nixon and Secretary of State Henry Kissinger. When Ford continued those policies and when petty insults came out of the Ford White House, Reagan had had enough. He challenged the incumbent of his own Party to a race for the 1976 nomination.

The primary campaign of 1976 was spirited and mean-spirited. Besides foreign and domestic policy issues, social issues were highlighted. While Ford favored overturning *Roe v. Wade*, and returning the issue of abortion to the states, Reagan favored a constitutional amendment, guaranteeing the right to life for the unborn. Worse, First Lady Betty Ford granted an interview in which she bragged about abortion rights.

Every state was hotly contested, with Reagan losing close fights one after another until North Carolina. Then a string of states went his way: Texas, Indiana, Georgia, Alabama, and more. At the convention in the Cow Palace in Kansas City, the defection of the Mississippi delegation took the wind out of the Reagan sails. He ended up with 1,070 Reagan delegates to Ford's 1,187.

That could have been the end of the story. After all, Ronald Reagan was already sixty-five years old. But Gerald Ford wanted to mend fences, so he beckoned Reagan and his wife to join him on the stage. When asked to speak, Reagan gave an impromptu address which riveted the convention. Many felt they had nominated the wrong man.

---

137 Lee Edwards. "The FBI Spied for LBJ's Campaign." *The Wall Street Journal*. May 25, 2018. P. A15.

Four years later, they corrected their mistake.

After winning the 1980 election, Ronald Reagan implemented policies sharply different from his predecessors, both Republican and Democrat. Domestically, he introduced Reaganomics, a combination of supply-side economics, Laffer-curve tax policy, and deregulation. The Federal Reserve, first under Paul Volcker and then Alan Greenspan, regulated the national money supply to control inflation.

Working with a Democratic majority in Congress, Reagan crafted a reduction in federal income tax by twenty-five percent over three years. The top marginal rate went from seventy percent to twenty-eight percent.

Reaganomics worked wonders on the American economy. Inflation dropped from 13.5% in 1980 to 4.32% four years later. Unemployment dipped from 8% in 1980 to 7.2% four years later. Despite a recession in the process, attitudes had improved. America seemed to be going in the right direction.

But not everyone participated. For Catholics on the northside of Saint Louis, a crisis was brewing. Too many old churches, rectories, and schools dotted the landscape, and most of the old parishioners had left years before. These institutions were inherited by tiny African American communities which could not fill the churches or support the schools.

Adding to this dilemma, housing stock disintegrated. Crime raged. Nuclear families suffered. Public schools were in a free-fall. Regardless, hope and initiative were not in short supply.

The Archdiocesan Human Rights Office established an education committee in 1981 to study the situation on the northside. A proposal was made in 1982 that the parishes of "the Urban Apostolate" band together, using the staff of the Human Rights Office as a resource.

Parishes and organizations were not waiting for a top-down solution, though. As early as 1976, Catholic parishes, Protestant congregations, businesses, and individuals in North Saint Louis and on the near-south side, sought a way to come together and make a difference. They hired Tom Gaudette of Chicago, trained by Saul Alinsky, to come and help them organize. He set up the Saint Louis Association of Community Organizations (SLACO).

The churches were vital to the foundation of SLACO. Without churches, the organization lacked strength and credibility. But if the churches did not join in the effort, they would lack grassroots commitment and leadership. SLACO needed churches, and churches needed SLACO.

The SLACO staff all lived in the city, so they had a stake in the outcome. They were led by Sister Mary Dolan, O.P. from 1980 until her retirement in 1991. The accomplishments were remarkable. SLACO sought to board up or demolish abandoned houses by lobbying the Board of Aldermen. They sponsored community clean-up campaigns. Working with the Charles F. Vatterott Company, they developed low and moderate-income housing. By 1991, sixty single family homes were built as well as sixty-three apartment complexes. They were called Fairfax Court, Etzel Place Apartments, and Buder Place Homes.

Mustard Seed Revolving Loan Fund was set up in 1989 in cooperation with Citicorp Mortgage. SLACO sponsored housing tours and lobbied the Missouri legislature to regulate speculation at sheriff's auctions. They acted as a watchdog on proposed developments in the Greater Pruitt-Igoe area and Gate District around Lafayette Square. The goal was to prevent the poor and elderly residents from being forced to leave their homes.

When General Motors closed its large plant on the corner of Union and Natural Bridge, SLACO fought a proposal to put in a dog racetrack. Instead, what developed was the Union-70 Industrial Park which provided jobs for nearby residents.

SLACO received a $200,000 grant to revitalize Dr. Martin Luther King Boulevard. They lobbied for tighter liquor licensing in the city. They worked with the Police Mobile Reserve Unit to target high crime areas.

An undated SLACO progress report ended with the words of a Negro spiritual which expressed hope: "We've come this far by faith. Leaning on the Lord. Trusting in his holy Word. He's never failed us yet. Oh...can't turn around. We've come this far by faith."[138]

Reagan introduced increases in defense spending and sharp anti-communist rhetoric in foreign affairs. Defense spending was increased by twenty-five percent with the goal of a 600-ship Navy, the construction of the MX missile, and over five hundred Pershing II medium-range missiles. Money was put into research and development, leading to the Tomahawk cruise missile and the Patriot anti-missile missile.

---

138 Report. File History. O 4 E "North City Deanery Records: 1986 – 2005." Archives of the Archdiocese of Saint Louis.

These measures pleased many, but they shocked others. U. S. bishops voiced concern.

Archbishop May wrote a column recognizing the electoral victory as well as popularity of the new president, but he went on to say, "There are things that worry us (the bishops) in Washington today. The tone of heightened belligerency, the increased commitment to arming not just ourselves but even more of the world, the barely discernible efforts for bilateral disarmament – all this is ominous."[139]

Ronald Reagan believed the Soviet Union was not only illegitimate, but weak. His whole foreign policy was to deny the Soviets the hard currency they needed to prop up their regime and to drive them into bankruptcy. Along the way, he wanted to reverse the Yalta agreement which had handed over Eastern Europe to the Red Army.

This was more than politics for Reagan. He held this goal of freeing Eastern Europe, of driving the Soviet Union out of existence, and using America's restored might for good throughout the world. After the failed assassination attempt, the president met with Cardinal Terrance Cooke of New York who told him, "The hand of God was upon you." Reagan responded, "I know. I have decided that whatever time I have left is for Him."[140]

Reagan's aggressive posture put him at odds with Western allies who had negotiated a $35 billion deal with the Soviets to bring natural gas from Siberia to western Europe. Two 3,600-mile pipelines were to be built. Reagan pushed relentlessly against this.

Later, he scored a partial victory regarding the pipelines which he vehemently opposed. In May 1983 a G-7 economic summit was held at the College of William and Mary in Williamsburg, Virginia. Representatives from Britain, France, West Germany, Japan, Italy, and Canada joined the American delegation of Ronald Reagan, Secretary of State George Schultz, and Secretary of Treasury Donald Regan. It was agreed that only one pipeline would be built and that the other countries would restrict the sale of high-tech products to Russia. General Secretary Yuri Andropov was livid.[141]

It was well-known that Soviet spies were stealing technological secrets from America. Reagan wanted to thwart this. He put together a tiny, secret unit to design flawed equipment, defective plans

---

139 Archbishop John L. May. October 16, 1981. *With Pen and Staff.* Ligouri: Ligouri Publications. 1992. P. 305.
140 Paul Kengor. *The Crusader.* P. 76.
141 Ibid. P. 185.

for chemical plants, and software with bugs in them. The Soviets would steal these items, and then bad things would happen. In one dramatic event, faulty software worked for a while, regulating pressure on the pipeline in Siberia. But at one point, the software called for a massive increase in pressure which caused a huge explosion in 1982. No one was injured, but progress on building the pipeline was delayed considerably.[142]

While other nations were hesitant to engage in economic warfare with the Soviets, the U. S. went full force. During the Carter administration, as much as one-third of all U. S. exports to the Soviet Union were high-tech goods, as much as $219 million. By 1983, Reagan cut that to just $39 million.[143]

Poland captured the attention of Ronald Reagan. Shortly before the 1980 election, he delivered a speech in Dallas in which he lauded Pope John Paul II for his courageous pilgrimage to Poland. "It's been a long time since we've seen a leader of such courage and such uncompromising dedication to simple morality – to the belief that right does make might."[144]

The world was shocked when on December 13, 1981 General Wojciech Jarazelski declared martial law, raiding the headquarters of Solidarity. Seventy miners were shot in southeast Poland and four others in Krakow. Nearly a thousand arrests were made. Jarazelski did this to stave off a Warsaw Pact maneuver like the ones in 1956 Hungary and 1968 Czechoslovakia. The general had become aware of the Soviets staging Polish-speaking Russian troops near the border.

Monsignor Stanislaw Dziwisz, the pope's secretary, rushed to tell the pontiff of the crackdown. John Paul arranged to broadcast an address on Radio Free Europe, the Voice of America, the BBC, and Vatican Radio. He called for calm and the avoidance of any further bloodshed.

Later that day, the Pope received a phone call from Ronald Reagan who expressed his outrage at the martial law decree and promised to cooperate with the Vatican during the crisis. Reagan considered this moment a turning point in Soviet domination of Eastern Europe. He urged the Pope to use his influence to secure the release of Lech Walesa and others detained.

---

142 Archbishop John L. May. October 16, 1981. *With Pen and Staff.* Ligouri: Ligouri Publications. 1992. P. 155.
143 Ibid. P. 163.
144 Ibid. P. 88.

Reagan was not entirely blind to events in Poland, despite the press blackout. Washington was receiving information from a highly-placed Polish colonel, Ryszard Kuklinski. Acting as military liaison between Poland and the Soviet, he was privileged to highly-classified information. His secret hatred for the Soviets and his love for Poland caused him to be a U. S. mole. Just before the declaration of martial law in 1981, Kuklinski, his wife, and two sons were brought out of Poland by the CIA.

On December 23 Reagan met with the Polish ambassador to the United States, Romuald Spasowski. Just four days earlier, he and his wife had defected to the United States. During their Oval Office visit, Spasowski asked the president, "May I ask you a favor, Mister President? Would you light a candle and put it in the window tonight for the people of Poland?" Reagan did so immediately.[145] Pope John Paul II did the same thing on Christmas day.

Later, Reagan sent a scathing letter to Leonid Brezhnev, blaming the Soviets for causing martial law in Poland. He followed that by cancelling negotiations on a massive grain deal, banned Aeroflot flights to the United States, and took other measures to further hurt the U. S. S. R. Reagan was roundly criticized by Helmut Schmidt of West Germany and Pierre Trudeau of Canada. None of this affected Reagan's resolve.

In January 1982 the pressure was turned up. On January 10 the Pope spoke on Vatican Radio criticizing the martial law decree and heavy-handed treatment by the Polish government. On his part, Reagan declared January 30 as Solidarity Day and encouraged meetings and rallies and prayer services to show solidarity with the Polish people.

On June 7, 1982, Ronald Reagan met Pope John Paul II for the first time. They met one-on-one without interpreters for fifty minutes. Both agreed that the days of the Yalta agreement were numbered. They both agreed to share information even more closely. Reagan was good to his word. Vernon Walters and William Casey made at least fifteen visits to John Paul, sharing with him satellite photos and other sensitive information.

The President and the Pope spoke of their common destiny, both nearly assassinated within weeks of each other. Reagan told the pope,

---

145 Paul Kengor. *The Crusader*. P. 100.

"Look at the evil forces that were put in our way and how Providence intervened."[146]

When the Pope complained that the sanctions were hurting the Polish people, Reagan offered to resume regular flights for the Polish national airlines, LOT, and to restore a travel fund which had been suspended.

On March 8, 1983, Reagan dropped a rhetorical bombshell. Speaking at an assembly of evangelicals in Orlando, Florida, he told them the Soviet Union was the "focus of evil in the modern world." Fifteen days later he dropped another one. "I call upon the scientific community which gave us nuclear weapons to turn their talents to the cause of mankind and world peace; to give us the means of rendering these weapons impotent and obsolete."

The Strategic Defense Initiative (SDI) was meant to be a space-based missile defense system. It was more than that. It was meant to be the fiscal nail in the Soviet coffin. They certainly could not compete toe-to-toe with the United States in this phase of an arms race.

Reagan was not without his critics, including the Catholic bishops of America. Archbishop May reacted to letters critical of the bishops and defending Reagan and his rhetoric. In an article in the Archdiocesan paper, he wrote, "We all like to feel good about America. I know that sometimes Catholics are a bit disturbed to hear Church criticism of our President or our country. We are a patriotic people. There have been critical articles in past months in the Catholic press about the Reagan administration – about civil rights, cutbacks on social programs, Central American policy, and mostly about the arms race."

May continued, "Especially has Catholic criticism deplored the rhetoric of our president, the secretary of state, and other administration spokesmen. They used such ominous phrases – 'first strike capability' and 'limited nuclear warfare.'" After describing some of the arms buildup, the Archbishop added, "Our tough-talk approach has been criticized in the Catholic press across the world as diametrically opposed to the position of the Pope in his repeated pleas for reduction in threats and arms."[147]

---

146 Carl Bernstein and Marco Politi. *His Holiness: John Paul II and the Hidden History of Our Time*. New York: Doubleday. 1996. P. 357.
147 John L. May. *With Staff and Pen*. Ligouri: Ligouri Press. 1992. P. 305.

The Archdiocesan Human Rights Office had established a World Peace Committee. The minutes of the WPC of November 13, 1984 showed that between fifty and one hundred people came to a rededication vigil on November 11. They suggested selling Freeze Bonds as a 'trust' fund. "With each Bond purchased, a name of a person in the Soviet Union will be given for correspondence in an effort of communication."[148]

On June 8, 1986, they staged what they called a Walkathon Here to Back Freeze, a call to freeze nuclear armaments and reenter into negotiations with the Soviet Union. The World Peace Committee minutes of June 24 called the walk "less than a success," as only two hundred people showed up and they raised between $4,000 and $6,000.

The World Peace Committee (WPC) was interested in other matters also. Amnesty International, Haiti, and Guatemala were targeted. Reagan's foreign policy in Central America was of particular concern.

On August 8, 1986, the riverboat Delta Queen docked in Saint Louis. It had left Saint Paul, Minnesota a week earlier and was a floating symposium on issues of peace conducted by forty-six Soviet citizens and one hundred twenty-seven Americans. As the "peace cruise" docked, a man carried a big sign which read, "A good planet is hard to find."

On November 14, 1986, a group calling itself "Pledge of Resistance" demonstrated in front of the Federal Courthouse. When elderly Mary Auer entered the building to warm herself, she was forcibly removed. Angie O' Gorman and William Ramsey tried to come to her assistance. Ramsey was pulled into the building by two federal agents and choked with a nightstick. He fell to the ground unconscious. When he regained consciousness, he was charged with trespassing and given three summons. A lawyer with the group witnessed the entire encounter.[149]

The Human Rights Office wrote letters of protest to the offices of Senator Thomas Eagleton and Representatives Richard Gebhardt and William Emerson.

---

148 Human Rights Office. Correspondence 1983-1985. A281. Archives of the Archdiocese of Saint Louis.
149 "Statement by William Ramsey. November 15, 1986. RG O3c)5 Human Rights: World Peace Committee Correspondence 1986 – 1990. Archives of the Archdiocese of Saint Louis.

The WPC also launched a multi-year campaign to introduce people to the 1983 NCCB pastoral letter, "Challenge of Peace." Their records show they gave presentations to sixteen parish groups, sometimes as small as ten. But in October 1984 over two hundred fifty gathered at the Church of the Magdalen on South Kingshighway to hear their presentation.

They also spoke to eight parish school faculties, two eighth grade classes and eight high schools: Saint Dominic in January 1984 to an audience of over five hundred, only to be exceeded in October 1984 by an audience of six hundred at Notre Dame High School.[150]

What the WPC did not know was Reagan hated the idea of nuclear war every bit as much as he hated communists. Mutually Assured Destruction was just as the acronym said, MAD. He even hinted that he would share SDI with the Soviets, truly making nuclear war a thing of the past.

Senator Ted Kennedy of Massachusetts derided SDI and called it "Star Wars," after a recent blockbuster film. The Soviet press picked up on the term and used it endlessly.

In June 1984 SDI was tested publicly. A missile was launched from California, and an anti-missile missile was launched from the Pacific Ocean. The California missile was blown out of the sky. The test sent shockwaves through the Kremlin and among Reagan critics. What was not revealed until 1993 was that the missile had a homing device on it and the anti-missile missile had a receiver to home in on it.[151]

The year 1984 was an election year. Reagan received a letter from Father S. C. Rokicki from Detroit who had spent six weeks in Poland. He wrote, "They want me to tell you that 80% of Poland is praying for your reelection. The Polish people are very proud that you stand up to communists... The Polish people know weeks in advance that you will be re-elected."[152]

Indeed, Ronald Reagan won a second term with the Electoral College vote at 525 to 13.

Previously, John Paul had paid a second visit to Poland. He met with General Jaruzelski. The prime minister was clearly nervous, his

---

150 "Report on Activities Related to "The Challenge of Peace" within the Archdiocese of Saint Louis." GR)3c)5 Human Rights: World Peace Committee Minutes 1985 – 1987. Archives of the Archdiocese of Saint Louis.
151 Paul Kengor. *The Crusader*. P. 210.
152 Ibid. P. 213.

right hand shaking uncontrollably. John Paul spoke carefully and quietly about the pain caused by martial law and the arrests.

Before leaving Poland, the Pope met privately with Lech Walesa. He became aware that though the Solidarity movement had been crushed, an underground network still existed, fueled by CIA money.

At least two things made it difficult for the Soviets to act decisively in Poland. Their invasion of Afghanistan was proving to be a disaster, both for the Afghan people and for the Soviet army. Second, with the death of Leonid Brezhnev, the top post in the Kremlin became a revolving door. Yuri Andropov, former head of the KGB, served less than eight months before his death. He was followed by Konstantin Chernenko who lasted only thirteen months. The Central Committee chose fifty-four-year-old Mikhail Gorbachev. He was the fourth general secretary in just three years.

Gorbachev was a hard-core communist, which he had made clear in his book *Perestroika*. He intended to update the Soviet Union, not to destroy it. He believed that Marxism-Leninism was the wave of the future. He was not about to let the Soviet empire crumble at its seams.

It became more difficult for Soviet Jews to leave. And those who did had to pay exorbitant fees for the privilege. Most wanted to move to Israel, but their plight was taken up by the National Conference on Soviet Jews. The executive director, Jerry Goodman, drew a crowd to the Jewish Community Center Association and asked them to write President Reagan. He told them, "I am convinced the president would be at a better position to deal with Gorbachev if he knew there were people out there – Jews and non-Jews – who cared."[153]

Catholics were very much engaged in this issue. In 1973 the National Catholic Conference of Interracial Justice sponsored a petition featured in an ad in the *Chicago Tribune*. Thirty-three of the fifty signers were prominent Catholics.

Gorbachev authorized the use of chemical weapons in Afghanistan in 1986. The Quran was confiscated and burned. Imams were imprisoned. The Afghan resistance, the Mujahedin, was hard pressed. Half the country's population was displaced.

CIA director William Casey arranged for arms shipments to the rebels via Egypt, Saudi Arabia, Pakistan, and even China. When Reagan wrote National Security Decision Directive 166, it was a

---

153 September 20, 1985. "Americas Urged to Support Reagan Talks on Soviet Jews." *Saint Louis Post-Dispatch*.

game-changer. The president got $450 million from Congress and added another $200 million from Defense Department accounts for the rebels. In 1985 alone, the CIA delivered 10,000 rocket-propelled grenades and 200,000 rockets to the Mujahedin.[154] The CIA worked closely with Pakistani intelligence, the ISI.

In the end, the U. S. sent over two billion dollars in funds and weapons to the rebels which caused the Soviets to invest between three and eight billion in funds they could not afford. Making matters more dire, Ronald Reagan convinced the Saudis to increase oil production, flooding the world market and driving down prices, further denying the Soviets hard currency.

It was in a meeting with General Jaruzelski that Gorbachev began to reassess the future of communism. Much of the conversation revolved around the role of the Catholic Church in Poland and more specifically, the Polish pope.

"What kind of a man is he?" Gorbachev asked. "What is his intellectual training? Is he a fanatic? Or is he a man with his feet on the ground?" Years later, Jaruzelski reported replying to the general secretary that the pope was "an outstanding personality, a great humanist, a great patriot."[155]

Acting as a go-between for Gorbachev and the Church, Jaruzelski began to make reforms in Poland. John Paul reciprocated with an encyclical, *Slavorum Apostoli*, Apostles to the Slavs. It called for dialogue. On September 11, 1986, martial law was lifted in Poland. Prisoners were released. Solidarity was again meeting in public.

On January 13, 1987, General Jaruzelski came to the Vatican to describe Gorbachev to the pope, as he had earlier described the pope to Gorbachev.

On June 8 the pope made his third visit to Poland. It was not a friendly visit. John Paul pressed hard for changes. The government responded by cutting off television coverage, making mass arrests, and deploying riot police. At the pope's departure, Jaruzelski was cold and his remarks biting. The forces of change were nonetheless set in motion. Massive strikes were followed by political change. Solidarity won the first free election in Poland since World War II. Yalta was dead.

When Hungary opened its borders with Austria, tens of thousands

---

154 Paul Kengor. *The Crusader*. P. 233.
155 Carl Bernstein and Marco Politi. *His Holiness*. P. 451.

of East Germans "went on vacation" in Hungary and crossed into Austria. Others did the same to Poland.

In October, massive protests took place in East Berlin and in Leipzig. The Honecker regime fell, and borders with West Germany were opened. Bulgaria fell next, then Czechoslovakia. Romania fell too, but not without considerable bloodshed.

Then the unthinkable happened. On December 1, 1989, General Secretary Gorbachev and his wife came to the Vatican for a one-on-one meeting with the pope. Two years later on December 31, 1991, thousands thronged into Red Square celebrating the end of the Soviet Union. During the changing of the guard at Lenin's tomb, a man rushed forward with a statue of Our Lady of Fatima. He held it there as a silent rebuke to all that Lenin stood for.

Ronald Reagan was out of office, back at his Rancho del Cielo. John Paul would reign as supreme pontiff for another fourteen years. The two together had changed the world.

Back in Saint Louis a different tempest was brewing. Judge James H. Meredith died in 1981. Ten years earlier he had ruled against black parents who sued the Saint Louis Board of Education for its desegregation plan which did little to change the racial mix in the public schools. Children were given the option of "continuation transfer," which meant they could stay in their neighborhood school until graduation, or choose "intact busing," in which whole classes of black students were transferred to white schools if they had room for them.

Meredith was overruled by the U. S. Eighth District Court, and Edward T. Foote was ordered to devise a plan for the 1980-81 school year which would include county as well as city schools. He was given sixty days. When too few county schools opted into the plan, the court hinted that it would establish a metropolitan school district. More county districts then bought into the system.

The court argued that setting up magnet schools and transferring some teachers were not enough. Each city school was instructed to have a black student population of at least thirty percent. Twenty-six of the one hundred fifty-three schools fell short. These included Cleveland High School and twenty-five grade schools in the system.

An attorney for Concerned Parents for Neighborhood Schools, Anthony J. Sestric, argued, "You can figure off the top that 35% of the kids – black and white – just will not show up for the bus. Parents have the ability to opt out of the city system too easily if you do not involve the county schools in the plan."[156] They did.

By 1983, the courts ordered the county school districts to increase their racial mix by way of busing. The plan now called for a mix of at least fifteen percent of the student population to be African American. County students could engage voluntarily and were to be attracted into the city with magnet schools, with specialty programs. Money was to be set aside for infrastructure improvements in the urban schools. All of this would be funded by the state of Missouri. The implementation of the plan was pushed back to the 1983-84 school year.

The *Post-Dispatch* interviewed students at Beaumont High School, an all-black school. Thirteen students were asked about busing. Ten said they were in favor of it, but only if it were voluntary. One student noted, "I don't see how students will get a better education because of integration, and besides, there is the chance that there will be lots of fights."[157]

To intercede before things got out of hand, a group calling itself "Interfaith Coalition for Peaceful Integration" formed with representatives from Church Women United, National Council of Christians and Jews, the Archdiocese of Saint Louis, Carondolet Ecumenical Council of Churches, and Southside Ministerial Association. They played no role in the desegregation of the schools but pledged to get accurate and timely information to stake-holders in the neighborhoods.

Things developed differently in the urban Catholic schools. Northside parishes were seeking ways to collaborate. In 1972, Saint Edward's closed its school with 149 children and merged it with Most Blessed Sacrament, creating Bishop Healy School.[158] The school was governed by a board elected from both parishes. The school was staffed by laity and Sisters of Saint Joseph under the leadership of Sister Elizabeth Aherns. She announced the merger saying everyone was "getting together and learning to work together and play together and it has all gone rather smoothly."

The school was unique in that it used a "non-grade system" in order "to place children at their ability level." There would be visiting

---

156 March 4, 1980. "Plea for Support on School Ruling." *Saint Louis Post-Dispatch*.
157 March 4, 1980. "Students Views on Decision." *Saint Louis Post-Dispatch*.
158 Both parishes had experienced a decline of enrollment. Most Blessed Sacrament went from 321 in 1969 to 309 in 1971 while Saint Edward went from 194 in 1969 to 181 in 1971. When the schools were combined the enrollment at Bishop Healy School was 330 with nine religious sisters and seven lay faculty.

music specialists as well as language lessons and visiting speech specialists provided by the Sisters of Saint Joseph.[159]

A North Deanery School Planning Committee was established in 1987. Auxiliary Bishop J. Terry Steib announced, "What we're trying to do is to look ahead in a positive manner and begin creating some kind of vision."[160] There was concern about enrollment in the schools and in funding. It was projected that enrollment would dip from 2,294 to around 2,024 by 1990, and the per-pupil costs would rise by twenty-five percent. Already, nine of the thirteen parish schools received archdiocesan subsidies of a million dollars a year.

Catholic enrollment in these schools ranged from seventeen percent to fifty-seven percent, the average being thirty-seven. Over eighty percent of the teachers and administrators were lay.

The answer was the creation of FOCUS, the Federation of Catholic Urban Schools. These included Bishop Healy on the grounds of Most Blessed Sacrament parish, Cathedral, Central Catholic-Northside Catholic-Saint Nicholas which merged a year later, De Porres which closed, Holy Cross in Baden, Holy Guardian Angels, Most Holy Trinity, Our Lady of Mount Carmel, Saint Engelbert, Saint Francis Xavier which closed, and Saint Peter Claver.

The director of FOCUS was Sister Margaret McCulloch, BVM. She announced, "There are a lot of programs that are just beginning, and we are realistically trying to work at them and take them to completion, but there is a lot to be done."[161]

The FOCUS schools would use varied learning environments and methods to meet the needs of their student population. They would engage in interracial and multicultural experiences like visits to the Saint Louis Zoo and Art Museum. They offered before- and after-school care, hot breakfasts and hot lunches, and hands-on science programs. The federation shared art, music, and physical ed teachers. They applied for a major grant for computers but were turned down. The Archdiocesan Education Office promised to seek other avenues for funding. Sister Mary Ann Eckhoff, a School Sister of Notre Dame, assistant superintendent, noted "In the 1980s we lost fifty percent of the children. It is absolutely essential that the Church's presence in the North Deanery be seen with a viable future."

---

159 September 24, 1989. *Saint Louis Review*.
160 November 20, 1987. *Saint Louis Review*.
161 August 18, 1989. *Saint Louis Review*.

The next year Holy Cross withdrew from FOCUS and raised $78,000 to keep its school open. Cathedral School opted to restrict enrollment to parishioners only. The remaining federation schools staged a math contest at Cardinal Ritter Prep. They fielded seventeen teams of five students each. It was such a success that it became an annual affair.

Archbishop May was aware that white families would seek to avoid the chaos that was sure to follow in the public schools by transferring their children to Catholic schools. He saw this happen when he was bishop of Mobile. There he had developed a "no transfer" policy. In August 1970 he told his diocese, "Our schools must not be used as havens from integration; nor do we intend to use the public-school crisis to boost our school enrollment." The only exception to this "no transfer" policy was for people moving to Mobile from out of town.[162]

In July 1980 he said the same thing to Saint Louis. Students, even if they were Catholic, even if they were members of a parish, if they had been enrolled in a public school during the 1979-80 school year, they could not transfer into a Catholic school. One exception was made. If the public-school student was entering either the first or ninth grade, a transfer would be permitted. These were called "normal entrance points."

A three-part series appeared in the *Saint Louis Review* in May 1980. The author was staff writer Paul Pennich, Jr. The first article, "Catholic Integration Efforts Began in 1947" noted "There were no National Guardsmen to bar the schoolhouse door that September morning. There were no court orders, no presidential initiatives asked for or needed."[163] Pennich outlined the steps Cardinal Ritter took to bring about integration in Catholic schools. He also tied school segregation to housing segregation and spoke of the landmark Supreme Court decision which outlawed property covenants. The disagreement had been between the Kraemer family, white, and the Shelly family, black, over the property at 4610 Labadie.

The second article came to the heart of the matter regarding Catholic schools and the archdiocesan decision not to be a safety valve for whites fleeing public schools because of integration. Entitled "'No Transfer' Policy Marks New Era," the article cites a 1974 decision by the board of education, with the blessings of Cardinal Carberry. "The

---

162 John L. May. *With Staff and Pen.* P.287.
163 May 16, 1980. "Catholic Integration Efforts Began in 1947." *Saint Louis Review.*

Catholic schools of the Archdiocese of Saint Louis shall not become havens or even give the appearance of becoming havens for any student who may be seeking to avoid pressures brought about by current efforts to integrate public schools in various areas of the archdiocese."[164]

Despite enrollment decline, loss of religious order teachers, and negotiations with teacher groups, Catholic schools would not be opened to an influx of white students avoiding the changes in public schools, said Msgr. John J. Leibrecht, superintendent of Catholic education. It was the "no transfer" policy.

Archbishop May backed up this decision with a pastoral letter in which he declared, "All of us in our Saint Louis metropolitan and neighboring areas will be affected for better or for worse by the overall response to this court order. We cannot ever say to any group here, I have no need of you. To have a stable, prosperous, peaceful community, we simply have to live and work together."

May also told the *Globe-Democrat*, "We're not going to allow our schools to be used to undercut the law."[165]

This stand on principle came with costs. It denied the potential for several hundred students to enter the Catholic school system, and it included minority students, most of whom were not Catholic and many of whom could not pay the full tuition. This brought financial challenges.

Pennich included in his article some telling statistics. Of the 67,700 children enrolled in archdiocesan schools, 7,200 were minorities. Urban schools were more integrated than county schools. Of the forty urban parochial schools, twenty-two of them had minority populations which ran from six to ninety percent. In Saint Louis County, sixty-three of the eighty-eight schools had minority populations greater than five percent.

Five of the eight urban high schools had minority populations higher than five percent. Highest were Rosati-Kain, ranging from twenty-one to thirty-five percent depending on the year, Mercy in University City, thirty-six to fifty percent, and Cardinal Ritter Prep with ninety percent.

The article noted that of the minority students enrolled in the Catholic schools, ninety percent were non-Catholic. Many could not pay the

164 May 23, 1980. "'No Transfer' Policy Marks New Era." *Saint Louis Review*.
165 October 4-5, 1980 "Archbishop Says Schools Can't Escape Integration. *Globe-Democrat*.

full tuition, so city parishes found themselves subsidizing them.

Pennich highlighted one teacher to show the system in flux. Joe Wiley began his teaching career at Most Blessed Sacrament in 1957 when it had a ninth grade. Between 1962 and 1966 he taught at De Andreis and then became principal of Providence High School for Boys before it closed. He returned to De Andreis until it closed in 1976. Then Wiley became a counselor at Mercy. He observed, "We have the numbers; we don't have the interaction." He noted that black students did not participate in after-school activities except in football and basketball. He judged the relations between black and white students as "coexistence."

Pennich's third article highlighted the Upward Bound program, started by Saint Louis University High School. The objective was to recruit inner city youth by offering a four-week intensive academic program between seventh and eighth grades. Two African American SLUH students were featured. They joined the Organization of Black Achievement at school and felt the experience was positive.

At Saint Francis Xavier School, Sister Margaret Mullin took an active hand in recruiting minority students. When she arrived, the school had only ninety students enrolled. Sixteen years later the enrollment stood at 304; seventy-seven percent were black. That year there were thirty-nine graduating, eight going to Rosati-Kain, four to SLUH, and twelve to Cardinal Ritter Prep.

During the summer of 1980, the Education Office teamed up with the Archdiocesan Human Rights Office to sponsor the "Racial Climate Study." Msgr. John Shocklee, executive director of the Human Rights Office, was cautiously optimistic but noted that there was much work to be done.

By October the Archdiocese had developed a three-part plan to further integrate the Catholic schools. First, they would establish a "Contact Program." These would be extra-curricular and educational contacts between schools of different racial makeup. By 1980 twenty schools were already involved in such programs. The goal was to get the other one hundred fifty-eight involved.

The second initiative was under the direction of Sister Sarah Page, OSF, director of curriculum. She was given the task of meeting with principals and directors of education to review materials to introduce students to multicultural programs. These could include seminars and workshops on integration.

The third part was to send to all 3,300 teachers in the system a copy of the National Conference of Catholic Bishops' 1979 booklet, "Brothers and Sisters to Us." How many read it and took it to heart is unknowable. Regardless, the Archdiocese of Saint Louis, its archbishop, its Human Rights Office and its Education Office made a commitment to do the right thing, even as public schools lurched into an uncertain future.

Busing was a hot political topic and played a major role in the gubernatorial election of 1984. John Ashcroft, Missouri attorney general, campaigned on the platform that the Saint Louis desegregation plan was "illegal and immoral." He won both the Republican nomination and the governor's race.

The next Attorney General, Democrat Jay Nixon, also opposed the plan, claiming it cost too much. He suggested using the money to fix up the urban schools and establish high quality curriculum, letting the children stay in their neighborhoods. His proposal was seconded by Saint Louis' first black mayor, Freeman Bosley, Jr.

In the end, the burden of desegregation fell mainly on black students who left home early in the morning to take long bus rides to schools where they often felt alienated. The city schools also suffered, as the best students and best athletes opted for an education in a county school. The state of Missouri shaved back its financial commitment by funding only city magnet schools and the voluntary transfer program.

As much as Archbishop May was concerned about Catholic education and racial equality, he was equally passionate about pro-life issues. As early as 1971, in Mobile, he staked out his position, aware that states were relaxing their abortion laws. He declared, "Any Catholic directly responsible for the crime of abortion is automatically excommunicated according to the traditional law of the Church. Changes in state law do not affect Catholic doctrine in this manner."[166]

The Archbishop laid out in detail his pro-life position in a series of *Saint Louis Review* articles which ran between August 29 and September 12, 1980. In 1987 they would again be published in the *Review*.

May began by setting straight the medical facts. He described the development of a fetus from week-to-week from the first detection of a heartbeat just four weeks after conception. He drew a contrast

---

166 John L. May. *With Staff and Pen.* P. 245.

between animals and humans. "Killing methods as cruel as these are forbidden by law in every animal slaughterhouse in the country. The same laws (and often the same individuals) that go to extraordinary lengths to protect snail darters, burnished louseworts, and peregrine falcons (endangered animal species), consider this cruel mass slaughter of the unborn a sign of human progress and of women's liberation."[167]

He spoke of "the clever use of language." Words like "fetus," "procedure," "evacuating the results of conception," and "improving delivery to the target organs" desensitize people to the reality of what was happening.

The archbishop took on the argument that "choice should be respected and honored." He pointed to the fact that before civil rights legislation, motel and restaurant owners claimed their right to choose who would be their customer and who would not be, choosing to exclude blacks. He used the parallel of slavery and said slaveowners could have parroted the pro-choice argument. "If you think slavery is wrong, then nobody is forcing you to be a slave owner. But don't try to impose your morality on others."

When critics claimed that pro-lifers are one-issue voters, Archbishop May pointed out that there are many one-issue voters. Some vote only regarding the war in Vietnam. Some vote only to advance the Equal Rights Amendment or to bring aid to Israel.

Nor were pro-life issues only Catholic issues. May pointed to prominent non-Catholics who were pro-life. He mentioned Senator John Danforth, Surgeon General Dr. C. Everett Koop, the Lutheran Church Missouri Synod, the Southern Baptist Convention, the Union of Orthodox Jewish congregations, the Mormon Church, and Dr. Bernard N. Nathanson who was a former abortionist, a secular Jew who professed atheism.

One of the issues for the pro-life side was to find ways to support women and families who turn to abortion in desperation. May noted, "If we are a community that cares, we must find ways to help carry the burdens of all." There is a choice that must be made. "Will ours be a society that values and protects each and every human life, born or unborn, or will it be a society that considers some human lives expendable? That choice is ours to make."[168]

---

167 John L. May. *With Staff and Pen.* P. 252.
168 Ibid. P. 261.

This concern was not only to prevent abortions, but caring for both mother and child dates back early in the pro-life movement. Saint Louis held its first pro-life convention at the Busch Memorial Center on the grounds of Saint Louis University in October 1977. Representative Henry Hyde of Illinois told the five hundred attending that the pro-life movement was looking for "human solutions" for "the human problems in unwanted pregnancies," not the violent solution of abortion.

Outside the Center were two hundred pro-choice protesters. An impromptu protest against the protesters erupted when SLU students began shouting, "We like Hyde," and made makeshift banners reading "SLU is Pro-Life."[169]

At the October 25, 1987 convention, Father Michael Mannion, Director of the Glassboro State College Newman Center in New Jersey asked, "How can we ask a woman to see her child within her as sacred if she does not see herself as sacred? We must stand with her, so she will choose life." Father Mannion had written two books, the first on abortion and the second on ways to support expectant mothers.

He warned against violent and even graphic protests. "I've never counseled a woman who was deterred by a sign that said, 'baby killer.'"[170]

That theme had also appeared on May 13 of that year, when the Archdiocesan Pro-Life Committee brought around one hundred people to participate in the Missouri Catholic Conference (MCC) Citizenship Day. At the capitol, they lobbied representatives and senators to pass House Bill 518 and its partner bill, Senate Bill 299. Both called for a raise in Medicare income eligibility for pregnant women and their children from thirty-six percent to one hundred percent of the federal poverty level.

The House passed the bill the next day. It was then taken up by the Senate Budget Committee. Carl Landwehr, MCC director, called them "Birthright bills," because they impacted women getting Birthright counseling. He pointed out the financial incentives of a poor pregnant woman, where she could get an abortion for around $250, but

---

169 October 21, 1977. *Saint Louis Review*.
170 October 30, 1987. "Priest Tells Group Compassion is Key to Pro-Life Work." *Saint Louis Review*.

birthing and caring for her newborn could run as high as $3,000.[171]

As early as 1986, the archdiocese was exploring ways to address the question of crisis pregnancies directly. They received a manual from Robert J. Pearson entitled, "How to Start and Operate Your Own Pro-Life Outreach Crisis Pregnancy Center."

Actually, the archdiocese already had one. The Villa Maria Maternity Home was established by Catholic Charities and opened in August 1983 at 1340 Partridge in University City. It cared for pregnant women and had a foster family care center for infants. It also offered counseling. The 1985 statistics were impressive. That year 718 clients were served, sixty-three given residence, and another eighty-two attended educational programs.[172]

On January 21, 1986, the archbishop called for a coalition to address the issue of crisis pregnancies. He called it the Life-Line coalition. If a woman was pregnant and in trouble, she should call the local rectory. The staff would be coordinated by Father Joseph Naumann. Or they could call Birthright or contact the Villa Maria Center. Birthright had been in Saint Louis since 1971 and had offices in Ballwin, Saint Charles, Hampton Avenue South, Bridgeton, Eureka, and Hillsboro.

The Life-Line coalition would be headed by Monsignor Robert Slattery, executive director of Catholic Charities and would include Mrs. Jane Mehan, president of Birthright Counseling Saint Louis; Doctors for Life, represented by Drs. Anne Bannon and Jerome Shen; the Saint Vincent de Paul Society, represented by Sister Eileen Donovan, SSND; and representatives from Saint John Mercy, Saint Mary's, Saint Anthony's, Saint Joseph's in Kirkwood, Saint Joseph in Saint Charles, and De Paul, the Catholic hospitals of Saint Louis.

One way the Archbishop kept in contact with his priests was a periodic newsletter entitled *Notanda*, nicknamed "The Blue Notes" because it was always printed on blue paper. The first *Notanda* came out November 10, 1980. Archbishop May wrote, "Henceforth you will be receiving this publication from time to time. It will be a clergy bulletin – an informal message from the Ordinary to all priests and deacons... I will write whenever I feel the need to do so."

It is telling that the archbishop included deacons in the Blue Notes. Over the twelve years of sending out these bulletins, May seldom ad-

---

171 May 22, 1987. "State Legislators Receive Visit from Pro-Life Groups." *Saint Louis Review.*

172 "Villa Maria Center. RG III C 8. Archives of the Archdiocese of Saint Louis.

dressed the deacons or diaconate issues directly, but he was quick to tell his priests that these men were full clerics also.

On May 22, 1981, May sent out a *Notanda* with an article entitled, "Our Deacons (Permanent Types)." He said, "In going around to our parishes I have been surprised to see permanent deacons assisting at Mass as laymen or filling some minor role in the liturgy. Our permanent deacons are clergy with major orders with the priests and bishops. They should take their rightful place in the liturgy as the Church prescribes. It is sad to see these men who reached ordination as deacons not functioning fully in the parishes where they are assigned."[173]

The archbishop concluded by saying how edifying it is for the laity to see bishop, priest, and deacon function in solemn liturgy.

In early October 1983 the third annual All-State Diaconate Conference was held at Saint Anselm Parish in Creve Coeur. The main speaker was a professor from Notre Dame University, John Houck. He told the deacons that their vocation mixed religious values and a corporate outlook. "Permanent Deacons, ordained ministers working and living in the lay world, are the 'experts' at how to make sense of the two worlds. They can show others how to examine the things we value – like time, justice and power."

Houck described three corporate types: the millionaire syndrome, the king of the mountain type, and the company man type. These are all modified. "The religious perspective can be put to use by rediscovering the meaning of the stories of the Bible."

The second speaker was Monsignor Ernest Fiedler, executive director of the U. S. Bishops' Committee on the Permanent Diaconate. He shared statistics with the assembly. There were over six thousand deacons in the United States. One hundred forty-five dioceses, of one hundred seventy-seven, had a Permanent Diaconate program. Ninety-six percent were fully employed in secular jobs; ninety-five percent were married.[174]

The 1980s saw considerable growth in the number of permanent deacons serving in the Archdiocese of Saint Louis. After the initial ordination of twelve men, there was a brief pause to evaluate the pro-

---

173 *Notanda* Volume II #4 May 22, 1981. RG I H6 "*Notanda* Blue Notes." Archives of the Archdiocese of Saint Louis.
174 October 7, 1983. "Permanent Diaconate Described as Bridge Linking Dual Values." *Saint Louis Review*.

gram. Then a class of 13 came in 1981; 11 in 1982. In 1983, 22 candidates came as ten were ordained.

In 1985 twenty-four men were ordained to the permanent diaconate. Their careers showed their diversity. The class of 1985 included an assistant advertising director, three insurance salesmen, an attorney, a mortgage banker, a farmer, two printers, a purchasing director, a personnel manager, a vice president of United Way, a pharmaceutical firm employee, an engineer, a banker, a dental technician, an architectural engineer, four retirees, and the director of education for the National Museum of Transportation.

The Diaconate director, Father John M. Costello, sought out other ministries for deacons. He said ninety-nine percent served in parishes. He was assembling a survey to study the academic, spiritual, and pastoral areas of their lives as well as the effect the diaconate had on family life.

On September 8, 1988, the first Archdiocesan Convocation of Deacons took place at the old Kenrick building. Its offices were now housed there. The new director was a permanent deacon, Gerry Quinn. The manager of the building was a permanent deacon, Robert Snyder. Around two hundred attended. Father Costello was invited back to celebrate the Mass.

There were sensitive issues beginning to emerge in the diaconate program, and Gerry Quinn was a canon lawyer, the perfect man for the job.

Some applicants had been civilly divorced. Could they be accepted as candidates? Deacon Quinn wrote to Bishop Terry Steib, the episcopal vicar for the diaconate, citing canon law. Canon 1029 said that for a licit celebration of ordination, "the candidate is one who is well respected in the community and not a cause of any scandal or wonderment in the community."

In such a case there would have to be a thorough investigation, a declaration of nullity from a tribunal, and assurances that a second marriage had been canonically recognized.[175]

By October 1989 at least two non-parochial appointments went to permanent deacons, airport ministry and Catholic Charities.

A milestone was marked when the Office of the Permanent Diaconate released a compiled handbook, The Report on the Perma-

---

175 April 19, 1989. Deacon Gerry Quinn to Bishop Steib. RG III 13.4 "Permanent Diaconate Correspondence: 1989-90. Archives of the Archdiocese of Saint Louis.

nent Diaconate 1990. It began by describing the governing bodies starting with the episcopal moderator, the Committee on the Permanent Diaconate, established in 1984, the Office of the Permanent Diaconate, and the Council of Deacons.

Other topics described the faculties of a deacon, active ministries, retirement, assignments, and transfers. It described the Annual Ministry Agreement Form signed by the deacon and his immediate ecclesial superior. The procedures for incardination, coming into the archdiocese, excardination, and leaving the diocese for another assignment were defined.

There was a section on the occasion of a marital separation or divorce, and how the deacon would be assessed as to his culpability.

Guidelines were given for the course of studies necessary before a deacon would receive the faculties to preach.

Regarding attire, "Clerical shirt or dress of any kind is not authorized. A badge or name tag to identify the deacon is encouraged."

Even funeral arrangements were included. When a deacon died, the family should notify the Diaconate Office. During the funeral Mass, the coffin is to be directed in such a way that the head of the deceased is pointing toward the altar, as is done for a priest, for the deacon is also ordained. His is to be clothed as the family wishes, and is permitted to be buried in a dalmatic, his liturgical vestment.[176]

Developments in the permanent diaconate were among the most fruitful in the archdiocese in the 1980s. In 1986, 21 were ordained. In 1987, 22 were ordained. Each year following, no fewer than nine were ordained.

Archbishop May wanted to revitalize parish life in his archdiocese. He found a program developed in New Jersey and brought it to Saint Louis.

RENEW was a three-year program introduced in dioceses in the United States. It was parish-based and was intended to be worked in small groups. It had been fifteen years since Cardinal Ritter had introduced Operation Renewal, another parish-based program to introduce the changes of the Second Vatican Council to the people of the archdiocese. In that program, some 40,000 people participated. There, parish assemblies were held, representatives elected, and proposals were made for the parishes and for the archdiocese. Some

---

176 "Report on the Permanent Diaconate: 1990." RG 03E13. Archives of the Archdiocese of Saint Louis.

dealt with liturgical changes and others with pastoral planning.

RENEW was different from Ritter's Operation Renewal. It was implemented nation-wide. Its focus was on the person and ties to the parish. It began as a diocesan project in Newark, New Jersey. Archbishop Peter Gerety wanted to revitalize his parishes. Eventually, eighty-six dioceses introduced the program. It sought to "enable people to love their church even in the midst of enormous institutional change and confusion."

After the program was completed, James R. Kelly, a professor of sociology at Fordham University, conducted a study of RENEW for the Lilly Endowment and published his observations in *America Magazine*. He was surprised that the program avoided doctrinal and moral issues. "I quickly came to see that, indeed, this nonjudgmental characteristic of Renew is one of the major reasons for its success. Amid the clamor of church controversy, many men and women seek mostly to deepen their attachment to the core elements of the average Christian life: Scriptures, the Mass, prayer, uncomplicated fellowship and support."[177]

For the Archdiocese of Saint Louis, leadership for RENEW was given to Father John Jay Hughes. He was a native of New York and had followed in his father's footsteps to become an Episcopalian priest. Indeed, his father had been the precentor, or director of liturgy, at the Cathedral of Saint John the Divine. Father Hughes was named after John Jay, the first chief justice of the United States, an ancestor.

Father Hughes had converted to Catholicism while studying in Germany. He was provisionally ordained by the bishop of Münster and came to Saint Louis to take a teaching position at Saint Louis University's Divinity School. He and many others on the faculty were terminated shortly before the program closed in 1974.

Rather than return to Germany, Father Hughes took up residence at Mother of Good Counsel Nursing Home, where he said Mass daily for the sisters and wrote articles, including book reviews for the *Post-Dispatch*. He appealed to Cardinal Carberry for a position, but he was still incardinated in the Diocese of Münster, and the Cardinal "could see no way of inserting me into a system that works basically by seniority without upsetting the whole pecking order." He lament-

---

177 Kenneth A. Briggs. *Holy Siege: The Year that Shook Catholic America.* San Francisco: HarperCollins. 1992. P. 253.

ed, "I was like an army officer who got detached from his regiment."[178]

The first step to implement RENEW was to invite volunteers to be trained. Sister Mary Ann Klohr, CSJ was named director of training. She left her post as principal at Our Lady of Lourdes in University City and gathered nine hundred people at the Mercy Center for a Mass celebrated by Archbishop May and a commissioning service. That was in January 1981.

On May 1, the *Saint Louis Review* ran a major article entitled "RE-NEW! RENEW! RENEW!" by staff writer Teresa Coyle. She described the program as lasting three years, broken up into a training semester and five semesters of programs. The kick-off would come in a fall meeting with pastors. Each participating parish would send four delegates: the pastor, the associate and/or a staff member, and two lay members. After an overnight workshop, the parish team was expected to recruit another eight volunteers, making up a core team of twelve.

After four training sessions, ten special committees would be set up to provide publicity, a phone tree, make home visits, and do other tasks. The target was a Sign-Up Sunday set for October 1982. After that, small groups of ten or twelve would meet each "semester" for six-week courses.

Eventually, RENEW in Saint Louis involved fifty thousand Catholics from almost all of the parishes, the highest percentage of any diocese in the United States. It came to an end in the fall of 1984. A survey showed considerable success. Two hundred thirty-two parishes participated.

One person reported, "It brought parishioners out of their shells – now working for parish unity, greater participation at Mass." Another said RENEW had brought the parish together as a community. "It has helped to rearrange some of our priorities." Others pointed to concrete actions which came out of RENEW: food collections for the unemployed, lobbying for tax reform, increased membership in Saint Vincent de Paul conferences, a program of pen pals for learning disabled children, and home improvements for the elderly by parish volunteers.[179]

One disappointment was that only fifteen percent of the presbyterate responded to the survey. Regardless, of those who did, six-

---

178 John Jay Hughes. *No Ordinary Fool: A Testimony to Grace.* Mustang: Tate Publishing & Enterprise. 2008. P. 263.
179 January 13, 1984. "RENEW Survey Indicates Success." *Saint Louis Review.*

ty-eight percent rated the program as strong and positive or good.

On November 23, 1984, RENEW ended with a Mass at the cathe-dral. It was attended by fifteen hundred people. Concelebrants in-cluded Auxiliary Bishop Edward J. O'Donnell and the RENEW co-di-rectors, Fathers John Jay Hughes and William Scheid.

During his homily, Father Hughes noted, "As we leave the map (as RENEW ends) God gives us something better – a guide. He is the same guide his Son gave to 11 frightened men huddled in a locked upper room in Jerusalem the evening of the first Easter Day, when he breathed on them and said: 'Receive the Holy Spirit.' Those 11 very ordinary men went out from that room to change the world. Today, in this hour, the risen Lord is challenging us to do the same."[180]

In December 1986 a committee of three bishops evaluated the RENEW program: Bishops William Levada, auxiliary of Los Ange-les, Donald Wuerl of Seattle, and Elden Curtiss of Helena, Montana. They criticized it as a "tendency toward generic Christianity." They observed it lacked "a clearer presentation of the distinctive nature of the Catholic church, not merely as a community of faith but as a structured, hierarchical, visible, sacramental community bound to-gether in the tradition that includes Scripture as a font of faith but also the authoritative development and interpretation of the doc-trine of faith by the magisterium of the church."[181]

This criticism should not come as a surprise. Catholicism was de-veloping differently in different parts of the country. One observer noted, "Going from East to West in Catholic America was to experi-ence, in general, a steady moderating of church tradition and a drift toward less formality and legalism. Thus, Catholics on the East Coast tended to adhere more closely to prescribed practices and pattern, the Midwest less, the West Coast least."[182]

The two West Coast bishops on the committee were experienc-ing great flux in Catholic traditions and beliefs. They took a hard line while the Montanan was only slightly more moderate.

Archbishop May seemed well pleased with the outcome and told Father Hughes, "We never expected that RENEW was going to be so

---

180 November 23, 1984. "Mass at Cathedral Marks Conclusion of RENEW Here. *Saint Louis Review*.

181 Kenneth A. Briggs. *Holy Siege*. P. 129.

182 Ibid. P. 415.

big." But Father Hughes considered the comment more a complaint than a compliment.[183]

Another area of development came out of the Charismatic Renewal Office. Paul Masek, a graduate of Benedictine College in Atchison, Kansas, began working in the office while also working for Saints Joachim and Anne parish in Saint Charles. In 1988 the Charismatic Renewal Office sent Paul to a six-week program called National Evangelization Team to receive formal training in youth ministry. He returned to Saint Louis with a different idea.

While NET required a person between eighteen and twenty-seven to leave home and job or school for a full year, taking and giving retreats, Paul sought to build a home-based program. He would rely heavily on volunteers whom he would train and direct to bring the Gospel message to youth, both in the Saint Louis Archdiocese and dioceses nearby in Illinois. He opened his group up to youth as young as thirteen and set no outer bounds of age. As the functions would include retreat and evangelization and include prayer, Masek called his endeavor REAP, with deep biblical implications.

REAP became a mission in search of a home. First, it was sponsored by the Charismatic Renewal Office, but as REAP teams worked in schools, it came to be part of the Catholic Education Department, Religious Education office. But then it dealt mainly with youth, so REAP got moved to the Office of Youth Ministry, until it became an office of its own within the Catholic Youth Apostolate.

Paul Masek was the only paid employee of REAP. The first year he recruited nineteen volunteers who led forty-three retreats for nearly two thousand retreatants.[184]

Through a donor's gift, Masek was able to hire a second staff member, Heather Gallagher. Her focus was on speaking to high school groups about chastity. The virtue was not confined to religious implications. It was seen as part of a healthy lifestyle and included frank talk about sexually transmitted diseases as well as self-respect and respect for those with whom a teen might have close relations.

One highlight came when the REAP team was invited to have a retreat entitled, "Let's Talk About Abstinence," to a public high school in Madison, Illinois in 2001.

---

183 John Jay Hughes. *No Ordinary Fool.* 274.
184 By 2018, REAP has sponsored over four thousand events, with more than 265,000 participants. Reapteam.org/history.

Programs like REAP and RENEW brought vitality to the Catholic community of the Archdiocese of Saint Louis. Soon, its archbishop would have other things to demand his attention. He was about to take a vital role in developments on the national stage.

Cardinal John J. Carberry hands the crozier to the newly-installed Archbishop John L. May at his Installation Mass on March 25, 1980. Apostolic Delegate Archbishop Jean Jadot is looking on from behind. Photographer Richard Finke. From the Archdiocese of St. Louis Archives.

Archbishop John L. May greets a well-wisher as he processes to the Cathedral with Permanent Deacon Daniel Austin of Blessed Sacrament Parish (left), and Transitional Deacon James Byrnes from Kenrick Seminary (right). Photographer Richard Finke, 1980. From the Archdiocese of St. Louis Archives.

This Freeze the Arms Race panel was organized by the Human Rights Office on April 6, 1984. From the Archdiocese of St. Louis Archives.

Msgr. John A. Shocklee, co-chairperson of the Archdiocesan Commission on Human Rights, spoke at a Memorial Day convocation for Peace and Justice in Central America on May 28, 1984 at Memorial Plaza in downtown St. Louis. The event was sponsored by the Interfaith Committee on Latin America. Pictured sitting on stage from left to right are: Rev. Otis Woodard, Joe Connolly, Marilyn Lorenz-Weinkauff, and Sister Betty Campbell. Photographer Richard Finke. From the Archdiocese of St. Louis Archives.

Pauline Humphrey introduces a meeting of SLACO in June 1986 at Saint Louis University. From the Human Rights Office Records at the Archdiocese of St. Louis Archives.

BELOW: On August 2, 1986, passengers of the riverboat Delta Queen disembarked at the St. Louis levee during the Mississippi River "peace cruise." The weeklong shipboard symposium of 46 Soviet and 127 U.S. citizens began at St. Paul, Minnesota. Photographer Richard Finke. From the Archdiocese of St. Louis Archives.

At a high school Teachers' Institute held by the Archdiocesan School Office in 1980, Archbishop May stands with Sister Mary Ann Eckhoff, SSND, the then-assistant superintendent for secondary schools; Mr. Floyd Hacker, administrator at DuBourg High School; and Msgr. John J. Leibrecht, superintendent of secondary schools. Photographer Richard Finke. From the Archdiocese of St. Louis Archives.

Catince Gorman of St. Nicholas School and Joann Allen of St. Stephen Protomartyr School roller skated together at the St. Nicholas roller rink during an event through the Archdiocesan School's Contact Program. The program sought to connect Catholic students of different races through school visits, a pen pal exchange, and other events. Photographer Richard Finke, 1981. From the Archdiocese of St. Louis Archives.

Students make art with Sr. Alma Zacharias, D.C., at Central Catholic Community School in 1970, which enrolled seventh and eighth graders from four inner city parishes: St. Bridget, St. Patrick, St. Alphonsus, and St. Theresa. The school later merged with St. Nicholas and closed in 2010. Photographer Richard Finke. From the Archdiocese of St. Louis Archives.

Sister Margaret McCulloch, BVM, was the director of the Federation of Catholic Urban Schools (FOCUS). Photographer Richard Finke, 1989. From the Archdiocese of St. Louis Archives.

Joe Wiley was honored by Msgr. John Shocklee at an unknown event around 1984. From the Archdiocese of St. Louis Archives.

Archbishop John L. May visited with the Guardian Angel Settlement in 1980. The child care facility was originally founded by the Daughters of Charity of St. Vincent de Paul in 1859. Photographer Richard Finke. From the Archdiocese of St. Louis Archives.

Archbishop John L. May walked with pro-life picketers after protesting at Barnes hospital on January 22, 1989, the anniversary of Roe v Wade. The march continued to the St. Louis Cathedral where the Archbishop celebrated Mass. On May's left is then-Father Joseph F. Naumann, who was coordinator of the Archdiocesan Pro-Life Committee. Photographer Richard Finke. From the Archdiocese of St. Louis Archives.

Deacon Robert J. Snyder was appointed as the administrative director of the "Kenrick Center" in 1987. He oversaw renovations to the building and its use as a conference center. The building is now the Cardinal Rigali Center. Photograph dated 1999. From the Archdiocese of St. Louis Archives.

Deacon Gerald Quinn was appointed as the first deacon to head the Permanent Diaconate Office in 1988. From the Archdiocese of St. Louis Archives.

ABOVE: Fr. John Hughes coordinates events on RENEW Sunday at the Cathedral Basilica. Representatives from 230 parishes came to the inaugural liturgy for the program on September 26, 1982 to offer their commitment to prayer. Photographer Richard Finke. From the Archdiocese of St. Louis Archives.

Heather Gallagher worked with Paul Masek and the REAP youth ministry. Photographer Mark Kempf, 2000. From the Archdiocese of St. Louis Archives.

Chapter Seven

JOHN L. MAY AND THE NCCB

John L. May held two offices which gave him national and international exposure, meeting Vatican officials, Pope John Paul II, two presidents, and several other national leaders.

In 1983 May was nominated as president of the National Conference of Catholic Bishops. He came in third. However, the more important vote was for vice president, as the vice president was almost always elected president the next time around. May won on the third ballot, 156 to his rival's 82.

Archbishop May's role as vice president was an active one. In 1983 he attended a theological conference of some ninety U. S. bishops in one-on-one sessions with members of the curia. All agreed that it was a valuable experience to get to know each other. Prior, there had been some distrust and rumors. May noted, "'Some cardinal or archbishop heard from a friend in Rome this or that.' The idea was to 'clear the smoke away,' and 'lay everything on the table.' The results of these meetings were often relayed to the Administrative committee or to all the bishops in meetings from which the press is barred."[185]

In 1984 the Archbishop led a U. S. delegation of bishops to the Pan-African Bishops' Symposium in Kinshasa, Zaire. Other delegations came from Europe, Canada, and Latin America. May was amazed at the beautiful liturgies set in an African mode, the fact that fifty percent of Zaire was Catholic, and that the African bishops had to grapple with "grinding poverty, illiteracy, corruption and inefficiency, tribal divisions, scores of different native languages in every country, unbelievably poor transportation and communications." Regardless, he saw great hope and booming vocations and predicted, "Undoubtably, the Church in Africa will be one of the greatest in the universal Catholic community."[186]

President Reagan invited Archbishop May and other bishops of the NCCB to the White House. May reported back to the Conference,

---

185 Thomas J. Reese, S. J. *A Flock of Shepherds: The National Conference of Catholic Bishops*. Kansas City: Sheed & Ward. P. 231.
186 John L. May. *With Staff and Pen*. P. 202.

"He invited us to say whatever we liked. (Cardinal) Szoka brought up the whole question of race relations in this country, and he spoke, of course, of the situation in Detroit. He told the President, very honestly, that black people don't look for much from him, that that's their feeling and that's his image with them. And we would like to help in any way we can."[187]

Reagan was getting used to receiving harsh criticism from the U. S. bishops. In 1983 the NCCB issued a pastoral letter, "The Challenge of Peace," which set out to use scripture and Catholic theological principles to argue for strategies of peace, not confrontation. After nearly one hundred forty votes on better wording or amendments, the final draft was prepared. The bishops had come very close to condemning any nuclear first strike when they were reminded that that would remove deterrence, which was a key element to the *Pax Atomica* which kept nations from using nuclear weapons since 1945.

Later in 1984 the NCCB issued another pastoral letter critical of Reagan's economic policies, "Economic Justice for All." In all, the NCCB issued thirty-one major statements during the Reagan era. Some spoke to social issues; some dealt with purely ecclesiastical matters. These statements perplexed politicians as well as media. They could not figure out if the conference was dominated by the Left or the Right. John Carr, an NCCB staffer, summed it up best. "Anybody who watches us closely knows that neither political party likes us at all. They shouldn't... We're very unpredictable. Reporters can't make head nor tail of this outfit. That is the way it should be because our agenda is not ideological or political, it comes from the teaching."[188]

The bishops took fire from the Right and from the Left. In a column, Archbishop May said it was open season on the bishops. He defended himself and his fellow bishops. "Some days when you read the mail and certain publications, it seems that the American Bishops are nincompoops or charlatans or perhaps a combination of both. So, it is really quite disappointing to attend a meeting of the Bishops' Conference and find the participants not at all that colorful. From my sixteen years of such meetings, I have found the bishops a hardworking, wise, and concerned group of clergy. I have always felt humble to be one of them."[189]

Archbishop May led National Conference visits to Mexico and

---

187 Thomas J. Reese, S. J. *A Flock of Shepherds.* P. 188.
188 Ibid. P. 306.
189 John L. May. *With Staff and Pen.* P. 200.

Cuba. Both countries had strained relations with their respective episcopal conferences. The Americans insisted that they would meet only with Carlos Salinas of Mexico and Fidel Castro of Cuba if the leadership of their episcopal conferences were included. Both Mexico and Cuba conceded. This heightened the stature of the Mexican and Cuban episcopal conferences, both of which were appreciative of the American concern.

In 1986 John L. May was elected president of the NCCB on the second ballot with 164 votes, 74 more than his closest competitor. He was the first president to have served as a pastor. Earlier, May had served as head of the Catholic Extension Society which raised funds for missionary work within the United States. This had given him many contacts and a broad vision of the national needs. His ten years as bishop of Mobile, and now his position as archbishop of Saint Louis, gave him administrative experience without losing his pastoral touch.

John May was a quiet man, something of an introvert, but he was not to be underestimated. Monsignor Daniel Hoye, former general secretary of the United States Catholic Conference observed, "May is stronger than people think. If it is a matter of principle, he will not move."[190]

Another observer was Monsignor George Higgins. He noted, "He's slow on his feet. He's a Luxemburger, he digs in, but he's been very good, much better than I thought he would be. His great quality is he's an honest guy. Not brilliant, but he tells you exactly what he is thinking." He later added, "John May has not an iota of the Roman in him."[191]

Russell Shaw, an NCCB staffer, was quoted, "He is considerate. If he has a fault, it is that he is not very assertive." Auxiliary Bishop Timothy Lyne of Chicago, a classmate, said, "He is a strong person in a quiet way."

Even the secular press saw these qualities in Archbishop May. *The New York Times* quoted him as saying, "There is some tension with some people and not with others. We are members of the universal Church." *The Times* observed a "growing and dangerous disaffection between some American bishops and the Vatican during the presidency of Bishop James W. Malone. These included the recent removal of Archbishop Raymond Hunthausen of Seattle."

The Times used as an example of May's diplomacy the request by the gay organization Dignity to open the cathedral for a Mass. May replied,

---

190 Thomas J. Reese, S. J. *A Flock of Shepherds*. P. 59.
191 Ibid. P. 60.

"I will pray with anyone. But not communion." *The Times* reacted, "Archbishop May has earned a reputation as a low-key leader who is bright but not overly ideological, according to Church officials who know him."

The Times article ended by noting that every week Archbishop May invited ten priests for an informal dinner or barbeque.[192]

On May 12, 1987, the archdiocese sponsored an information night at the Slattery Center on the grounds of Saint Anselm parish. It was called "AIDS: An Overview for the Catholic Community," and was the first event sponsored by the Catholic Task Force on AIDS. Later, in July the same Task Force petitioned the State of Missouri to provide Retrovir (AZT) in the Medicaid program to ameliorate the symptoms of AIDS. It had been done in forty-four other states.

The Missouri Department of Social Services replied that it would require legislation, but the Task Force appealed directly to Governor John Ashcroft for an executive order. In the letter, Ashcroft was praised for having expanded Medicaid coverage to all needy preschool children and pregnant women.

Archbishop May had established the Catholic Task Force on AIDS in January 1987 "for broad-based community support for a plan to help people with AIDS."[193] Monsignor Robert M. Krawinkel was named coordinator of health affairs for the archdiocese. There were four priests, one sister, and three doctors on the Task Force as well as representatives from SSM Health Care System, Alexian Brothers Hospital, and Catholic Charities.

The Task Force had two objectives: to educate people on the issues of AIDS in archdiocesan schools and agencies and to address the housing needs for people in the last stages of dying. Sister Michele O'Brian, a Sister of Charity of the Incarnate Word, became the coordinator of the Archdiocesan Health Outreach Program. She expressed her frustration. "It's almost impossible to find a nursing home that will take a person with AIDS. The ignorance of their attitude is unbelievable."[194]

At that time, twenty-eight cases had been identified in Saint Louis, with another twenty-five cases yet to be confirmed. The Saint Louis City Health Department estimated there would be between eight hundred and two thousand cases by 1991.

---

192 *New York Times.* November 12, 1986.
193 April 3, 1987. "Task Force on AIDS to Start Work Here." *Saint Louis Review.*
194 Ibid.

Doorways was an interfaith program supported by the archdiocese and six other church bodies. It began in 1988. By 1990 two hundred sixty people received housing assistance through Doorways. They received a donation of an eleven-unit building. One was used for offices while the other ten were prepared for ten homeless men with AIDS. Sister Lynne Cooper, CSJ was the director and solicited help from the Southeast Deanery for the renovations.[195]

In 1988 the Vatican issued a strong draft statement intending to limit the role of national conferences. Archbishop May assembled an ad hoc committee of former presidents of the conference. These included Cardinal John Krol of Philadelphia, a close friend of Pope John Paul II. They hammered out a measured response, one which the bishops could approve, thus defusing a potential nightmare.

Archbishop May was fond of saying, "It is commonly seen as unwise in the NCCB to raise three issues: holy days of obligation, age of confirmation, and new special collections."[196]

He also kept in private session topics which were sensitive to the Vatican. May enumerated these as first Communion before first confession, women lectors and acolytes, the annulment procedure, Catholics joining Masonic societies, pastoral care for the divorced and remarried, the process for selecting bishops, papal finances, a mandate for theology professors, Archbishop Raymond Hunthausen, and the reintroduction of the Tridentine Mass.[197]

It was the issue regarding permission to celebrate the 1962 Latin Mass which showed May's diplomacy without surrendering his opinion. The Vatican wanted bishops to grant priests the right to celebrate the Latin Mass, but most American bishops refused. Their excuse was that those people who sought the Latin Mass were usually the same ones who were divisive on other issues.

Regardless, the Vatican began granting permission on a case-by-case basis. Swiss, German, and English episcopal conferences launched public protests. Most American bishops at this point kept their opinions to themselves. The European conference presidents

---

195 In 1992, Doorways got a Housing and Urban Development grant for $2,928,900 to build and subsidize two independent living facilities and in 1995 received another grant of $2,000,000 to renovate a hundred-year old building in the 4300 block of Maryland. This created a thirty-six-bed facility for people in the latter stages of AIDS.
196 Thomas J. Reese, S. J. *A Flock of Shepherds*. P. 143.
197 Ibid. P. 177.

were summoned to the Vatican. The American was not. However, May sent a private letter to the Vatican, expressing his concern.

Actually, Archbishop May had expressed his views on the Latin Mass a few years earlier to his priests in a Blue Note. He wrote, "Letters requesting a Latin Mass have been few and far between lately. I don't really know what that means. Have folks gradually lost their desire for that good old feeling? Are they satisfied because there is a Latin Mass available to them on occasion? Or have they just given up because their requests have fallen on deaf ears?"

After this speculation, he continued, "As you know the Holy See did ask the Bishops some time back their thoughts in regard since some Catholics in the U.S.A. have apparently been writing to Rome about this."

By way of encouragement, May added, "Once again I remind you that no permission is needed to offer the Mass in Latin and that you should do so occasionally if you are fulfilling a pastoral need. I would especially encourage the use of some of the grand old Latin choral music whenever appropriate along with English liturgy. Why not bring forth from your storehouse and use all the best – nova et vetera?"[198]

On the other side of the liturgical spectrum, the Vatican was concerned with ongoing experiments with the liturgy. Archbishop May noted in meeting after meeting that the issue of clown ministries— priests dressing as clowns at Mass—kept arising. "Somebody put that bug in their ear."

Archbishop May took the liturgy very seriously. When he learned that a priest celebrating Mass interrupted Communion to announce that another priest helping with Communion was celebrating his birthday, the organist through a pre-arranged signal broke out into "Happy Birthday to You."

The Archbishop wrote in his *Notanda*, the Blue Notes, a private communication with his priests: "Despite the good intention (showing priestly solidarity), it is a grave abuse to use the liturgy for personal purposes, especially its most sacred moment when we should be concentrating on the Lord, present in his body and blood."[199]

Vocations, especially to the diocesan priesthood, were a constant

---

198 *Notanda*. Volume II # 5 July 1, 1981. "Latin Mass." Archives of the Archdiocese of Saint Louis.
199 John L. May. *With Staff and Pen*. P. 41.

concern during the 1980s. The archdiocese had four large facilities: Kenrick Seminary, Cardinal Glennon College, Prep South, and Prep North. Most of them were half-empty. The archbishop lamented, "This overall seminary situation is my most worrisome problem. Therefore, it is also your problem. What are your thoughts?"

In 1985 the Archbishop reported that there were one hundred fifty-four students enrolled in Prep South, with all of them declared to be studying for the priesthood. But Prep North had only eighty-three studying to become priests, while another one hundred fifty-five filled in the enrollment, attending as if the junior seminary were a private school.

Cardinal Glennon College had an enrollment of seventy-five, but only fifty were studying to become priests for the archdiocese. Kenrick Seminary had just forty Saint Louis men, out of an enrollment of seventy-six. There was one Saint Louis man studying in Rome.

Archbishop May made these dire observations: "The number of claimed seminarians in our minor seminaries shrinks remarkably when they graduate. Our Saint Louis college seminarians are much fewer. Kenrick's Saint Louis seminarian enrollment is grim indeed. There is no indication of foreseeable ordinations in numbers adequate to continue our traditional priestly service here."[200]

The Archbishop then explored three reasons for the plummet in priestly vocations and four reasons why some dioceses had seen an uptick in vocations.

First, he cited the present culture of our modern society. He saw "a total conspiracy against anyone accepting an absolute value and against anyone being willing to give up anything for a good cause." It was what modern media was calling "The Me-Generation."

Next, he took aim at Catholic families. "We are no longer supporting the chance of a priestly vocation." There were too many anecdotal instances of teenagers being discouraged by parents if they expressed an interest in the seminary or a religious community. In one case, a student at De Smet Jesuit High School expressed an interest in the Society of Jesus and was transferred by his parents to Parkway North.

The third reason given was the massive decline in the use of the confessional. When people, including Catholic youth, gave up on the Sacrament of Penance, they stopped looking at their interior and

---

200 *Notanda.* Volume VI #5 November 12, 1985. "Vocation Crisis." Archives of the Archdiocese of Saint Louis.

moral life. They became worldlier and more in tune with that secular culture of our modern society.

Archbishop May saw remedies being employed in other dioceses. Priests in those dioceses preached about priesthood. They "make the vocation to the priesthood attractive." They do not shy away from the fact that the life is demanding, and challenges are attractive to many young people, despite the overall attitude of hedonism in society.

In those dioceses, priests get directly involved in youth work. Children and teens can see that these priests are real people. But above all, these dioceses engage in intense prayer for vocations.

Finances were pushing events. Something had to be done. An Inter-Office Communication observed that the reserve in the general funds of a million dollars had been used up in just three years. "We will begin using up the endowment fund for operations this year and can anticipate the depletion of all such funds by the time the present first theologians approach ordination."[201]

The Communication suggested that Kenrick Seminary be relocated to the campus of Cardinal Glennon College and Prep South. Several suggestions were given for possible tenants of the old seminary building. In March 1987 a Seminary Utilization Committee was established and suggested that the building be used for a conference center and/or retreat house.

Archbishop May asked Bishop Terry Steib to study the problem and make recommendations. What would result would be the "New Start" program, which would close the two minor seminaries and consolidate Kenrick and Glennon on the Glennon campus, creating Kenrick-Glennon Seminary. The target date was the 1987-88 academic year. The transition would be spearheaded by Bishop Edward O'Donnell.

On May 14, 1987, letters were sent to the Paul VI Pontifical Institute, the Vocation Office and the Permanent Diaconate Office from Bishop O'Donnell, offering them space in the old building. Later in the summer, it was made public that the old Kenrick building would be managed by Permanent Deacon Robert Snyder, who would also schedule all events there.

The transition of the "New Start" would not be smooth. Bishop O'Donnell wrote Frank Cognata of the Development Office that en-

---

201 "Draft II – Consideration about the Seminary Situation." Undated. RG 03D09 "Archbishop" Seminary Files: 1985-86. Archives of the Archdiocese of Saint Louis.

gineers found "several life-threatening situations" in the Glennon building. Specifically, faulty wiring in some of the student rooms, crumbling insulation, and a need to upgrade the fire escapes beyond the Building Code of 1930. The bishop appealed to Cognata to find ways to increase the 1987 Christmas Collection by at least twenty-five percent, an addition of around $150,000.

On July 31, 1987, the Blue Notes headlined, "Neither Cardinal Glennon College or Kenrick Seminary Has Closed." It explained that the two programs would simply be located on the same campus.

A bulletin was sent out to archdiocesan priests in August 1987. Its title was in bold capital letters, "A NEW START." It told of the electrical upgrades, the safety concerns addressed like new fire stairs, new fire-retardant doors, and smoke alarms in every room. The Vocation Office was relocated to the first floor of Saint Joseph Hall on the west end of the Glennon building while the second and third floors were set aside for the convent.

It described the academic arrangement for the college men to attend Saint Louis University. This was the work of Monsignors Timothy Dolan and Edward Reilly. The seminary faculty would remain the same. Prep South, now called Saint Louis Preparatory Seminary, would serve the whole archdiocese. Already thirty-six freshmen had applied.

Earlier, Dolan, still an associate pastor at Little Flower parish in Richmond Heights, had been given the task to negotiate the relationship with Saint Louis University. He told the *Saint Louis Review* there were two considerations. First, "the best priestly formation we can get, but secondly to do that as economically as possible. We couldn't keep up those two massive buildings so this is going to enhance our seminary formation. It's going to expand it." He assured the readership that the Glennon building was built to house two hundred, and the combined programs would not amount to one hundred and twenty.[202]

The new seminary rector, Rev. Ronald Ransom, C. M., sent a letter to Archbishop May in January 1988 stating that the theologate had fifty-four resident seminarians, eight on acolyte internship, one newly-ordained, and one about to be ordained.

In another missive, the rector reported that Albers Construction Company and James Mayer Architects were behind schedule. The seminarians had all moved in by August 1987, but lounges and meet-

---

202 October 3, 1986. "Archbishop's Representative optimistic on Kenrick Plan." *Saint Louis Review*.

ing rooms were incomplete, the interior stairwells were unfinished, as well as the college oratory. The kitchen renovations would be delayed until the summer of 1988.

Aided by Bishops O'Donnell and Steib and Monsignor Dolan, Archbishop May was able to concentrate on the New Start as well as other archdiocesan matters. As it happened, he was spared one very big headache.

A papal visit had been arranged for the second week of September 1987, and one would have thought that, as president of the NCCB, Archbishop May would have been heavily engaged. As it was, he was not. The Vatican had decided to downplay the role of national conferences, and so this affair was strictly between the Vatican and the ten cities to be visited.

Both 1986 and 1987 were difficult years in Vatican relations with the Church in America. Two sore points stood out. In August 1986 Reverend Charles E. Curran was told that he could no longer present himself as a Catholic theologian. His dissent, beginning with *Humanae Vitae*, had continued full force. Archbishop James A. Hickey forbad him to teach any subject at Catholic University of America. The next June, Curran received the backing of the Catholic Theological Society of America, though Curran had accepted a post at Cornell University as visiting professor.

Just weeks after the Curran removal, Archbishop Raymond Hunthausen of Seattle announced that he was receiving an unwelcomed auxiliary bishop, Donald Wuerl, who would supervise five areas of archdiocesan life in which the Vatican found Hunthausen lax in performing his duties.

Later, a panel of three bishops investigated Hunthausen and attempted to find a compromise, which he resisted. Seattle was still in chaos during the papal visit.

Between March 16 and 21, the ten ordinaries of the dioceses to be visited met with Vatican officials and with the pope. There was a general feeling among the bishops that the previous papal visit had not entirely been a success. And Catholic America was even edgier now. Gays were angry with a papal document which, while trying to affirm the human and civil rights of homosexuals, repeated the Catholic position that homosexual acts were gravely sinful.

Feminists were angry. American Jews were angry that Pope John Paul II had welcomed Austrian president Kurt Waldheim to the Vatican, despite accusations that Waldheim had cooperated with the Nazis during World War II.

The bishops laid out the issues and problems the pope would face in coming to America. It was agreed that the visit would include "dialogue sessions," and representatives would be selected to speak directly to the pope about certain issues. These would be submitted prior to the trip. The pope then would offer a prepared response.

The first test of this approach took place in Miami on September 10. First to speak was Father Francis McNulty, representing the diocesan priests of America. He spoke of the heavy demands on priests' schedules, and the harsher tone coming from the Holy See as contrasted to the pastoral approach of John XXIII. He wondered if mandatory celibacy was the cause of the shortage of vocations to the priesthood. He spoke about the important charism of theologians, a reference to Charles Curran, perhaps. And then went even further to speak about a greater role of women in the Church, hinting at ordination.

McNulty ended his presentation by reciting a poem, "Thought's Resistance to Words," written by John Paul himself. The pope embraced the priest and whispered into his ear, "You found good words."

Before reading his prepared remarks, John Paul made the enigmatic comment, "I remember a song. 'It's a Long Way to Tipperary.'"

The pope reassured the attending priests that whatever difficulties faced the Church, the Holy Spirit would see us through. Christ would fill the seminaries, if seminaries needed to be filled. John Paul did not directly address the issues McNulty brought up.

That afternoon the pope met with a delegation of American Jews. Some had boycotted because of the Waldheim visit. Others were pleased with what they saw and heard. This was the only instance where the remarks of a delegation were not sent to the Vatican ahead of the visit. They were spontaneous, as was the pope's reply.

Weeks earlier John Paul had written a letter to Archbishop May outlining his concern for a full and open historical exploration of the Church at the time of the Holocaust. The letter was made public and was well-received in the Jewish community. The pope, in his response, spoke of the great spiritual debt that Christianity had to Judaism.

The next event was a meeting with twenty-six representatives of American Protestants and Eastern Orthodox. Their spokesman was Bishop Philip Cousin from the African Methodist Episcopal Church.

Miami was followed the next day by a trip to Columbia, South Carolina where the pope met with Protestant leaders. On his first trip to America, John Paul met with Protestant leaders briefly. He talked; they listened. This time around there was more dialogue.

On September 12, it was New Orleans. There he addressed black Catholics, many of whom had met just four months earlier in the National Black Catholic Congress. He was enthusiastically received. From there he met with forty thousand students in the Superdome. A Mass was planned for the afternoon but got rained out with violent winds and lightning. Later, the pope met at Xavier University with college administrators and presidents, trying to assure them that the upcoming papal document on higher education would not be oppressive.

The next day, the Pope was in San Antonio celebrating Hispanic Catholicism. Seventy percent of San Antonio's Catholics were Hispanic. Its mayor, Henry Cisneros and its archbishop, Patrick Flores, were also Hispanic. But two issues plagued the community. Nearly forty percent of Hispanic Catholics eventually left for Protestant denominations. And many had illegal status, which kept them away from the center of society.

John Paul caused eyebrows to be raised when he remarked during a homily, "Among you there are people of great courage and generosity who have been doing much on behalf of suffering brothers and sisters arriving from the south. They have sought to show compassion in the face of complex human, social, and political realities." Some took this as a reference to the sanctuary movement which was hiding and aiding illegals.

The Immigration and Naturalization Service asked for a clarification, and the papal spokesman, Dr. Joaquin Navarro-Valls, assured them that the pope was not endorsing any illegal practices.

Early the next morning, John Paul was serenaded by a sixty-piece Mariachi band. His motorcade was accompanied by fifty more musical groups on his way to the airport. The next stop was Phoenix.

Three issues dominated his stay in Arizona: health care, AIDS, and Native Americans. The dialogue presentation was given by John E. Curley, Jr., president of the Catholic Health Association. He spoke of challenges due to the loss of religious as nurses and administrators. He spoke of finances and said, "Our institutions and services are increasingly caught in a tension between our call to care and the need to survive in a potentially ruinous economic climate."

He spoke of the need for moral guidance in areas such as genetic

engineering, technically-assisted human reproduction, organ pro-
curement and transplants, life-sustaining medical treatment, and
even human experimentation.[203]

The papal response was to emphasize the practical, continuing to
provide services while putting forth the pedagogical. It was important for Catholic health care to defend the dignity of human life and to
judge all new technologies in that light.

Later, John Paul met with ten thousand Native American Catholics who had gathered for the Tekakwitha Conference. There were an
estimated 285,000 Catholic Indians, but only twenty-five priests and
one bishop, Donald Pelotte, his father being Abenaki and his mother
French-Canadian. He was forty-two years old at the time, a bishop
only two years. Bishop Pelotte joined the pope as they entered the
coliseum in a long procession with colorful vestments.

The longest stay would be in California, September 15 to 18. The
first stop was in Los Angeles, with its nearly three million Catholics.
Again, Hispanic Catholicism was showcased. One parish, Our Lady
Queen of Angels, typically celebrated eleven Masses on a weekend
with an attendance averaging ten thousand. It was not uncommon to
baptize two hundred babies on a weekend.

Beyond the sacraments, Our Lady Queen of Angels was heavily engaged in social work for the neighborhood. Besides providing food to
the needy, the parish also offered job counseling and housing, especially for those arriving from Central and South America.

After going to the cathedral, Pope John Paul went to the Universal Amphitheater where he spoke to six thousand teenagers and
another twelve thousand by way of satellite to teens in Saint Louis,
Denver, and Portland. He was emotionally overwhelmed when he
was serenaded by a young man with no arms, playing a guitar with
his feet.

From there the pope went to the Registry Hotel to meet with movie
stars and television and movie executives. He told them he recognized
the incredible influence they had on culture but warned them, "... communications can appeal to and promote what is debased in people:
dehumanized sex through pornography or through a casual attitude
toward sex and human life; greed through materialism and consum-
erism or irresponsible individualism; anger and vengefulness through

---

203 Kenneth A. Brigg. *Holy Siege*. P. 525.

violence or self-righteousness. All the media of popular culture which you represent can build up or destroy, uplift or cast down."[204]

In the evening, the pope celebrated Mass at the Los Angeles Coliseum.

The next day, Tuesday, September 16, Pope John Paul II heard speeches from four leading American prelates. The first was Cardinal Bernardin of Chicago, speaking on the relationship between the Church in America and Rome. He recognized that poll after poll showed the Catholic population stood at odds with Vatican positions on many issues. He reminded the pope that Americans cherished their freedom to think and to speak and that this led to "two unfortunate tendencies." One was for American Catholics to view Vatican direction as regressive and unreasonable. The other was the Vatican's view that questioning was a form of dissent and even apostasy. Bernardine called for greater collegiality among bishops and the pope.

Archbishop Quinn of San Francisco spoke of the moral challenges facing American Catholics. Issues like increasing divorce rates, greater affluence and education giving Catholics more independence in thought and action, medical technology, greater concern over human sexuality, and increased questioning of the role of women in society were all needing to be addressed.

The third speaker was Archbishop Weakland of Milwaukee. He spoke of the laity and the need to develop a spirituality both for the workplace and for the home. He also spoke of an increased role for women in society and in the Church.

Finally, Archbishop Pilarczyk of Cincinnati spoke of vocations and the increased role of laity in Church affairs.

The pope's response was to call for unity with the papacy, both among the clergy and the laity. He was unequivocal when he spoke. "It is sometimes reported that a large number of Catholics do not adhere to the teachings of the Church on a number of questions, notably sexual and conjugal morality, divorce and remarriage. Some are reported as not accepting the Church's clear position on abortion"

The pope continued, "It is sometimes claimed that dissent from the Magisterium is totally compatible with being 'a good Catholic' and poses no obstacle to the reception of the Sacraments. This is a

---

204 Ibid. P. 533.

grave error that challenges the teaching office of the Bishops of the United States and elsewhere."[205]

He further warned the bishops to keep a keen eye on their seminaries, to root out the use of general absolution at penance services, and to express clarity on the Church's teaching regarding homosexuality.

That evening John Paul celebrated Mass at Dodger Stadium with sixty-three thousand people. Several times in his homily he switched to Spanish which the large number of Hispanics attending the Mass greatly appreciated .

The next day was a brief visit to Monterey, mainly to visit the tomb of Blessed Junipero Serra. Seventy thousand joined the pope who spoke of the dignity of farm work. President Reagan had provided him with a helicopter which he used first to visit Carmel Mission and then to take the short flight to San Francisco.

At Mission Dolores the pope met with nine hundred people, most of them victims of AIDS. His presence brought out demonstrators, some two thousand gays, lesbians, and others protesting the Church's position on homosexuality. They were joined by one hundred fifty Dignity members and another one hundred fifty protesting the Waldheim visit.

Later at the Cathedral, the pope heard from two representatives, a Vincentian priest and a religious sister. The priest spoke in rather vague terms about the "rightful role of women... in the Church in the United States." Sister Helen Garvey, president of the Leadership Conference of Women Religious, was more pointed on the topic and received enthusiastic applause several times during her presentation.

As the day ended, John Paul retired to the archbishop's residence a short distance from the cathedral.

Friday morning began back at the cathedral with some three thousand laity from throughout the country. The first speaker was Donna Hanson, the director of social ministries for the Diocese of Spokane. She told the pope that Americans believe that raising challenging questions is a healthy practice. Again, there were bursts of applause throughout her speech.

The next speaker was the director of pastoral ministries for the Archdiocese of San Francisco, Patrick Hughes. He called for greater recognition of the good work that the laity were doing in the Church, and for equitable pay.

---

205 Kenneth A. Brigg. *Holy Siege*. P. 540.

John Paul did not directly address either speaker. Instead, he reminded his audience that the Church has various functions whose areas needed to be respected and honored. He drew a distinction between the ordained and those not ordained and reminded his listeners that the Catholic Church was by nature hierarchical. He extolled the increased role of the laity in the Church. He also received several bursts of applause.

That night, his last in California, he celebrated Mass with seventy thousand people. Clearly exhausted from the ten-day marathon, Pope John Paul II boarded *Shepherd One* to fly to his last stop, Detroit. He arrived shortly before 9:00 PM, Eastern Time and flew by helicopter to Sacred Heart Seminary and then the cathedral. Archbishop Edmund Szoka greeted the pope, a dear friend, and was overwhelmed with emotion.

On Saturday, the Polish pope met with Detroit Poles, speaking in Polish under the banner of Our Lady of Czestochowa. He then went to Ford Auditorium to meet with permanent deacons, some 2,800 of them, and their wives. There were eight thousand deacons in the United States. It was the only ecclesial body—among priests, seminarians, religious sisters and brothers—which saw remarkable growth in the 1980s. The pope had high compliments for the deacons and their wives for taking up the call to follow Jesus and serve the Church in this unique way.

The visit ended with a gathering at Hart Plaza and a speech on social justice. John Paul ended by saying, "I hope, and I wish that this visit will be spiritually fruitful." At the airport, he met briefly with Vice President George H. W. Bush.

Archbishop Hunthausen was still stewing in Seattle. Charles Curran was still unable to teach on a Catholic campus. Dignity was still indignant over the Church's teachings on homosexuality. Women were still ineligible to be ordained. But the pope had heard from his wayward flock, and those in the flock who were not wayward certainly found his presence among them to be spiritually fruitful.

Two other positive developments happened in the last years of May's episcopacy in Saint Louis: One was the result of concerned citizens; the other he had a direct hand in.

Kent Hedlund was the executive director of Operation Food Search. Founded in 1981, it began by going to local hospitals and begging for the food they had not used that day. Operation Food Search then took the surplus food, much of it perishable, to over two hundred community services for distribution to the hungry. Hedlund figured that in 1988 alone he had received $414,000 worth of food from the hospitals.

Earlier, Operation Food Search had teamed up with Catholic Charities and Food Crisis to coordinate efforts to feed the hungry. Catholic Charities had a 12,500 square foot warehouse in the midtown area. Food Crisis had an 11,000 square foot facility downtown. Operation Food Search acted as a broker, arranging volunteers at pantries to pick up "outdated, surplus or 'distressed' food from area food companies."[206]

Among the three organizations, it was estimated that $5,000,000 had been donated in 1983 alone to two hundred food pantries, twenty soup kitchens, and one hundred centers preparing meals for the needy.

In 1984 the executive director of Operation Food Search was Marcia Mellitz. She conducted a survey of 5,800 people, representing twenty-six thousand family members, neighbors, and friends. She found that forty-one percent of charity recipients were white, and forty-three percent were black. The remainder were not determined. Eighty-six percent of the households surveyed had at least one child while twenty percent had at least one person over sixty.

Perhaps the most telling discovery was that elderly white women in South Saint Louis were the most neglected.[207]

Despite the establishment of FOCUS schools in North Saint Louis and the founding of Cardinal Ritter Prep High School, the trends in urban education were not bright. Kevin Short summed it up. "In the 1980s, Catholic schools began transitioning from a majority religious to a principally lay faculty, and the cost of attendance began to skyrocket. It changed the dynamics of these schools. Faith-based education was no longer available to parts of the middle class, and definitely not to the poor."[208]

Archbishop May met with Sister Mary Ann Eckhoff, SSND superintendent of Catholic schools, and several local Catholic leaders to found the Today and Tomorrow Educational Foundation in 1991. The objective was to raise funds which would be distributed in lump sum grants to the various parochial schools in the City of Saint Lou-

---

206 November 20, 1984. "Many Go Hungry Despite Food Aid." *Globe-Democrat*.
207 Ibid.
208 March 22, 2018. "Today and Tomorrow Educational Foundation: Sky's the Limit.
Ladue News.

is. In turn, this would make faith-based education more affordable for elementary students in need. TTEF grew year by year and has become one of the largest charitable foundations in Saint Louis.[209]

On November 22, 1992, the Archdiocese of Saint Louis celebrated an anniversary Mass for Archbishop John L. May. He had been a bishop for twenty-five years. It was held at the Arena and was attended by seventeen thousand people. The occasion was bittersweet. Archbishop May had been diagnosed with brain cancer. In July a small tumor had been removed, and he was undergoing aggressive treatments of chemotherapy and radiation. He was weak. His right arm was limp. He would not be able to join his fellow bishops at Mundelein Seminary to celebrate their anniversary together.

The Mass began with the processional, "To Jesus Christ Our Sovereign King," by Monsignor Martin Hellriegel. The recessional was by Marty Haugen, "Let Justice Roll Like a River," which included the line "...and wash all oppression away."

Bishop Edward O'Donnell read the archbishop's homily for him. "When will the Lord knock on your door? And on mine? None of us knows. For me, he is likely to come sooner than you. When he knocks on my door, and on yours, it will be not an end, but a beginning. Someone is waiting for you at the end of life's road – and for me."

At the end of Mass, Archbishop May was presented with a large green and white quilt. Four symbols were featured: his coat of arms, the Saint Louis Arch with a cross, and his two favorite hobbies, golf and bicycling. He got up the strength to say into the microphone, "The best gift today is all of you. I won't forget. Thank you."

Bishop O'Donnell responded, "Twelve years ago, into Saint Louis came a man of God whose name was John. Like John the Baptist, John May has never proclaimed himself, but always only the Lord, whose prophet he is."[210]

John L. May resigned as archbishop of Saint Louis three weeks later on December 9. He died on March 24, 1994, at the age of seventy-one. He was buried in the Cathedral.

---

209 In 2017, TTEF provided scholarship awards to 4,300 children. It is the fourth largest elementary school scholarship organization in the U.S.A. and has granted more than $90 million since 1991. Ninety-eight percent of TTEF seniors graduate from high school and ninety-nine percent of those go on to post-secondary education, often being the first in their family to do so.

210 "May's Episcopal Celebration." R G I H 9a. Archives of the Archdiocese of Saint Louis.

ABOVE: Archbishop John May met with President Ronald Reagan in 1983. As president of the NCCB, Archbishop May was critical of the Reagan administration's stances on economic policy and the arms race. White House Photograph. From the Archdiocese of St. Louis Archives.

Kenrick Seminary Rector Fr. Ronald Ransom, CM, talked at the Serra Club district convention in St. Louis, 1986. Photographer Richard Finke. From the Archdiocese of St. Louis Archives.

Tim Guthridge and Barb Prosser at Cass House helped stock the pantry of the largest of three Catholic Worker Houses in the St. Louis Area. Cass House provided housing for around 50 people nightly, and ran a daily soup kitchen that could accommodate 70 more people. Photographer Richard Finke, 1982. From the Archdiocese of St. Louis Archives.

The episcopal seat at the New Cathedral sits empty with a votive candle and a sign in front reading, "For the health of Archbishop May, we pray to the Lord." The Archbishop's brain cancer and surgery were announced publicly on July 20, 1992. Photographer Richard Finke. From the Archdiocese of St. Louis Archives.

After undergoing brain surgery, Archbishop May gives a thumbs up to photographer Richard Finke to say he's doing okay, 1992. From the Archdiocese of St. Louis Archives.

On World Day of the Sick, Auxiliary Bishop Edward J. O'Donnell, archdiocesan administrator, anointed retired Archbishop John L. May at the Cathedral Basilica Mass on February 11, 1993. The archbishop was among hundreds that day receiving the Sacrament of the Anointing of the Sick. Photographer Richard Finke. From the Archdiocese of St. Louis Archives.

Archbishop John L. May's casket was taken down to the crypt entrance at the Cathedral Basilica after his funeral on March 30, 1994. Photographer Richard Finke. From the Archdiocese of St. Louis Archives.

Cardinal Ritter High School senior Cameron Caldwell was able to attend school through the help of the Today and Tomorrow Foundation. Here, he talks with student Samira Alwazir in a British Literature class. Photographer Lisa Johnston, 2015. Courtesy of St. Louis Review.

Chapter Eight

JUSTIN RIGALI

"First of all, I know nothing." That was the opening line Msgr. John Gaydos wrote to the Installation Committee members on December 30, 1993. Archbishop John L. May had resigned as archbishop of Saint Louis over a year earlier. The archdiocese was being led by Auxiliary Bishop Edward O'Donnell, but it seemed that Rome was taking extraordinary time to appoint a successor. Nonetheless, Gaydos continued, "It might be prudent, however, for us to plan on having a meeting."

On January 6, 1994, the committee did meet, but the minutes showed again a mild irritation at the delay. "General observation: As you can see, there are lots of questions – no answers! Nothing can really be decided definitely until a new archbishop is named, and we can begin scheduling events, liturgies, music, etc."[211]

Once the announcement was made two weeks later, the committee sprang into action. On January 28, it set the installation for March 16, 1994 at 2 P.M. A Vespers service was set for the night before at the cathedral at 7 P.M. Invitations, program booklets, receptions, hotel accommodations, and banners were discussed.

A week later, the committee turned its attention to transportation, music, the new archbishop's coat of arms, and his official photograph. Everything was coming together rapidly. This would be an installation unlike any other in Saint Louis history, for the subject of the installation was unlike any other bishop sent to the archdiocese. Justin Francis Rigali was secretary of the Sacred Congregation of Bishops and secretary of the College of Cardinals.

Days earlier, rumors were floating the name of Justin Rigali. Sister Charlotte Rigali, C.S.J., serving on the archdiocesan tribunal as a canon lawyer, was asked by the *Post-Dispatch* which reported, "entirely possible that a bishop of her brother's status and prestige would leave the Vatican and come to St. Louis." She added, "This is an important see."[212]

---

211 "Programs – Installation Committee – Archbishop Rigali." Folder 26. RG 03L01. Saint Louis Archdiocesan Archives.
212 "Rumors Fly about May's Successor. *St. Louis Post-Dispatch*. January 22, 1994.

While the *Post-Dispatch* ran a headline, "To the City and the World: Pope Sends Trusted Adviser to Guide St. Louis," the *Chicago Tribune* called out, "A Vatican Insider Sent to St. Louis." The conservative paper *The Wanderer* ran an exhaustive biography of the new archbishop under the title, "Called 'Doctrinally Conservative:' Archbishop Rigali Appointed to St. Louis."

Father John Jay Hughes told columnist Jerry Berger that he had recently written to Rigali recommending that the next archbishop of Saint Louis should "be someone capable of raising our sights from local concerns to the great worldwide family of which we are proud to be a part."

Justin Rigali was born on April 19, 1935 to Henry and Frances (White) Rigali. He was the youngest of seven. He was ordained April 25, 1961 for the Los Angeles Archdiocese by Cardinal McIntyre and served as associate pastor of two parishes before being sent to Rome to take a doctorate in canon law at the Pontifical Gregorian University. From 1964 to 1966 he studied at the Pontifical Ecclesiastical Academy, a school for Vatican diplomats, and served in the English language department of the Secretariat of State. For four years, Rigali was assigned as papal nuncio to Madagascar and returned to Rome in 1970 to become the director of the English language department of the Secretariat of State. Meanwhile, he taught at the Pontifical Ecclesiastical Academy and acted as English translator for Pope Paul VI.

Pope John Paul II kept Rigali as director of the English-language department of the Secretariat of State. He accompanied the pope on numerous papal trips, including the 1979 and 1987 visits to the United States. In 1985 Rigali was consecrated an archbishop by John Paul II and was named president of the Pontifical Ecclesiastical Academy. In 1989 he received his post at the Congregation for Bishops and in 1990 his post at the College of Cardinals.

While most Saint Louisans, whether Catholic or not, were overwhelmed to have such a luminary as the new archbishop, a few voiced concern that Archbishop Rigali would be a wooden bureaucrat, aloof from the people. These, it seemed, paid attention to Rigali's titles but not to the man. While carrying all of his Vatican responsibilities, Archbishop Rigali regularly availed himself to do pastoral work in Roman parishes. He also acted as chaplain for cloistered nuns at the Monastery of Saint Joseph in Rome.

The installation of Archbishop Rigali was everything it was touted to be. Attendants included Cardinal William Baum, the Prefect for the Apostolic Penitentiary, Cardinal Edmund Szoka, President of the Prefecture for the Economic Affairs, Cardinals Joseph Bernardin of Chicago, Bernard Law of Boston, John O'Connor of New York, James Hickey of Washington, D.C., Roger Mahoney of Los Angeles, and Anthony Bevelacqua of Philadelphia. Over a hundred bishops attended, and it was estimated that five hundred priests were there, as well as representatives of the ecumenical and interfaith communities.

Cardinal Bernardin Gantin, Prefect of the Congregation for Bishops, Rigali's immediate superior, presented the crozier which had been used by every Saint Louis archbishop since 1903. Archbishop Agostino Caccevillan, the papal nuncio to the United States, read the notice of appointment by Pope John Paul II.

Sitting with the Rigali family were three Swiss guards, representing their comrades. They played no formal role and did not wear the distinctive uniforms. The three had paid their own airfare in order to attend the installation. When interviewed by a reporter, Alistair Lanz said, "Archbishop Rigali is our friend. He befriended the guard. He'd say Mass for us, take us to dinner and come to our Christmas parties."[213]

Not attending was Archbishop May. He had continued to weaken and at the time of the installation had lapsed into a coma. Archbishop Rigali would say his funeral Mass fourteen days later.

After the installation Mass there was a reception held next door at Rosati-Kain High School. Other receptions followed, but Archbishop Rigali proved to be a virtual dynamo, a man whose secretaries and assistants found it difficult to keep up with him.

On April 28 lightning struck old Saint Anthony of Padua Church during the 8 A.M. Mass. It had been a South Saint Louis landmark since 1864. The fire department arrived immediately and set streams of water on the burning roof. Right behind them was Archbishop Rigali, assuring the Franciscan community of his support to rebuild what had been lost.

Rigali stirred a controversy in early August 1994 when he appealed for clemency for Christopher S. Simmons who had just been convicted of the murder of Shirley Ann Crook. His sentence was capital punishment. The archbishop wrote that killing even a convicted

---

213 "Special Detail: 3 Swiss Guards Attend as Tribute to Rigali." *Post-Dispatch*. March 16, 1994.

murderer cheapened life all the more. He pleaded for a sentence of life without the possibility of parole.

While the family of Shirley Crook was angry at the request and wrote letters to the *Post-Dispatch*, the judge denied Rigali's request and Simmons was executed.

The day after Christmas, Archbishop Rigali drove to Farmington to celebrate Mass with fifty inmates of the Farmington Correctional Center. Around a dozen staff also attended. He sought to ensure the prisoners of their goodness in the eyes of God.

A month later, Archbishop Rigali attended a funeral service for a fifteen-year-old girl from Sacred Heart Parish in Florissant. She had been sexually assaulted and murdered in a girls' restroom at McCluer North High School.

One local historian referred to late nineteenth century Saint Louis as "a cradle for bishops." The same might be said about the 1990's. Edward O'Donnell and Terry Steib were consecrated on the same day in Saint Louis in 1984. Both would serve as auxiliary bishops, joining George J. Gottwald and Charles R. Koester. For the archdiocese to have an archbishop and four auxiliaries was extraordinary. But Bishop Gottwald would retire just four years later, and Bishop Koester continued to serve until his resignation in 1991.

Edward O'Donnell gave many years of leadership service to the archdiocese. He was ordained in 1957 after attending Prep Seminary and Kenrick Seminary. He served as associate pastor at three parishes, took part in the Selma Voters' Rights Demonstration in 1965, and was a board member of the Urban League of Saint Louis and member of the Saint Louis branch of the NAACP.

O'Donnell was made the head of the Archdiocesan Radio and TV Office in 1966 and was named the editor of the *Saint Louis Review* upon the death of Father Thomas Hederman in an automobile accident. Cardinal Carberry made O'Donnell the director of the Archdiocesan Respect Life Program which he ran from 1972 to 1973 and then was made the coordinator of the Pro-Life Committee.

A veritable dynamo of activity, O'Donnell left the *Review* to become vicar general of the archdiocese while serving as pastor of Saint Peter's Parish in Kirkwood. Somehow, he found time to write a book published by Ligouri, *Priestly People – A Practical Guide to Lay Ministry*.

In November 1994 a *Post-Dispatch* article announced, "Bishop O'Donnell Gets Own Diocese." It spoke of the sixty-three-year-old bishop who had administered the archdiocese for twenty-one months before Archbishop Rigali arrived, and of his work freeing up Archbishop May to concentrate on his work at the NCCB. O'Donnell said he would miss Saint Louis, but "I want to put my feet under my own table." He was heading off to Lafayette, Louisiana.

It was not a plum assignment. The diocese was still reeling from the revelations of the pedophile Gilbert Gauthe. A lot of healing would be needed. O'Donnell served the Lafayette diocese for eight years before retiring at age seventy-one in 2002. The previous years had been physically demanding. He "had a series of health problems for the past five years and just last year was diagnosed with Parkinson's disease." He had also suffered a mild stroke and was experiencing the beginnings of diabetes.

To the people of his diocese, O'Donnell wrote, "I cannot say I have accomplished as much as I would have wanted to do. I only wish I had been given more years of good health so that I could work as I had become accustomed to with energy, with joy and with effectiveness."

He added, "At a time when the Church needs aggressive and more energetic leadership, these are dangerous weaknesses in dealing with the serious and immediate problems we face."[214]

No doubt Bishop O'Donnell was referring to another article in the diocesan newspaper, "Clergy Sexual Abuse Dominates Bishops' Nov. Meeting."

Bishop O'Donnell returned to Saint Louis to take up residence at Saint Agnes Home in Kirkwood. He died there on February 1, 2009 at the age of seventy-seven.

J. Terry Steib, S.V.D. was ordained for the Divine Word Missionaries on January 6, 1967. He served his community as provincial superior for three terms from 1976 to 1983 and was vice president of the Conference of Major Superiors of Men from 1979 to 1983. He was consecrated as bishop along with Edward O'Donnell to serve as auxiliary bishop of Saint Louis. Bishop Steib was the first African American bishop in the history of the archdiocese. He served as executive director of the National Black Clergy Caucus and worked diligently with the black Catholic community in the archdiocese and took a special interest in Catholic education in North Saint Louis.

---

214 *Acadia Catholic*. December 2002.

In May 1993 Bishop Terry Steib was made the fourth bishop of Memphis. The installation took place at the Cook Convention Center and was attended by ailing Archbishop May as well as the second bishop, J. Francis Stafford, and third bishop, Daniel Buechlein, O.S.B.

The next Saint Louisan to be named a bishop was Paul Zipfel. He seemed never to be far from home. Zipfel was born September 22, 1935 of Albert J. and Leona (Rau) Zipfel and attended Saint Michael's Parish school in Shrewsbury. For high school he went to Prep South, within walking distance of his home. He attended nearby Kenrick Seminary from 1955 to 1957. Two of his uncles, retired, were part-time employees of the seminary, one a carpenter and the other overseeing the boilers. He finished his studies at Catholic University of America and was ordained on March 18, 1961.

While completing an MA in education at Saint Louis University, Father Zipfel served as associate pastor in several parishes, most notably at Holy Cross where he was heavily influenced by Monsignor Martin Hellriegel. He was administrator of high schools and pastor of parishes and was consecrated a bishop on May 16, 1989. The consecrating bishops were Archbishop May and Bishops O'Donnell and Steib.

On December 31, 1996, Bishop Zipfel was named the sixth bishop of Bismarck, North Dakota.

The *Dakota Catholic Action* introduced their new bishop to the Catholics of Bismarck with an article entitled, "Bishop Zipfel's Lifelong Hobby Makes Friends – Like Magic." It told of his interest in magic tricks since the age of nine and how he belonged to two major magician organizations. His magic tricks were icebreakers and gave him an instant rapport with those he met.

Bishop Zipfel retired in October 2011, moving to the University of Mary where he intended to be a spiritual director. Sadly, within a year he developed dementia and moved back to Saint Louis to Our Mother of Good Counsel Home in Normandy. He died on July 14, 2019. The funeral was celebrated at the cathedral by Bishop Edward Rice, concelebrated by several bishops, many clergy, and was attended by the faithful, especially former members of Holy Family Parish in South Saint Louis, where he was so beloved.

The loss to Memphis of Bishop Steib in 1993 and the loss to Lafayette of Bishop O'Donnell, the retirement of Bishop Gottwald in 1988 and that of Bishop Koester in 1991, left the archdiocese short of auxiliaries. That would be corrected with the consecration of Edward Braxton, 50, of Chicago, Illinois.

Braxton had been pastor of Saint Catherine of Siena and Saint Lucy in Oak Park. The third child of five of Cullen and Evelyn Braxton, the bishop-elect had a stellar educational background. He studied at Loyola University of Chicago, took his seminary training at Saint Mary of the Lake, and studied at Catholic University of Louvain, Belgium. He taught courses at the University of Notre Dame and Harvard Divinity School

Cardinal Bernardin commented, "Chicago is sending one of its most capable priests to Saint Louis. I know Bishop-designate Braxton to be a priest of deep faith, courage and conviction. He has a keen mind, great pastoral sensibilities and proven leadership ability."[215]

From the beginning, Bishop Braxton showed concern for the black community and about the role of black Catholics. He was not shy about observations. He expressed alarm at the number of black pregnancies outside of marriage. "A pattern of three generations of unwed mothers in a single family may be the single greatest internal obstacle to the growth and economic stability of the Black family in America."

And his critique of black Catholics was severe. The Church was seen as "the special home of the great ethnic and national groups of Europe. It is the custodian of their customs, their traditions and their mores – and is in some way incompatible with the Black experience in America. When we reflect on the scars of the past, we need no longer wonder why there are so few Black Catholics. The wonder is that there are so many."[216]

Bishop Braxton was a frequent lecturer nationwide on racism and wrote articles for *America* and the *National Catholic Reporter*.

After six years as auxiliary bishop in Saint Louis, Edward Braxton was given his own diocese, Lake Charles, Louisiana. It was an experience he had not been trained for. Accustomed to large city life, universities, libraries, and concert halls, the bishop found himself in a small, Southern city of 70,000, half of whom were black. The city itself was half Catholic, and while the rest of the five counties or parishes were less Catholic, the Catholic population of the diocese still constituted nearly thirty percent of the whole. The diocese had one high school,

---

215 "Welcome: Fr. Braxton Appointed New Aux Bishop." *St. Louis Review*. March 31, 1995.
216 "New Bishop Traces Various Ties to St. Louis." *St. Louis Review*. March 31, 1995.

Saint Louis. The city had one institution of higher learning, McNeese State University. Lake Charles was over a two-hour drive from Houston and over a three-hour drive to New Orleans.

Five years later, Bishop Braxton was given the diocese of Belleville, Illinois. While the move brought him closer to his family and back to a large metropolitan area, it proved to be a major headache. When Bishop Wilton Gregory was assigned to become the archbishop of Atlanta, and the Belleville see became vacant, the Presbyterial Council met and wanted to influence the decision of their new ordinary by consulting with Cardinal Francis George, archbishop of Chicago and metropolitan for Illinois.

The appointment came so quickly that a meeting with Cardinal George could not take place. Some Belleville priests reacted angrily. "We were very much taken aback," one stated. Another said anonymously, "The clergy is convinced that if the process had been followed at all, this name would not have emerged. Obviously, he knows someone in Rome."[217]

Things did not improve. At the bishop's installation, there was a small protest outside the Cathedral. One news article claimed that seventy-five percent of the diocesan priests had signed a letter to Cardinal George expressing displeasure at the appointment.

Things had become so vitriolic that Bishop Braxton addressed an open letter to be read at every Mass. He explained that upon his arrival, he had met with several priests who urged him to cancel the installation and refuse the post. He said, "They had incriminating information against me which might be released, if I did not heed their words." He told of an anonymous phone call on his private line which threatened, "We will not rest until we get rid of you."[218]

One month later, a local millionaire, Frank Ladner, took out a $10,000 ad in *USA Today*, calling upon Pope Benedict XVI to remove Bishop Braxton. Regardless of ongoing opposition, Bishop Braxton served as Bishop of Belleville for fourteen years and submitted his resignation when he turned seventy-five.

In 1997 three Saint Louis priests were consecrated as bishops, one to serve as bishop of the Jefferson City Diocese and two as auxiliaries in Saint Louis.

---

217 "Priests Say They Weren't Consulted on New Bishop." *Post-Dispatch*. May 1, 2005.
218 "Braxton: Priests Blackmailed Me." *Post-Dispatch*. March 21, 2008.

Monsignor John Gaydos had served as secretary to both Cardinal Carberry and Archbishop May. He had accompanied Carberry to both conclaves of 1978 and served as chancellor of the archdiocese from 1981 to 1990 when he was made pastor of Saint Gerard Majella in Kirkwood. He was made vicar general the year before being consecrated as the third bishop of Jefferson City.

The Jefferson City Diocese was created in 1956 along with Springfield-Cape Girardeau. Its founding bishop was Joseph M. Marling, C.PP.S. He had served as auxiliary bishop of Kansas City, Missouri since 1947. During his tenure, Marling built the new cathedral, nearly two dozen churches, rectories, and schools and invited the Carmelites to establish a monastery in his diocese. He established the diocesan newspaper, sent missionaries to Peru, and attended the Second Vatican Council. Marling brought the Christian Brothers to staff Helias High School in 1956.

Bishop Marling retired in 1969 at the age of sixty-four. His successor was Michael Francis McAuliffe, a priest of the diocese of Kansas City, Missouri. He built on Marling's foundation and emphasized Catholic education, establishing the Diocesan Religious Education Office and sought ways to increase the salaries of lay teachers. He brought the Permanent Diaconate to his diocese as well as programs like Charismatic Renewal, Marriage Encounter, Teens Encounter Christ and many others. He was responsible for the founding of twenty-one more churches and ordained 78 priests and 84 permanent deacons before his retirement in 1997.

Michael Sheridan was consecrated bishop on September 3, 1997. He had a successful career as a priest. Ordained on May 29, 1971, he furthered his academic career by taking a doctorate in sacred theology at the Pontifical University of Saint Thomas Aquinas in Rome in 1980. Previously, Sheridan had earned a Masters in Divinity from Kenrick-Glennon Seminary and an MA in historical theology from Saint Louis University.

Father Sheridan served on the faculty at Kenrick-Glennon Seminary while pastoring first Christ the King Parish in University City and then Immaculata in Richmond Heights. After consecration, Bishop Sheridan served as auxiliary bishop for just over four years when he was asked to become coadjutor Bishop of Colorado Springs. The founding bishop Richard C. Hanifen was suffering from diabetes. He resigned on January 30, 2003, nineteen years from the date of his installation.

Bishop Sheridan made the schools and parish faith formation key goals of his episcopacy, as well as appointing a vocation director. Under Hanifen, the number of Catholics doubled in the diocese. But it was a pastoral letter dated May 1, 2004, which brought Sheridan national attention.

Regarding Catholic voters, the bishop wrote that they should absent themselves from Communion "if they back politicians who support abortion rights, stem cell research, euthanasia or gay marriage."

The letter brought a storm of protest. Michael Merrifield, a Democratic state legislator, told the *Post-Dispatch*, "I think it is an outrageous intrusion into what is supposed to be a separation of Church and state. It is frightening." The bishop retorted anything less would mean "the well-formed conscience of religious people should not be brought to bear on their political choices."[219]

Consecrated the same day as Bishop Sheridan was Joseph F. Naumann. His priestly formation was typical of Saint Louis priests: Prep South was followed by Cardinal Glennon College for a degree in Philosophy and completion of studies at Kenrick Seminary. Naumann was ordained on May 24, 1975.

Naumann's first two assignments were as associate pastor at Saint Dominic Savio Parish in Afton and then Our Lady of Sorrows Parish in South Saint Louis. But in 1984 he was able to devote himself to a cause which was near to his heart, the pro-life movement. He was appointed coordinator of the Archdiocesan Pro-Life Committee and sent to reside at Most Blessed Sacrament Parish as a part-time associate. In 1989 he left North Saint Louis to become pastor of Ascension parish in Normandy while remaining at Pro-Life.

Father Naumann had three objectives for the committee. The first area was educational, coordinating local rallies, establishing a speakers' bureau, and creating programs for the schools. A second area was pastoral, caring for women who shunned abortion but who had difficulties providing for their babies. The committee coordinated efforts with Catholic Charities, Birthright, and Our Lady's Inn in that regard. The third was that of community action. Out-going coordinator, Father Robert Boisaubin, who led the committee for six years, noted, "It has largely been their input that has been

219 "Bishop Says Certain Voters Shouldn't Receive Communion." *Post-Dispatch*. May 13, 2004.

instrumental in making Missouri the pro-life state that it is."[220]

That political action paid off. In 1990 a House amendment prohibiting the use of state funds for school nurses to encourage abortions or to refer students to providers passed in a 111 to 42 vote. The amendment had been fought by Speaker Bob F. Griffin (D-Cameron) and Senate President Pro-Tempore James L. Matthewson (D-Sedalia). Naumann noted that the vote proved "what we've contended all along, that what's happening this year is not the will of the legislative body. It's simply the decision of two people in leadership." Senator John D. Schneider (D-Florissant) looked to the future. "The primary item now is the caregiving bill," which would bring state aid to pregnant women who chose childbirth.[221]

At the age of fifty-four, Bishop Naumann was given administrative responsibilities over the archdiocese when Archbishop Rigali became archbishop of Philadelphia. He had served as vicar general of the archdiocese from 1994 to 2003. Seven weeks after the arrival of Archbishop Raymond Burke, Bishop Naumann was given a new assignment, coadjutor of Kansas City, Kansas.

Naumann served in that capacity for one year until Archbishop James Patrick Keleher resigned on January 15, 2005. Joseph Naumann became the next archbishop that day.

Like Bishop Sheridan in Colorado Springs, Archbishop Naumann caused controversy when he refused Communion to Kansas Governor Kathleen Sebelius, a nominal Catholic. Sebelius was a strong supporter of abortion rights and had received the endorsement of Planned Parenthood. She opposed a state amendment which would outlaw same-sex marriages, though it passed by 70% of Kansas voters. Later Kathleen Sebelius would serve the Obama Administration as head of Health and Human Services, implementing the Affordable Care Act, including its abortion and contraception provisions, which threatened the freedom of conscience of health care providers who opposed such practices.

After repeated attempts to get Sebelius to moderate her position on life issues, Archbishop Naumann issued a statement that she should not receive Communion from any priest in Kansas. His May 2008 statement was supported by then-Archbishop Raymond Burke,

---

220 "Fr. Naumann Named Head of Pro-Life Committee." *Saint Louis Review*. DATE? 1984.
221 "Pro-Life Forces Win Vote in Mo House." *Saint Louis Review*. May 18, 1990.

Prefect of the Apostolic Signatura, the Church's highest court, extending the prohibition nationwide. "After pastoral admonition, she obstinately persists in serious sin," Burke said.[222]

Priestly vocations flourished during Archbishop Naumann's tenure in Kansas City, Kansas.

Next to be consecrated was George Lucas as bishop of Springfield, Illinois. He, too, followed the typical path of Saint Louis priestly formation: Prep Seminary, Cardinal Glennon College, Kenrick Seminary. After ordination on May 24, 1975, Lucas served as associate pastor at several parishes, while pursuing a master's degree in history at Saint Louis University, which he was awarded in 1986.

In 1987 Father Lucas began teaching at Prep South and was made dean of students. Thereafter, he served as chancellor, then vicar general, and was pastor at All Saints Parish in University City for one year, 1994. The next year, now-Monsignor Lucas was named president-rector of Kenrick-Glennon Seminary. That year saw a significant change in the seminary, as all but two Vincentians left the faculty. The gaps were filled by lay faculty and archdiocesan priests with advanced degrees. Monsignor Dennis Delaney would replace Lucas as president-rector when he became bishop of Springfield.

The just under ten years spent in Illinois were fruitful. Bishop Lucas introduced the Permanent Diaconate to the diocese in 2001. In 2002, he instituted "Harvest of Thanks, Springtime of Hope," a major fundraiser for Catholic education and Catholic Charities. It raised over $22 million. His last act as bishop of Springfield was an $11 million restoration of Immaculate Conception cathedral.

On June 3, 2009, Archbishop Pietro Sambi, apostolic delegate to the United States, installed Lucas as archbishop of Omaha, Nebraska. In attendance were his predecessor Archbishop Curtiss, his previous Illinois superior Cardinal George, and his previous Saint Louis superior Cardinal Rigali.

A year-and-a-half into his administration, Archbishop Lucas had the unpleasant duty of suppressing the Intercessors of the Lamb, an Association of the Faithful with a charism of prayer and sacrifice. There had been a canonical investigation which revealed serious irregularities. When their board refused to reform, the archbishop acted. The superior, Mother Nadine Brown, resigned. She died in 2013. Several mem-

222 "Sebelius in Trouble with Catholic Church." *Washington Times*. March 24, 2009.

bers left while a majority stayed, forming Intercessor Relief, under the guidance and protection of the archbishop of Omaha.

As with Archbishop Naumann in Kansas City, Kansas, Archbishop Lucas fostered priestly vocations for Omaha.

The last of the era to receive episcopal red was Timothy Michael Dolan. He began his priestly formation like so many others: Prep South, Cardinal Glennon College, but then was sent off for studies at Catholic University of America. After four years there, Dolan was ordained on June 19, 1976. He received an STB from the Pontifical University of Saint Thomas Aquinas in Rome. He returned to Catholic University to study from 1979 to 1983 Church history under Monsignor John Tracy Ellis. Dolan earned a Ph.D. in 1985 and published his dissertation as a biography of Archbishop Edwin V. O'Hara.

For five years, from 1987 to 1992, Father Dolan served as secretary to the Apostolic Nunciature in Washington, D.C. He returned to Saint Louis for two years, acting as vice-rector of Kenrick-Glennon Seminary and professor of Church history. Dolan would not see the transition of the seminary from Vincentian to Archdiocesan, as he was made a monsignor and named rector of the North American College in Rome where he served from 1994 to 2001. During that time, he wrote *Priests for the Third Millennium*.

Dolan's return to Saint Louis was intense, but brief. Archbishop Rigali tasked him to oversee the exploding clergy sex abuse scandal. As vicar for priests, he dealt with each accusation case personally. He worked with the Office for Continuing Formation of Priests in setting up workshops for priests and developed a list of sixteen "Dolan's Don'ts," activities that acted as red flags for abuse.

Bishop Dolan set aside a June overnight for priests ordained five years or less to let them vent their frustrations and concerns and to counsel them. It was called on short notice, and fewer than half the eligible priests came. What was more shocking was that a dozen of them failed to respond to phone calls and emails from the Office of Continuing Formation. Bishop Dolan vowed to call each of them in for an explanation, but June 25, 2002 intervened. He had other fish to fry.

It was on June 25 that Bishop Dolan was called to become archbishop of Milwaukee. The archdiocese needed his steady hand. Later it was claimed by lawyer Jeffrey Anderson, who made a career out of representing those who came forward as victims of clerical abuse, that as many as 8,000 children had been abused by over one hundred priests in the Archdiocese of Milwaukee. He himself represented 570 of them.[223]

Archbishop Dolan served six-and-a-half years as Archbishop of Milwaukee. On February 23, 2009, he was named as the next archbishop of New York and was installed April 15, 2009.

The clergy sex abuse scandal would not leave Archbishop Dolan alone. He took part in an apostolic visitation to Ireland after a government investigation into the history of sex abuse in Irish Catholic institutions was published. In 2011 he joined others in investigating the Pontifical Irish College in Rome. There he reported that the seminarians were more orthodox and more pious than the faculty. The study was not well received by the Irish bishops.

In November 2010 Archbishop Dolan was elected as president of the United States Catholic Conference of Bishops. It was in that role that he led the vocal opposition to the HHS Mandate within the Affordable Care Act. The Mandate was a direct assault on religious conscience and liberty, as it would force Catholic health care institutions to provide contraception, abortifacients, and abortion coverage to their employees.

Dolan's stature in the fight was enhanced, as he was made a cardinal of the Church by Pope Benedict XVI on February 18, 2012.

Cardinal Dolan continued to be a popular speaker and opinion-maker. He led the invocation at the inauguration of President Donald Trump. Vaticanologist John L. Allen, Jr. noted that Dolan was one of those Benedict appointees "who are basically conservative in both their politics and their theology, but also upbeat pastoral figures given to dialogue."[224]

Archbishop Rigali was also in the forefront for promoting lay leadership in his archdiocese. In 1995 Molly Kertz was given the post of executive director of the Pro-Life Committee, a position held by priests until that time. That same year, George Henry was promoted to superintendent of schools, replacing Sister Mary Ann Eckhoff, SSND when she transferred to Rome to work for her congregation.

In 1999 Archbishop Rigali named Jennifer Stanard the archdiocesan director of Catholic Relief Services.

The number of activities and events during Archbishop Rigali's

---

223 Radio interview on WTAQ NewsTalk 97.5 FM and 1360 AM. February 10, 2012.
224 "Benedict's U S Appointments Follow a Pattern." *National Catholic Reporter*. February 13, 2009.

tenure in Saint Louis was staggering, culminating in the papal visit of 1999. He showed that he would not be tied to a desk early on when Saint Anthony of Padua Parish was hit by lightning, as he arrived on the scene immediately after the firefighters came. He oversaw the opening of a new Regina Cleri retirement home on the grounds of the old Kenrick Seminary, a building he renovated to become office space for archdiocesan agencies.

One of the most significant losses following the Second Vatican Council was public Eucharistic Adoration. Archbishop Rigali vigorously encouraged its restoration. He sent a January 1, 1998 letter to the priests telling them that several new Chapels of Perpetual Eucharistic Adoration had been opened and that many parishes had begun Eucharistic Adoration weekly or monthly. He wrote that this was an excellent way to begin to prepare for the new millennium.

In the letter, the archbishop announced that a Eucharistic Workbook was being assembled and that the February 2 meeting with priests at Saint Raymond Maronite Church would deal specifically with that topic. He concluded, "It is my hope that our renewed efforts to provide the opportunity for Eucharistic Adoration will result in an increase of vocations to the priesthood and consecrated life. May this intention be our priority in prayer before the Blessed Sacrament!"[225]

The Archbishop's Conference on February 2 for priests and deacons was led by Archbishop Harry J. Flynn, archbishop of Saint Paul and Minneapolis. His topic was "The Eucharistic Vocation." After lunch, Rev. James Moroney, executive secretary of the NCCB Office of Liturgy, spoke on "The Mass and Eucharistic Adoration." That was followed by a talk, "Priests' Role in Encouraging Vocations," delivered by the director of the Archdiocesan Vocation Office, Rev. Michael Butler.

Actions followed quickly. On February 7 Rigali led the Archbishop's Conference on Eucharistic Renewal and Vocations for Lay Coordinators. Between March 14 and March 18, Father Martin Lucia, author of *Come to Me in the Blessed Sacrament*, met with priests in regional meetings.

By April 12 each parish was to submit a plan to the archbishop, show a video on Eucharistic Adoration in their parish during the month of May, implement their plan by May 31, and set aside June 14, the feast of Corpus Christi, with a Mass for Eucharistic Adoration Renewal.

---

225 Archbishop Justin Rigali to Priests. Archives of the Archdiocese of Saint Louis. RG01I09, Box # A177.

Heading the effort was Rev. Edward Rice, aided by a ten-member committee, including George Knollmeyer and Ed Meiners who had been in the forefront of petitioning for a restoration of Eucharistic Adoration.

Other resources were recommended, including literature available from Pauline Books & Media, especially Pope Paul VI's encyclical, *Mystery of Faith*, and Cardinal John Joseph Carberry's *Reflections and Prayers for Visits with Our Eucharistic Lord*.

Two early examples for parishes to follow were Our Lady of Lourdes in University City and Saint Anselm in Creve Coeur. The pastors were aided by a head coordinator, four division leaders, twenty-four prayer teams with twenty-four-hours coordinators, so that the Blessed Sacrament would be attended to twenty-four hours a day.

In 1996 and 1997, "Returning God's Gifts – Sharing Our Hope" became the first-ever capital campaign for the archdiocese as a whole. The goal was to raise $55 million to be placed in endowments. Even before the campaign began, $11.1 million had already been secured, six through the sale of Cardinal Glennon Children's Hospital and the rest through large donations averaging over $650,000 each. Eight hundred fifty attended the Parish Leadership Team Coordination Meeting at Saint Raymond on May 27, 1997.

Addressing doubts that so much money could be raised, even before the May 27 meeting, Archbishop Rigali set up two Block Pilot Parish groups, thirteen parishes in all, some large, others small and rural. By November 1996 the pilot parishes had $15,500,000 in pledges and by February 1997, they came in 125% of target, with eighteen million pledged.

The campaign co-chairs were Anthony Sansone and Deacon Robert Brooks. Rev. John Leykam was chair of the Campaign Clergy Committee.

By December 1997, $50 million had been pledged with seventy-seven parishes over their targets.

The success of the campaign was celebrated in a publication, "Returning God's Gifts – Sharing Our Hope: A Report on the Good News Accomplished in Our Community, 1996 – 2006." By that time, $66 million had not just been pledged, but had been received.[226]

The money had been invested in conservative portfolios of stocks

---

226 "Returning God's Gifts Material" RG 0 3K, Box # A2109, Archives of the Archdiocese of Saint Louis.

and bonds, overseen by the Investments Committee of the Finance Council of the Archdiocese. After ten years, it had earned another $10 million and had granted out $8.4 million.

The seminary endowment of $4 million had dispersed $700,000. The Clergy Continuing Education fund of $2.2 million had given out $237,000, much of it for convocations and sabbaticals. The Catholic Family Tuition fund of $13.7 million had granted $2.7 million to nearly 13,500 children. And the High School endowment of $6.8 million dispersed $1.3 million over those ten years.

There were sixty-eight parish grants, besides the $5 million which was returned to the parishes as a ten percent portion of the money they raised for the campaign. A Parish Viability Endowment was established with $19.8 million, with $3 million dispersed.

A priests' retirement and health endowment were set up with $11.8 million, and $2.9 million was set aside for cathedral needs.

Annual marches on January 22 highlighted the pro-life opposition to the Supreme Court decision of *Roe v. Wade*. Saint Louis participants continued to grow in numbers each year. By 1983 Saint Louis sent sixteen busloads to Washington, D. C. Each bus had an average of fifty riders. The next year there were seventeen buses, and by 1986 eighteen buses.

The year 1987 was a bust. The capital was blanketed with eleven inches of snow. Regardless, 1988 saw twenty-three busloads from the Archdiocese of Saint Louis.

The March for Life was cancelled in 1991 due to security concerns, as the United States had entered into the Persian Gulf War.

The March for Life took a major turn in 1997. Archbishop Rigali took a direct interest in the March. He flew to Washington with Rev. Vincent Bommarito, coordinator of the Pro-Life Committee, Molly Kertz, Pro-Life Chair, and her husband and several others. They met with Senator John Ashcroft of Missouri on the afternoon of January 21 and later with Senator Kit Bond. After dinner, the delegation attended a concert at Archbishop Carroll High School.

The 22nd began with a 7:00 A. M. Mass at the Shrine of the Immaculate Conception, an hour-long meeting with the Missouri congressional delegation, and at noon, they joined the rally and March at the Ellipse. From there an estimated 125,000 marched down Constitution Avenue to the Supreme Court.

The weather was crisp, but the political atmosphere was grim. President Bill Clinton had just been re-elected the past November.

He vetoed the "partial birth abortion bill," and the Senate failed to override his veto. People at the rally were calling him "the abortion president," and "an enemy of life."

After the March, the Saint Louis delegation met with Representatives Kenny Hulshof of the Ninth District and Jo Ann Emerson of the Eighth.

After that, the otherwise flawless visit went sour. The six waited for their scheduled shuttle ride to Baltimore/Washington International Airport for their return flight to Saint Louis. When it did not arrive on time, a phone call was made to the company. Assurances were made that the shuttle was on the way. After more calls and a delay of an hour-and-a-half, Father Bommarito flagged down a taxicab. The six piled in and he paid out of pocket for the ride to the airport, arriving just in time to catch the flight.

In 1998 the chief celebrant and homilist at the Immaculate Conception Shrine Mass was Archbishop Rigali. Of the 150,000 attending the March, 2,000 came from the Saint Louis Archdiocese. In his sermon, the archbishop outlined the challenges ahead. "The 'culture of death' has grown stronger during these last twenty-five years," but he concluded with hope. "Dear friends: though the forces supporting the culture of death may seem so powerful and strong, let us remain undaunted. In our Eucharist, we possess the full power of the Risen Christ who tells us to have confidence because He has overcome the world."[227]

In July 1999 there was a glimmer of hope. The Supreme Court ruled in the Webster case, which originated in Missouri, that states had the right to put some restrictions on abortions.

Other activities abounded. During Lent 1997 Catholics were encouraged to return to their baptismal churches as a form of pilgrimage. Cardinal Ritter Prep, a predominately African American high school with a great reputation, got a new home in the Grand Center.

Both 1997 and 1998 saw the titanic struggle over the ownership of Saint Louis University Hospital.

The 1990s were not kind to SLU Hospital. In 1991 they were concerned about losing $1.2 million in a federal contract which had been awarded them when Stanford University had been denied. The university sued and won in court. A *Post-Dispatch* article sounded the alarm, "SLU Hospital May Lose Research Grant."

---

227 "Homily, January 22, 1998, Shrine of the Immaculate Conception." RG 03 C8
"March for Life: 1997-1998." Archives of the Archdiocese of Saint Louis.

By 1994 the hospital had to let go seventy-seven employees. Though their bed-count was better than most area hospitals, revenues were down, as "managed care" health programs were squeezing them. Temporary workers had already been dismissed, and operating costs were carefully scrutinized, but it was not enough.

The hospital had been founded in June 1931 with a gift of the Desloge family. It was called Firmin Desloge Hospital and was co-owned by Saint Louis University and the Franciscan Sisters of Saint Mary, who staffed the hospital. Emerging in the depths of the Great Depression, the hospital was practically free for patients. The admission fee was twenty-five cents for those who could pay it, and a hospital stay was just $2.00 a day. A second large bequest was made in 1935 by Mrs. Blanche Bordley.

In 1959 the Sisters of Saint Mary gifted their portion to Saint Louis University. A document sent to Archbishop Rigali by the sisters noted, "The transition was made with the approval of His Excellency, Most Reverend Joseph E. Ritter and Mr. Joseph Desloge. Since it was His Excellency's wish that the hospital retains its character as a Catholic hospital, about 35 Sisters remained in various departments as semi-salaried personnel under contract for one year."[228]

But it was while Ritter was archbishop of Saint Louis that the university established a board of trustees, and the university and its hospital were no longer under the control of the archbishop. The board grew to fifty-two members, only ten of whom were Jesuits.

By the late 1990s the university was in the market to sell the hospital and invest the money to improve the medical school. Archbishop Rigali favored the purchase by a consortium of local Catholic hospitals which had made an offer of $200 million. However, Tenet Health Care, the second largest for-profit health provider in America, offered $300 million. Rigali vigorously opposed a sale to Tenet.

The archbishop had plenty of support. Cardinal Roger Mahony had opposed the sale to Tenet of Queen of Angels-Hollywood Presbyterian Medical Center in Los Angeles. Cardinals Bernard Law of Boston, John O'Connor of New York, and James Hickey of Washington each expressed outrage toward a sale of a Catholic hospital to a for-profit company. Even the liberal political action group, Americans

---

228 Mary Gabriel Henninger, SSM. "Sisters of St. Mary and Their Healing Mission." 1979. "Health Care – Proposal to Sell to Tenet Health Care – 1997." RG 0S Box # A 4174. Archives of the Archdiocese of Saint Louis.

for Democratic Action, wrote Archbishop Rigali, expressing support.

Tenet was not a good player. It was founded from the ruins of National Medical Enterprises. NME had been accused of bribing politicians as far back as 1985. Allegations resurfaced in 1991, leading to a Senate inquiry. NME lost a lawsuit for $10 million to the Texas Attorney General that same year.

In 1992 Dr. Robert Stuckey, long associated with an NME entity called the Psychiatric Institutes of America, died suddenly, days before he was scheduled to give evidence to a House committee. That same year the firm was sued by nineteen insurance companies, paying out $89 million in one case and $125 million in another. In 1994, National Medical Enterprises settled out of court for $379 million, the largest payout in U. S. history.

On September 29, 1997, Rev. Lawrence Biondi, SJ President of Saint Louis University, sent a letter to Mrs. Stephanie S. McCutcheon, President of SSM Health Care Central Region, and Mr. James F. Hardman, President of Unity Health, rejecting the offer of the consortium of Catholic hospitals. He expressed doubt that the consortium could maintain the hospital into the future. He also mentioned that the university's medical school would need an endowment of $360 million to "sustain our commitment to our Catholic, Jesuit health professions' education program."

By October 5, 1997, the dispute between the archbishop and the university president was public. In a *Post-Dispatch* article, Rigali said Lawrence Biondi "acted without my support and, to this point, without approval of the Holy See, which is regularly required by the Catholic Church whenever this type of 'alienation of Catholic property' is undertaken."[229]

In response, Father Biondi promised that Tenet would follow the directives of the United States Conference of Catholic Bishops and perform no abortions or euthanasia, as well as other life issues. They would maintain a pastoral care staff of thirteen, and daily Mass would continue to be offered in the chapel.

Archbishop Rigali received at least sixty-one letters of support during the controversy. They came from doctors, pastors, bishops, women religious, laity, lawyers, and Knights of Columbus councils. Some had been written to Father Biondi with the archbishop being copied.

---

229 "Archbishop: Mission of Hospital in Danger." *St. Louis Post-Dispatch*. October 5, 1997.

The most extensive letter came from Edward H. Adelstein, DVM, MD in Columbia, Missouri. He included with his letter an eighteen-page transcript of a radio interview he had done, four other pages of evidence, and a thirty-five-page transcript of a meeting with legislators on November 1, 1995 in which the lawmakers discussed Tenet Health Care. Adelstein said he had met with the Governor's office to warn them of Tenet's reputation. He told the archbishop that Tenet was "a ruthless, essentially amoral organization which sanctions abortions and where profits are placed far ahead of patient care."[230]

The archbishop received at least eleven letters supporting the sale of the hospital to Tenet. One lay board member said he did not want to see happen to Saint Louis University what happened a year earlier at Georgetown University. There the hospital failed financially, and the university had to take operating expenses out of its endowment.[231]

In the end, the battle was lost. The words of Cardinal Ritter would haunt the endeavor. In the late 1960s, the Jesuits at Saint Louis University established a Board which would make the university independent from the Church, and Catholic in name and in custom, but not in jurisdiction. Ritter wrote to Rev. Paul Reinert, the university president, "Be ensured of my enthusiasm and wholehearted support and approval of this proposal to enlarge your Board and involve laymen in the direction and policy-making responsibilities of the university. It is very much in keeping with the spirit of Vatican II."[232]

Regardless of the setback, Archbishop Rigali continued apace with a barrage of programs and initiatives. The archdiocese sponsored Reconciliation Weekends in 1999, 2001, and 2002. Parishes opened their doors for Catholics to go to confession, many of whom had not been in decades. Priests were pressed into service to hear confessions all weekend long.

Saint Louis sponsored the 2001 Eucharistic Congress. Cardinal Jan Pieter Schotte was sent by Pope John Paul II as his Special Envoy

---

230 Edward H. Adelstein to Archbishop F. Rigali. October 9, 1997. "Health Care – Proposal to sell to Tenet Health Care – 1997." RG 0S Box # A 4174. Archives of the Archdiocese of Saint Louis.
231 Kenneth F. Teasdale to Archbishop Justin Rigali. October 29, 1997. "Health Care – SLU Hospital proposal to sell to Tenet – Letters of Dissent." R G 0S Box # A 4174. Archives of the Archdiocese of Saint Louis.
232 Msgr. Nicholas Schneider. *Joseph Elmer Ritter: His Life and Times*. Ligouri: Ligouri Publication. 2008. P. 167.

to the Congress. Schotte was the secretary general of the Synod of Bishops. The Pope sent this message to the archdiocese: "Remembering with great pleasure our pastoral visit among the dear people of St. Louis and to their beloved Pastor, our Venerable Brother Justin Rigali, we recently learned of the celebration of the 100th anniversary of the Eucharistic Congress that had once happily taken place there for the entire nation."[233]

The Congress opened with Solemn Vespers at 6:30 in the evening at the America's Center. Archbishop Rigali delivered the homily, followed by Benediction of the Blessed Sacrament. Compline was celebrated at 9:15, ending with the chant *Salve Regina.*

The next day began with recitation of Lauds at 9:30 in the morning and Sext at 3:00 PM. In between those times, keynote speakers and break-out sessions were held throughout the building. Rev. Benedict J. Groeschel, CRF, a favorite guest on EWTN, was joined by the National Director of Priests for Life, Rev. Frank Pavone. In all, thirteen speakers were featured, including Bishop Edward K. Braxton, then-bishop of Lake Charles, Louisiana.

Throughout the day, confessions were available. Children were entertained with dress-ups as priests or nuns, each having their photo taken. Snacks were available. Teens attended a rock concert.

Mass was celebrated at 5:30 PM. Before Mass began the assembly was treated to twelve choirs singing gathering music. The homilist was Cardinal Schotte.

After Mass, tens of thousands of worshipers poured into the streets of downtown Saint Louis, trailing behind a monstrance and singing Eucharistic songs. Their destination was the Gateway Arch where they received a blessing with the Blessed Sacrament, followed by a riverfront fireworks display that could rival any Fourth of July celebration. It was a night to remember, the culmination of two days of conferences, keynote addresses, and worship.

That same year, the archdiocese purchased the Benedictine monastery on Morganford and turned it into the John XXIII Center. Many archdiocesan offices and agencies were relocated there as was Saint Mark's Parish, a consolidated parish of three others.

But the most significant event to take place during Archbishop Rigali's eleven years in Saint Louis was the 1999 visit by Pope John

---

233 "Pope Appoints Cdl. Schotte as Special Envoy to Congress." June 15, 2001. *St. Louis Review.*

Paul II. Karol Wojtyła had visited Saint Louis once before. In 1969 he was cardinal archbishop of Krakow and celebrated Mass in Polish at Saint Stanislaus Parish. Now, his visit would culminate in a Mass at the America's Center for 110,000 in attendance, arguably the largest indoor assembly of people in American history.

The planning committee included Monsignors Richard Stika, archdiocesan chancellor, ReverendsTed Wojcicki and Dennis Delany as well as Reverend Henry Breier, Jennifer Stanard, vice chancellor for Special Projects, and John M. Britt of the United States Secret Service. There were five venue chairs, Reverend Robert Finn to oversee the arrival and departure ceremonies, Reverend Paul Niemann to organize the evening prayer service, Reverend Robert Smoot for the youth gathering, and Vincentian Father James Swift in charge of the papal Mass. Monsignor James Telthorst was placed in charge of the Pre-Event Papal Mass.

There were another twenty-six committees which oversaw every aspect of the two-day visit.

Shepherd One landed on January 26, 1999, flying in from Mexico City where the pope had delivered the apostolic exhortation *Ecclesia in America*. Greeting him was a crowd of 2,300 along with Archbishop Rigali and President Bill Clinton. The contemplative communities of the archdiocese had been asked to pray for good weather, and God delivered. The sky was clear and bright, and the temperature reached 68 degrees.

Clinton spoke about the remarkable work John Paul had done in freeing Eastern Europe. The pope responded with a challenge. He recalled that the Dred Scott decision began here in Saint Louis and that it would deny constitutional protections to an entire class of people. He then tied that event to the current situation, challenging Americans to change their culture which still "seeks to declare entire groups of human beings – the unborn, the terminally ill, the handicapped, and others considered 'unuseful' – to be outside the boundaries of legal protection."[234]

After a brief meeting with President Clinton, the pope was transported to the archbishop's residence. To the crowd's dismay, what was meant to be a motorcade instead became a race down Skinker and Lindell Boulevards, reaching forty miles per hour.

---

234 *John Paul II: Pastoral Visit to St. Louis*. St. Louis: Archdiocese of St. Louis. 1999. P.17.

That evening some 20,000 young people gathered at the Kiel Center for a "Light of the World" Youth Gathering. Some had been there since 10:00 in the morning. Many had paraded from the Arch grounds fourteen blocks away to the Center, while others waited outside to greet the pope.

One of the highlights of the evening occurred when John Paul was presented with a hockey stick and a jersey with his name on it and the number "1." One of the athletic heroes of Saint Louis, Cardinal first baseman Mark McGwire, was introduced to the pope and kissed the papal ring. The story circulated later that that one kiss doubled the value of the ring!

The next day was set for the Papal Mass at America's Center. The enormous crowd had gathered, bussed in from various locations, by 7:30 A.M. There were thirty Masters of Ceremony who had to be in the building by 5:00 A.M. They were given instructions by Reverend Eugene Morris. Attending were nearly 1,000 priests, 500 bishops, hundreds of religious sisters and brothers, and over 100,000 lay faithful.

Through the extraordinary efforts of Reverend James Swift, CM the Mass was flawless. Communion stations were designated by gold and white umbrellas. It was practically a Eucharistic miracle that the 110,000 congregants received Communion in just twenty minutes!

Mass was over by noon, and the same buses which had delivered the crowds carried them away as quickly. Pope John Paul returned to the archbishop's residence for a few hours before attending an evening prayer service at the Cathedral. The Cathedral was packed, and representatives of various religious bodies were present.

This service was attended by Governor Mel Carnahan. He had postponed the execution of Darrell Mease until after the pope had left Missouri. The governor was not in a good mood. He and his wife had invited Representative Chris Liese, a Catholic from Maryland Heights, to join him. Liese, though a fellow Democrat, had not been treated well by the governor. The young representative had refused to compromise on his strong pro-life stand.

The flight to Saint Louis was in stony silence. Arriving at the airport, a limousine took them to the cathedral. The governor looked out the window. More silence. Finally, he said to Liese, "Well, I guess you know what your pope is going to ask me to do." The representative said "yes." Carnahan continued, "You know that that man is a cold-blooded killer.

He deserves to die. What do you think I should do?"

Liese said quietly, "I'd do it. This pope is no ordinary man."

As Carnahan feared, after the service, the pope made his way over to Vice President Al Gore and his wife, Tipper. He greeted them and then turned to the governor and whispered, "Show mercy to Mr. Mease." The governor complied and commuted the sentence to life without a chance for parole.

Before leaving the cathedral, Pope John Paul met briefly with Rosa Parks, the 86-year-old civil rights icon.

From the cathedral the pope was driven to the airport. The departure ceremony was brief. He was clearly exhausted after his days in Mexico City and full schedule in Saint Louis. One final incident brought a special blessing to one of the onlookers.

A former secretary at Christian Brothers University in Memphis wanted to bring her nephew, living in Nashville, to the papal visit. They contacted a priest she knew. Shortly before the papal visit, the priest received a phone call from the office of Vice President Gore. Somehow, he had learned that these fellow Tennesseans would be in Saint Louis for the visit. He had arranged for the two of them to get tickets to the departure ceremony.

They took their place with hundreds of others, lining the corridor through which the pope would make his way to the airplane. Separating them from the pope was a police line. The teenage boy seemed to have impressed a police officer nearby with his soft southern drawl and use of formal "Yes, sir" and "Yes, ma'am." The officer turned and faced the boy and told him that when the pope walked past, he would step out of the way so he could see the pope clearly.

True to his word, the officer stepped aside as John Paul made his way through the corridor. The movement caught the eye of the pope who stopped briefly. The boy stepped forward and touched the pope's hand. This caused the pope to smile and nod briefly to the boy. Later his aunt assured everyone that that incident was the only thing the boy talked about all the way back to Nashville.

John Paul's final words before leaving the Cathedral summed up the papal visit and how it changed the Archdiocese of Saint Louis. He commented, "In particular I wish to say thanks to the local Church of St. Louis. I am indebted to all the many dedicated people – organizers, committee members and volunteers – who have labored long and hard behind the scenes. Nor do I forget the hidden but effective support of all who prayed for the spiritual outcome of this event, especially the contemplatives in their monasteries. A special word of thanks and appreciation is due to Archbishop Rigali, who just two days ago celebrated his fifth anniversary as your dedicated Pastor."

He added, "A few months ago, a pilgrimage from St. Louis came to Rome. We met on the steps of St. Peter's, where they sang to me: 'Meet me in St. Louis... meet me at the Dome!' With God's help, we have done it. I will always remember St. Louis. I will always remember all of you. God bless St. Louis! God bless America!"[235]

Archbishop Justin Rigali rushed to the scene of the fire at St. Anthony of Padua on April 28, 1994. Here, he comforts parishioners who were upset by the damage. Photographer Richard Finke. From the Archdiocese of St. Louis Archives and Records.

---

235 *John Paul II: Pastoral Visit to St. Louis.* St. Louis: Archdiocese of St. Louis. 1999. P. 150.

Sister Charlotte Rigali, CSJ, was a canon lawyer in the Archdiocesan Tribunal before Archbishop Justin Rigali was appointed to St. Louis. Photographer Richard Finke, 1994. From the Archdiocese of St. Louis Archives and Records.

After his consecration at the Cathedral Basilica, Bishop Edward Braxton walked with Fr. James Telthorst to the reception at Rosa-ti-Kain High School next door, 1995. Photographer Richard Finke. From the Archdiocese of St. Louis Archives and Records.

Bishops-Elect Joseph Naumann and Michael Sheridan bless Bishop-Elect John
Gaydos at a prayer service to honor the three men. It was sponsored by the Council
of Priests and held at St. Raymond Church. Photographer Richard Finke. From the
Archdiocese of St. Louis Archives and Records.

Msgr. George J. Lucas, president-rector of Kenrick-Glennon Seminary, offers his ideas on how to best prepare for the upcoming millennium at the National Conference of Diocesan Vocation Directors in St. Louis in 1999. He was consecrated Bishop of Springfield that same year. Photographer Richard Finke. From the Archdiocese of St. Louis Archives and Records.

Bishops stand in front of the chancery building on Lindell Boulevard in 1989. From left to right are pictured Bishop Edward J. O'Donnell, Archbishop John L. May, Bishop-Elect Paul A. Zipfel, and Bishop J. Terry Steib. Photographer Richard Finke. From the Archdiocese of St. Louis Archives and Records.

Auxiliary Bishop Paul A. Zipfel performed at the Midwest Magic Jubilee on August 1, 1991. Photographer Richard Finke. From the Archdiocese of St. Louis Archives and Records.

Standing beside Archbishop Rigali, Bishop Timothy Dolan joyfully greets well-wishers after his consecration at the Cathedral Basilica, 2001. Photographer Richard Finke. From the Archdiocese of St. Louis Archives and Records.

244

Molly Kertz was the first layperson to be appointed as executive director of the Archdiocesan Pro-Life Committee in 1995. Photographer Richard Finke. From the Archdiocese of St. Louis Archives and Records.

Archbishop Justin Rigali walks with his rosary in the annual March for Life in Washington, D.C. in 2001. Behind him at his right are Molly Kertz and Bishop Joseph F. Naumann. Bishop Michael J. Sheridan is behind Rigali on his left. From the Archdiocese of St. Louis Archives and Records.

George Henry was appointed Superintendent of Schools in 1995. Photographer Richard Finke, 1989. From the Archdiocese of St. Louis Archives and Records.

Jennifer Stanard was appointed Vice Chancellor for Special Projects in 1999. From the Archdiocese of St. Louis Archives and Records.

Archbishop Justin Rigali raises the monstrance during Eucharistic Adoration at an ADA event at St. Raymond's Maronite Church in 1999. Photographer Richard Finke. From the Archdiocese of St. Louis Archives and Records.

Anthony F. Sansone, Sr., was a co-chair for the "Returning God's Gift – Sharing Our Hope" campaign. Photographer Richard Finke, 1998. From the Archdiocese of St. Louis Archives and Records.

Deacon Robert Brooks was a co-chair for the "Returning God's Gift – Sharing Our Hope" campaign. Photographer Richard Finke, 1998. From the Archdiocese of St. Louis Archives and Records.

Archbishop Justin Rigali talks with Saint Louis University president Fr. Lawrence Biondi, SJ at the Liturgical Composers Forum on February 9, 1999. Photographer Richard Finke. From the Archdiocese of St. Louis Archives and Records.

Cardinal Jan Pieter Schotte, CICM, follows the procession to begin Mass at the Eucharistic Congress held at the Trans World Dome on June 15, 2001. Photographer Richard Finke. From the Archdiocese of St. Louis Archives and Records.

Chapter Nine

CRISES

In January 2002 the world learned of pedophile John Geoghan. An ex-priest, he was convicted and given a sentence of nine to ten years. The judge said, "He engaged in what this court can only characterize as reprehensible and depraved behavior."[236]

Geoghan was ordained in 1962, and he was accused of four molestations while his pastor complained to the Archdiocese of Boston. He was transferred in 1966, 1967, 1974, 1982 and 1984. It was recognized that he had a history of homosexual encounters with young boys, and after two more accusations, the archdiocese sent him to Saint Luke's Institute in Maryland where he was diagnosed as a homosexual pedophile, was treated, and returned to the archdiocese with the assurance that he was now of low risk.

The accusations continued, and Geoghan was sent to Regina Cleri, the clergy retirement home, and was assigned to visit aging priests. More accusations followed until in February 1998 he was dismissed from the priesthood. By then there were one hundred thirty claims against him, ranging over thirty-four years. The archdiocese had settled out of court with fifty accusers at an estimated $10,000,000. In 2003 Geoghan was strangled by his cell mate at the Souza-Baranowski Correctional Center in Massachusetts.

Boston had other disturbing priests. Father Paul Shanley was the archdiocesan representative on the Sexual Diversity Committee. He was a founding member of NAMBLS, the North American Man Boy Love Society, which advocated sexual relations between men and boys. He hung around with gangs of sadomasochist bikers.

Convicted of child abuse, Shanley was given a twelve-year sentence in February 2005, but he was granted a new trial in 2009 before the Massachusetts Supreme Court where his lawyers brought forth over one hundred experts to argue against "repressed memory" testimony. Regardless, Shanley's conviction was upheld, and he served in prison until his release in 2017.

---

236 "Ex-Priest Gets Maximum Sentence in Abuse Case." *Washington Post*. February 22, 2002.

These cases caused a national uproar, but in fact there had been two previous cases. The first, in Louisiana, caught national attention, but only briefly. The second caught the attention of the nation's bishops. Father Gilbert Gauthe began abusing boys as early as 1972. He was confronted in 1974 by Bishop Louis Frey. Gauthe admitted that the reports were true, but surprisingly, the bishop made him diocesan director of scouting.

In 1980 when Gauthe's sister-in-law caught her husband abusing one of their children, he told her that he and Gilbert had been abusing children for years. Dixie Diez went to the police to report the two brothers as pedophiles. Though her husband was eventually convicted of child molestation, nothing was done about Gilbert for five years. He was convicted in 1985, but his name had dropped out of national news.

Father James Porter was ordained in 1960. Over a three-year period, he molested sixty children until he was transferred to a parish in Fall River, Massachusetts. There were nearly a hundred reports until he was sent to a mental institution for thirteen months of treatment. When experts declared that Porter was cured, he returned to ministry only to be reported again and again.

In 1967 Porter was sent away for holistic psychotherapy. Again, Church authorities were assured that Porter had been cured. In the coming years, he served in parishes in Texas, New Mexico, and Minnesota until he was laicized in 1974.

Porter's case, and dozens of others, caught the attention of the American bishops. In 1984 they gathered at Saint John's Abbey in Minnesota to ponder a secret document entitled, "The Problem of Sexual Molestation by Roman Catholic Clergy: Meeting the Problem in a Comprehensive and Responsible Manner." It was authored by canon lawyer Father Thomas Doyle, Father Michael Peterson of Saint Luke's Institute, and lawyer Raymond Mouton, the man who had defended Gilbert Gauthe in his trials but who had become so disgusted that he wanted to bring an end to clergy abuse of children.

The report chronicled some thirty current cases and predicted that within ten years, the Church in America would have to spend a billion dollars on such cases. Regardless, the report added "with optimistic suggestion that secular experts on sexual behavior have been highly successful in treating sexual disorders and are indispensable to the Church."[237]

James Porter also caught the attention of the *Boston Globe* and ABC News in 1990. In 1992 he was convicted of child abuse, but the conviction was overturned by the Minnesota Supreme Court. A new conviction came in 1993 in which Porter was sentenced to eighteen to twenty years in prison where he died in 2005.

These three crises, propelled by Gauthe, Porter, and Geoghan led the general public to believe that the issue was pedophilia as regards clergy sex abuse of minors. But the survey by the John Jay College of Criminal Justice, released in February 2004 revealed something else.

Files of 110,000 Catholic priests who served in the United States between 1950 and 2002 were opened for inspection. The survey found that there had been around 11,000 accusations lodged, of which 6,700 were judged to be substantiated. Of the 110,000 priests studied, 4,450 were credibly accused, though only a few of these cases would be litigated in a court of law.

Most surprising was the role played by pedophiles. Of the 110,000 priests studied, 133 had credible accusations lodged against them at least ten times. As in the cases of Gauthe, Porter, and Geoghan, these accusations ran into three figures.

The damage done by these men, and by others to a lesser degree, was enormous. Lives of little children were harmed beyond repair. Some committed suicide. Others would develop deviant sexual behavior themselves.

Revelations flowed fast and furious into public view. Reports of clerical sexual activity with youth, mainly with teenage boys, flooded the pages of newspapers, dominated the nightly news reports, and became the grist for exposés like *60 Minutes, Geraldo, Sally Jesse Raphael, Donahue, Oprah Winfrey,* and *Prime Time Live.*

In Saint Louis, the first report came in the March 1, 2002 *St. Louis Post-Dispatch*. A headline on the front page read, "Archdiocese Outs Priest from Church." The next day, Saturday, a headline read, "St. Louis Archdiocese Removes Second Priest over Allegations of Past Child Abuse." But the priest was not named, adding to the suspense.

The Sunday paper featured two articles. "Archdiocese Sought a Quiet Way Out," and "Prominent Priest Is Removed From Parish."

---

237 The Linacre Institute. *After Asceticism: Sex, Prayer and Deviant Priests*. Bloomington: Authorhouse. 2006. P. 59.

The Post-Dispatch included three unsubstantiated accusations, one accusation against a prominent priest and author and the story of a conviction from 1964.

This began a barrage of articles. The one article in the Friday paper was followed by three on Saturday and six on Sunday. Monday the 4th of March had three articles, followed by two on Tuesday, one on Wednesday, two on Thursday, and five on Friday. One of the Friday articles argued loudly that none of this had to do with homosexuality.

Saturday the 8th had one article while Sunday had nine articles. The next week had at least one article a day regarding clergy sex abuse. A Saturday article, among the three, called into question the role of clerical celibacy and the same speculation appeared in one of the five articles in Sunday's paper. In the first three weeks of March, one priest had his name printed nine times, another eight times, and a Florida bishop who once served in the Jefferson City diocese was named eight times.

In the meantime, during that week the computer of one pastor was seized by the FBI in Operation Candyman. Archbishop Rigali called the priests of the archdiocese for a day of prayer and conversation at Saint Raymond's Maronite Church on the 13th.

Archbishop Rigali placed newly-consecrated Bishop Timothy Dolan in charge of overseeing the crisis and charged the Office of Continuing Formation to create a two-day conference for the priests which would cover theological, psychological, and legal issues regarding the crisis. One was held in May, but because of the short notice, many priests could not attend. A second conference was slated for October.

The first day began with a description of Pope John Paul II's theology of the body, delivered by a moral theologian from Kenrick-Glennon Seminary. That was followed by two sessions on the meaning of priestly celibacy and one session on the history of clerical celibacy in Church history, both delivered by seminary professors. A fifth session was a discussion on the scriptural understanding of celibacy, delivered by a renowned Johannine scholar.

The second day was less theological and more practical. Three sessions entitled "Healthy Sexual Development and Lifestyle" and "Deviations and Red Flags" were led by a seminary professor of Pastoral Counseling and an outside expert. They were joined by the archdiocesan lawyer for the last session entitled "Legal Issues and Definitions." That was followed by a vigorous question and answer period.

A complete study of the more than three thousand files of priests who had served in the Archdiocese of Saint Louis from 1950 to 2018 found sixty-one with substantiated allegations and three guilty of possessing child pornography. Eleven of these priests had been accused after they were deceased and could not defend themselves. Five had worked in the archdiocese but were incardinated elsewhere. All who were living had been removed from ministry, while fourteen had been laicized.[238]

The three convicted of possessing child pornography each went to prison. Of the other sixty-one, thirteen were convicted in court and two had their convictions overturned.

How could this have happened? While those on the left argue that the crisis was caused by mandatory celibacy, they ignored the fact that child sex abuse was present in Protestant denominations and among Jewish rabbis, too. It was present among public school personnel and in law enforcement. Having a wife does not prevent one from being a child molester.

There is greater evidence that homosexuality plays a role in clergy sex abuse. The John Jay Survey found that eighty percent of the credible accusations had been perpetrated against teenage boys.

Pope Benedict XVI reflected on the sexual abuse crisis among Catholic clergy in a lengthy letter which was published in the German monthly *Klerusblatt*, which was quickly translated by news agencies. It was his reflection on the recent papal summit on the same topic in which Pope Francis assembled the presidents of the Bishops' Conferences in February 2019.

Benedict pointed to the sexual revolution of 1968, which had its origins many years earlier, that caused in the Church "a moral collapse, and it is precisely from that revolution that the drama of the sexual abuse of minors originated." He pointed out, "Until the Second Vatican Council, Catholic moral theology was largely founded on natural law, while Sacred Scripture was only cited for background or substantiation. In the Council's struggle for a new understanding of Revelation, the natural law option was largely abandoned, and the moral theology based entirely on the Bible was demanded... the hy-

---

238 "Promise to Protect." July 26, 2019. www.archstl.org/promise-to-protect/list-release.

pothesis was expounded that the Church does not and cannot have her own morality."[239]

Doubts and uncertainties followed immediately after the Council. One incident at Kenrick Seminary in Spring 1968 spoke volumes about the chaos in seminary training at the time. Within just a few years, one quarter of the faculty priests had abandoned their vocations. Bishop George Gottwald, administrating the archdiocese at the time, was summoned to the seminary to meet an assembly of angry and confused seminarians and priests. The media were there to record the confrontation.

When the bishop tried to calm the situation, one priest burst out, "Hah! I dare you to tell me what we can possibly teach our students now that has not changed, that will not change, that can be stated with any amount of conviction at all! I dare you to tell me!"

All attention was centered on Bishop Gottwald. He calmly recited the Apostles' Creed.[240]

Besides doctrinal confusion, the Church suffered from a decline in ascetical discipline. One study concluded, "A spiritual malaise and the concurrent collapse of ascetical discipline in the middle of the twentieth century created psychologically untenable conditions for many priests and bishops." This malady was "the prime effect of the failure of religious purpose and discipline and its most visible signs were a defiance of religious authority, the precipitous decline in seminary enrollment, and the uniquely sexual features of the scandal."[241]

Holy habits were set aside along with religious habits. It became unfashionable to say the Rosary, to attend Perpetual Help devotions, Eucharistic adorations, or Forty Hour devotions. Hours of meditation or spiritual reading became rare. Frequent confessions, "mortification of senses," fasting, and abstinence were discouraged. Therapeutic psychology held that these practices were at the root of abnormal behavior, of a twisted mind. Religion makes one crazy.

Philip Rieff wrote in 1966 *Triumph of the Therapeutic*. He warned the modern Western world about the dangers of therapeutic psychology, saying it was "a secular evangelization for pagan hedonism; its

---

239 Pope Benedict XVI. As cited in Alessandro Zangrando. "Roman Landscape: Suddenly Benedict." *Latin Mass*. Vol. 28. No. 2. Summer, 2019.
240 Cardinal Timothy M. Dolan. *Priests for the Third Millennium*. Huntington: Our Sunday Visitor. 2000. P. 18.
241 The Linacre Institute. *After Asceticism*. P. 1.

goals and methods are in fundamental opposition to Christianity."[242]

Yet, as seen at the Bishops' Conference at Saint John's Abbey in 1984, therapeutic psychology was lauded, and the bishops were assured "that secular experts on sexual behavior have been highly successful in treating sexual disorders and are indispensable to the Church."

The wisdom of centuries of spiritual masters was set aside for something new and untried. Carl Rogers pioneered client-centered therapy. Others touted the theories of transactional analysis which argued that personalities are formed early in life. Of great influence was former priest, Eugene Kennedy, who wrote in his 2001 book, *The Unhealed Wound*, "The doctrine of original sin and the institutional structures of the Church that defend doctrine are the real culprits... Of course (so they say) God exists and He created man, but He made man to enjoy his sexual desires in a manner that, apart from their procreative purpose, can actually lead man to God if only the institutional structures would not stand in the way of man's spiritual fulfillment."[243]

A critic of this new approach was Father Benedict Groeschel, C.F.R., a professor of pastoral psychology. He wrote, "We have been absolved by psychology rather than the blood of Christ. We have substituted therapy (which has its legitimate place) for repentance. We have replaced the teaching of Sacred Scripture and Church tradition with our own opinions, and we have substituted the evening T.V. for the pronouncements of the Pope."

Father Groeschel, a frequent retreat master and a constant voice on the Eternal Word Television Network, did not go easy on his generation of Catholic leaders. "We have wasted the Church's vast patrimony, built up by poor Catholic immigrants of the past, and splurged the resources they left for the spread of the Gospel on foolish and self-indulgent things. We have given away scores of colleges, hospitals and other amenities. We have failed to preach and encourage chastity in and before marriage, as well as in entertainment. We have harvested bitter fruit in a shameful and deeply painful scandal."[244]

The moral, doctrinal, and disciplinary confusion that followed after the Second Vatican Council, the sometimes-frivolous experimentation in sacred liturgy, the rejection of asceticism, the embracing of

---

242 The Linacre Institute. *After Asceticism.* P. 39.
243 Ibid. P. 64.
244 Fr. Benedict J. Groeschel, C.F.R. *From Scandal to Hope.* Huntington: Our Sunday Visitor. 2002. P. 139.

therapeutic psychology, and the failure of seminary formation made too many individual priests vulnerable to the toxic sexual atmosphere of the 1960s and 1970s.

There was a shift in the sexual morals of America, including among minors. Between 1960 and 1991, unmarried teen pregnancies doubled. While teen brides were have having children, they were outnumbered two to one by unwed mothers. During that time, forty percent of all teen pregnancies ended in abortions. In many school districts, it was assumed that teen sex was unavoidable, and condom distribution became part of the school nurse's duties.

This trend was bolstered by television shows, sit-coms, and movies. *The Summer of '42* told the story of a young war widow who seduces a teenage boy and "gave him his manhood." That 1971 film was followed in 1980 with *The Blue Lagoon*. Here was a tale of a nineteenth century shipwreck. Three survived, a crusty old sailor who died early in the film, and two children, cousins. They were not rescued for many years, and as they grew into adolescence, they became sexually active. The film glorified this incestuous relationship.

The situation comedy, *Soap*, ran for nearly four years and pressed such themes as homosexuality, marital infidelity, incest, rape, and even student-teacher sexual relations. While the program was criticized for these excesses, the criticism drove viewership. *Soap* was abruptly canceled by ABC, perhaps pressured by sponsors threatening to withdraw their ads. But the bridge had been crossed, and other shows would take *Soap*'s place.

There was also a shift in sexual definitions. Many state legislatures decriminalized deviant behavior. Exhibitionism was normalized with young people "streaking" in public places, wearing nothing but a pair of tennis shoes.

By the time the Geoghan crisis had surpassed the Gauthe and Porter crises, and dioceses all over America were having their own calamities, the bishops realized the path set at Saint John's Abbey was inadequate to address what had become a national plague. They met in Dallas to pound out a charter. It was agreed that a single instance of a credible accusation against a priest or deacon should lead to his permanent removal from ministry.

The Dallas Charter offered a flawed solution. SNAP, the Survivors Network for those Abused by Priests, always critical, said it did not go far enough. Indeed, the Charter was mum on abusive bishops, which would result in a new wave of scandals surrounding Cardinal Theodore McCarrick in 2018.

The Charter offered no forgiveness, no redemption to a cleric guilty of a single misdeed, equating him with a serial pedophile. It did not address the homosexual culture in some seminaries and in some dioceses. This, too, would be uncovered in the Pennsylvania Grand Jury revelations of 2018, especially regarding a ring of offending priests in Pittsburgh who encouraged one another in their deviant ways. They gave gold crosses to boys they singled out, so as to signal their availability.[245]

But most remarkable about the Dallas Charter is that it ignored the spiritual dimensions of clerical chastity.

Father Groeschel criticized the bishops for being more like CEO's than shepherds. However, his little book ends on a note of hope. "Now is a time to move on wisely and well. We may be a leaner, cleaner, and more attacked Church, but Christ will be with us. His word will be heard. His sacraments given and received with devotion and humility, and His holy doctrine and teaching will be embraced. All this can happen if we embrace His cross, which has come on the Church in such a strange and unexpected way. Now is the time to turn to God."[246]

In the midst of the 2002 crisis in Saint Louis, Archbishop Rigali put it even more succinctly. Speaking to members of the Priests' Council, he noted, "Gentlemen, these days we cannot get away with anything less than holiness of life. And that's not bad."

---

245 Bishop Robert Barron. *Letter to a Suffering Church: A Bishop Speaks on the Sexual Abuse Crisis*. Park Ridge: Word On Fire. 2019. P 6.
246 Fr. Benedict J. Groeschel, C.F.R. *From Scandal to Hope*. P. 185.

In 2002, Archbishop Justin Rigali spoke to lay representatives from parishes at a meeting addressing issues related to clergy sexual abuse. Sitting, from left to right, are pictured Dr. Nancy Brown, Bernard Huger, Deacon Phil Hengen, and Dr. Susanne Harvath. Photographer Richard Finke. From the Archdiocese of St. Louis Archives and Records.

Jennifer Brinker, a reporter at the St. Louis Review, interviewed Bishop Mark Rivituso, Sandra Price and Archbishop Robert J. Carlson on Feb. 26, 2019 to discuss the Vatican Summit on the Protection of Minors in the Church, and the Archdiocese's work to address cases of abuse by clergy. Sandra Price is the executive director of the archdiocesan Office of Child and Youth Protection. Photographer Lisa Johnston. Courtesy of St. Louis Review.

Chapter Ten

RAYMOND LEO BURKE AND A PRIDE OF LIONS

The contrast in the press between coverage of the departure of Archbishop Justin Rigali and the anticipated arrival of his successor, Bishop Raymond Burke, could not have been starker. Patricia Rice, religion editor for the *Post-Dispatch*, gushed in an article, "Rigali's Gain is City's Loss." It was front page, above the fold, and contrasted the Archdiocese of Saint Louis, with its 555,000 Catholics and 401 diocesan priests, with Rigali's destination of Philadelphia, with its 1.5 million Catholics and 736 diocesan priests.[247]

Rice followed with another article, "One Day, He Could Vote on New Pope," confident that the move to Philadelphia would bring Rigali the cardinalate also. She speculated on his replacement and named six likely candidates, two of whom were African American. She quoted Father John Jay Hughes as he approved, saying "Many people think it's high time."

The Catholic newspaper for Philadelphia, *The Catholic Standard & Times*, headlined the following day, "God's Providence Brings Archbishop Rigali to Philadelphia."[248]

In less than ten weeks, Patricia Rice proved correct regarding the red hat. In an excited tone, in the article, "Rigali Tells of Call That He Would Be a Cardinal," she wrote, "Cardinal-delegate Justin Rigali laughed, joked and almost danced on the stage at the Archdiocesan Pastoral Center in Shrewsbury on Monday as he recalled hearing the news that he would become a cardinal." There would be thirty-one new cardinals; he was the only American.[249]

Finally, on October 6, 2003, the *Post-Dispatch* ran an article, "Rigali Says Last Mass Here." The day before, on Sunday afternoon, 1,800 people crowded into the Cathedral for Mass and listened to Mayor Francis Slay declare, "For us, it's a bittersweet occasion. It's bitter be-

247 Patricia Rice. "Rigali's Gain is City's Loss." *St. Louis Post-Dispatch*. July 16, 2003.

248 "God's Providence Brings Archbishop Rigali to Philadelphia." *The Catholic Standard & Times*. July 17, 2003.

249 Patricia Rice. "Rigali Tells of Call That He Would Be a Cardinal." *St. Louis Post-Dispatch*. September 30, 2003.

cause we're watching a wonderful leader be moved to a different diocese. But we can't forget the sweet part."[250] Interestingly, the mayor did not name the sweet part.

Rome moved swiftly. Auxiliary Bishop Joseph Naumann was designated administrator of the archdiocese but was himself named coadjutor bishop of Kansas City, Kansas. The announcement was made on January 8, 2004 that Bishop Raymond Burke of La Crosse, Wisconsin was named the next archbishop of Saint Louis. Nauman commented, "I knew that I would probably be moved once Cardinal (Justin) Rigali left for Philadelphia. But I was hoping for a longer period of time to help work with Archbishop-elect Burke."[251]

For Bishop Burke, the *Post-Dispatch* went negative from the first instant. An early January article noted that La Crosse was named among eighteen other dioceses by the United States Conference of Catholic Bishops Office of Child and Youth Protection as failing to complete its child protection program. Children, parents, and staff were to be trained to detect signs of child sex abuse and proper protocol for addressing abuse. La Crosse had completed between half and two-thirds according to the USCCB audit. Yet days later, the *Post-Dispatch* had to run an article stating that the USCCB reversed itself and removed La Crosse from the list.

The next day another article followed critical of the archbishop-elect. It headlined, "Burke Denied Communion to Lawmakers." The ban came after an exchange of letters and refusal by three Wisconsin politicians to meet with the bishop. Burke had written to them, "It is a grave contradiction to assume a public role and present yourself as a credible Catholic when your actions on the fundamental issues of human life are not in accord with Church teachings." Specifically, the bishop's concern was regarding their pro-abortion and pro-euthanasia stands.

Cited in the article was State Auditor Clare McCaskill, "the state's most recognized Catholic in favor of abortion rights."[252]

The article pointed out the high stakes involved. In the Missouri House of Representatives, fifty of the one hundred and sixty-three were Catholic. In the Senate, eight of the thirty-two identified as Catholic.

---

250 "Rigali says Last Mass Here." *St. Louis Post-Dispatch.* October 6, 2003.
251 "Bishop Naumann gets Post in Kansas." *St. Louis Post-Dispatch.* January 8, 2004.
252 "Burke Denied Communion to Lawmakers." *St. Louis Post-Dispatch.* January 9, 2004.

What the *Post-Dispatch* failed to mention was that bishops in Atlanta, Pensacola-Tallahassee and other dioceses were doing the same thing. The Code of Canon Law, 915, required Catholics who "obstinately persist in manifest grave sin are not to be admitted to Holy Communion."[253] Supporting abortion and euthanasia legislation would be manifest grave sin. A Catholic politician under those circumstances should not approach Communion.

Later in 2004, Archbishop Burke's position was further bolstered by the USCCB document, "Catholics in Political Life," and by a directive from then-Cardinal Ratzinger directing bishops to meet with offending politicians, instructing them on the Church's pro-life stand, and directing them not to present themselves for Communion if they persist in their position.

Another *Post-Dispatch* article written by Jo Mannis was entitled, "New Archbishop Makes Some Catholic Politicians Uneasy." One example was May Sheve, a former legislator from South County and a Catholic who was pro-abortion. Mayor Francis Slay, identified as a Catholic and pro-life, was quoted: "I'm not going to criticize the Archbishop. He's doing what he thinks best for the Catholic Church. Likewise, I do what I think is best for the city of St. Louis. I'm leader of a diverse city."[254]

State Representative Tom Villa, Democrat from Saint Louis, could "foresee potential conflicts," but added, "I think the newspaper reports may be digging this gentleman a hole before he gets here."

Villa had second thoughts a few days later when he said in a January 12th KMOV Channel 4 interview, "I would have a problem with anybody telling me I can't receive communion. Your faith is something that is personal."

Another *Post-Dispatch* article mentioned that Bishop Burke had directed the Central Wisconsin HIV/AIDS Ministry Project to skip the annual AIDS Walk when he became uncertain about how the money would be spent.

A January 26th article entitled, "St. Louis Gets Archbishop with High National Profile," but what seemed to be complimentary proved to be otherwise. The article called Burke the "fastest rising bishop in

253 James Coriden, Thomas J. Green, Donald E. Heintschel, ed. *The Code of Canon Law: A Text and Commentary*. New York: Paulist Press. 1985. P. 653.
254 "New Archbishop's Stance Makes Some Catholic Politicians Uneasy." *St. Louis Post-Dispatch*.

the US hierarchy," and that he was the first American appointed by a pope to argue appeals cases before the Church's highest court.

The article continued, "In the seven weeks since Pope John Paul II named him to head the Archdiocese of St. Louis, Burke has exploded onto the national stage through a series of bold pronouncements that have captured the attention of the nation's media and have inadvertently knocked some other bishops on their heels."

Two other critical remarks were made. Bishop Burke had pulled his diocese out of CROP Walk, a fund raiser by Church World Services when he discovered that some of the money would be directed toward buying condoms.

Burke was also criticized for launching a $25 million project to build a shrine to Our Lady of Guadalupe. Despite assuring the people of the La Crosse Diocese that no diocesan money would be used and that all funding would come from beyond the diocese, the *Post-Dispatch* said the shrine "created a huge schism, prompting a priest who heads two parishes to resign."[255]

After such a media barrage, Saint Louis Catholics might well wonder what firestorm was coming their way. But below the surface, many admired and respected the new archbishop for his clear and forceful stance. He argued that denying Communion for a pro-abortion Catholic politician was not meant to be a punishment, but rather a remedy. It was meant to touch their souls, to cause them to reevaluate their position which was contrary to every Catholic teaching all the way back to the first century, as witnessed in the *Didache*, a Christian handbook even older than the New Testament.

The little village of Windsor, Missouri in Henry County had one such supporter. Jack Krier wrote a column, "The Town Kri-er," for the *Windsor Review*. Krier called it "A Catholic to Admire," and stated, "His Excellency, the Most Rev. Raymond Burke of St. Louis Missouri has the admiration of many Catholics – including this writer – because of the courage to take a stand every Catholic priest and bishop should take."[256]

Just days earlier, the Democratic front-runner for the 2004 nomination, Catholic and pro-abortion John Kerry came to Saint Louis to campaign. Archbishop Burke announced that he should be denied Communion in Missouri because of his support for abortion. Later,

---

255 "St. Louis Gets Archbishop with High National Profile." *St. Louis Post-Dispatch.* January 26, 2004.
256 "A Catholic to Admire." *Windsor Review.* February 12, 2004.

Republican candidate Rudy Giuliani, another pro-abortion Catholic, received the same stern warning.

The year 2004 brought to a head another controversy which had been bubbling just below the surface. On August 4 Archbishop Burke removed the priests serving at Saint Stanislaus Kostka Parish in North Saint Louis. Life in the rectory had become untenable. The parish board had removed grocery privileges from the priests, insisting that grocery shopping would be done by board members. Never, in any parish, had such an absurd arrangement been tried. Saint Stanislaus would be a parish without a priest until the board would reconcile with the archdiocese.

The issue stemmed from the very dedication of the parish in 1891. Archbishop Peter Richard Kenrick helped Father Urban Stanowski incardinate as an archdiocesan priest and stay at Saint Stanislaus rather than return to his Franciscan monastery. Throughout the United States, Polish communities tended to join one camp or another. The Nationalists favored a trusteeship parish, independent of ecclesial authority. The Clericalists favored leadership by their pastors, appointed by their bishops. Saint Stanislaus proved to be a mix of the two.

Father Stanowski established a lay board on May 2, 1891, and incorporated the parish with the State of Missouri as "Polish Roman Catholic Saint Stanislaus Kostka Parish." The pastor was to serve as president and treasurer of the corporation. The bylaws called for five members of the board appointed by the archbishop.

The arrangement was challenged in court in 1909 by some disgruntled parishioners, but they lost their case. Regardless, two events changed all of that. First, a board in the 1980s altered its bylaws, and members of the board were to be elected by the parish itself. Why this was not challenged by Archbishop May is not clear. Perhaps the transition from one pastor who did not speak Polish to an elderly Polish-speaking pastor blurred any sense of urgency.

The second event came in reaction to the clergy sex abuse scandal and the extraordinary awards being given to plaintiffs. Traditionally, every diocesan property and assets were in the hands of the ordinary as corporate sole. This arrangement made these assets vulnerable to seizure, as an offending priest would be considered an agent of the bishop, and his misdeeds would make the bishop responsible for failing to supervise him.

Diocese after diocese altered this arrangement, creating a board responsible for all properties, detached from the bishop, though he would still be a member of the board. Every parish was expected to transfer its ownership of properties to this board. In 2003, as other parishes were complying with the order, the board at Saint Stanislaus refused, arguing that the archdiocese just wanted its assets to pay for clergy abuse cases.

Archbishop Burke sent Monsignor Richard Stika to meet with the parishioners of Saint Stanislaus to try to find a recourse. The timing was terrible. The meeting was set for August 1, a day held sacred by all Poles, as it commemorates the Warsaw Uprising of 1944. The meeting did not go well, and so the two priests were removed from the parish three days later.

When Archbishop Burke demanded that the board recognize the 1891 bylaws, the board appealed to Rome only to be rebuffed.

In a civil case, the archdiocese argued for the 1891 bylaws and that the archbishop should appoint the board members. Unlike the 1909 ruling, the District Court ruled for Saint Stanislaus.

On July 1, 2005, Archbishop Burke designated Saint Agatha Parish on the near south side as the personal parish for Polish Catholics. Around two hundred families then left Saint Stanislaus, many of them going to Saint Agatha, while the board dug in its heels. They went one step further into schism by hiring Father Marek Bozak as their pastor.

Marek Bozak began seminary studies in Hosianum Seminary in Poland. He had come under suspicion by the rector of the seminary, Father Jan Gusowski, and when homosexual pornographic material was found in his room, he was dismissed immediately. Strangely, Bozak's bishop sent a letter of recommendation to Bishop John Leibrecht of Springfield-Cape Girardeau diocese. Bozak was ordained two years later in 2002.

After serving two years in a parish in Neosho, Bozak was transferred to Saint Agnes Cathedral. When rumors circulated that Bozak was considering a move to Saint Stanislaus, Bishop Leibrecht pleaded with him, without success.

Saint Stanislaus Parish got its renegade priest on December 2, 2005. On December 16 the archdiocese announced that Bozak and the board members were excommunicated for schism.

Regardless, Father Bozak celebrated Midnight Mass at Saint Stanislaus with an estimated attendance of 2,000. With this, Archbishop Burke suppressed the parish. His decree was published on December 29, 2005 and read, "Having verified the act of schism of Saint Stanislaus Kostka Parish (canon 751), in accord with the prescriptions of the *Code of Canon Law* (canons 120.1, 121, and canon 515.2) and having consulted the Presbyterial Council, I hereby suppress Saint Stanislaus Kostka Parish in the city of Saint Louis, Missouri."[257]

In March 2006 Father Bozak took his case to Rome to appeal for a lifting of the excommunication. He was unsuccessful. In May 2008 the Congregation for the Doctrine of the Faith reconfirmed the excommunications, and in 2009 Pope Benedict XVI dismissed Bozak from the clerical state.

In the meantime, Bozak made public his "vision" for the Catholic Church, which included married priests, women priests, and openly homosexual priests. This further split the parish, as more traditional parishioners rejoined the archdiocese, while their places were taken by others responding to Bozak's outreach to the gay community.

Three members of the board recanted and were received back into the Church along with another parishioner. These three members, supported by the archdiocese, filed a lawsuit to restore the 1891 bylaws. The archdiocese also demanded an independent audit of the Saint Stanislaus books. Rumors were afloat that the board was hiding financial misconduct.

In a December 21, 2005 blog, apologist Jimmy Akin hinted at impropriety. "If it were exposed, misappropriation of funds (or other goods) could result in a loss of power for the individual directors or fines or (for all I know) even jail time. Those would be powerful incentives NOT to reconcile with the Church and allow the audit to be conducted."

Akin softened his tone slightly by adding, "I have no proof of any wrongdoing, and I am not making any allegations of wrongdoing. But my spider sense is tingling, and I am suspicious."[258]

Archbishop Burke's successor, Archbishop Robert Carlson, attempted to settle the Saint Stanislaus schism with a compromise. The parish would keep its property and assets and would be brought back into the fold with a new board being named by the archbishop and with the assignment of an archdiocesan priest to replace Marek Bozak. In August, the parish voted to reject the offer, 257 to 185.

The event was picked up by the *New York Times* which published an article. One dissenter was quoted as saying, "They gave the church

---

257 "Decree." St. Stanislaus Kostka Polish Roman Catholic Church (2003 – present). RG O1J Accession: 2014 – 032. Archives of the Archdiocese of Saint Louis.
258 Jimmy Akin. "The Schism of St. Stanislaus Kostka Parish." December 21, 2005. Jimmyakin.com/2005/the_schism_of_s.html.

to the devil. People are blind. They don't see what he's doing. This is belief in Bozak, not in God."[259]

The *New York Times* turned its attention to the schismatic parish in 2012 when Saint Louis Circuit Judge Hetterback ruled that the property and assets of the parish belonged to the Saint Stanislaus Parish Corporation, quipping that the souls of the parishioners may be owned by the archbishop, but the property belongs to the Corporation.[260]

On March 14, 2013, the archdiocese and the board signed a settlement in which the archdiocese recognized the property rights of the board, and the board agreed to not represent itself as affiliated with the Roman Catholic Church.

Thereafter, Saint Stanislaus began a search for another entity with which to affiliate. Joining the Polish National Catholic Church, itself in schism from Rome, proved to be unattractive as the Church demanded the same authority over parish property and assets which the board had refused to the archdiocese.

In August 2013 negotiations began with the Episcopal Diocese of Missouri. Bishop Wayne Smith announced that Saint Stanislaus would be the venue for the ordination of the eleventh bishop of the Episcopal diocese of Missouri. Everything seemed to be moving toward affiliation until the question of parish property and assets came up. Affiliation was dropped, and Saint Stanislaus Parish Corporation remained an entity to itself. Its website title reads, "Saint Stanislaus Kostka Polish Catholic Parish," careful to avoid calling itself Roman Catholic.

In December 2004 Father James Rodis, pastor of Saint Agatha Parish on the near south side, retired. Archbishop Burke invited the Order of Christ the King Sovereign Priest to take over the parish. The charism of the Order is to preserve the rites of the pre-1962 liturgy according to the moto proprio *Summorum Pontificum* of Pope Benedict XVI. The arrangement lasted only six months when the Order transferred to Saint Francis de Sales, which had been suppressed as a parish and established as an oratory.

Archbishop Burke then invited the Society of Christ Fathers for Poles Abroad to take over Saint Agatha. The first pastor was Father Czesław Litak, a native of Poland. Many parishioners were former

---

259 "Renegade Priest Leads a Split in St. Louis Parish." *New York Times*. August 13, 2010.
260 "Defiant St. Louis Church Wins Archdiocesan Suit." *New York Times*. March 17, 2012.

members of Saint Stanislaus Kostka Parish who left either at the time of the schism or when Father Bozak announced his "vision" of progressive Catholicism.

Saint Agatha offers Mass in Polish and in English, Polish twice on Sundays and once on Friday. Confessions are also available in Polish. The parish supports Saint John Paul II Polish School, offering Polish language courses as well as courses in Polish history and culture. The Saint Agatha Center continued as an outreach to the area poor, offering food assistance, job resources, and literacy and GED classes.

A great contrast to the Stanislaus experience was the founding of two new parishes, or oratories, grounded in the traditional Latin liturgy. When the Order of Christ the King Sovereign Priest left Saint Agatha, it was given Saint Francis de Sales to administer. The switch was perfect, as Saint Francis de Sales is one of the patrons of the Order, along with Saint Benedict and Saint Thomas Aquinas. The Order was founded in 1990 to promote the traditional Latin Mass and was raised to pontifical status in 2008. Its rector has a right to ordain men to the diaconate and priesthood.

The first rector of the Oratory of Saint Francis de Sales was Rev. Canon Karl Lenhardt. He and his small community introduced the Mass according to the 1962 Missal of Pope John XXIII. The challenges were great, as the church and rectory were in disrepair. The neighborhood had also deteriorated over the years. It was rumored that the magnificent bell tower was separating from the church building itself and would have to be demolished. Thankfully, this rumor proved to be inaccurate.

At the invitation of Archbishop Burke, Canon Lenhardt conducted a conference on the Latin Mass for archdiocesan priests who might want to learn it. Interestingly, it was mainly young priests and seminarians who showed the greatest interest. And the congregation at Saint Francis de Sales was remarkably young and enthusiastic. As an oratory, the parish was non-territorial, serving the interests and needs of Catholics throughout the archdiocese.

The traditional Latin Mass, also known as the Tridentine Mass, had not been entirely suppressed with the Vatican II Novus Ordo Mass. Priests were permitted to celebrate that Mass, but only privately. In the 1980s permission was given, upon the request of a bishop, to establish places where the Mass could be celebrated publicly, though fewer and fewer priests knew the liturgy or had an interest in celebrating it.

Strangely, the Tridentine Mass was kept alive by schismatic groups like the Priestly Fraternity of Saint Pius X. In 1988 twelve SSPX priests returned to the Catholic Church to form The Priestly Fraternity of Saint Peter, founded to promote the Tridentine Mass.

The catalyst for this movement to restore the old liturgy came with Pope Benedict's 2007 moto proprio *Summorum Pontificum*, which allowed for the widespread use of the Tridentine Mass, as well as the celebration of other sacraments in forms used prior to the Second Vatican Council. Bishops were allowed to establish personal parishes which would be based on the ancient liturgy. It was in anticipation of this provision that Archbishop Burke invited the Order of Christ the King Sovereign Priest to come to his archdiocese.

At the same time, Archbishop Burke invited another traditional Latin Mass community, the Canons Regular of the New Jerusalem, to come to Saint Louis. He knew of this group which had been founded in 2002 in La Crosse, Wisconsin by Canon Daniel Oppenheimer while Raymond Burke was bishop there.

Located in West County, Canon Oppenheimer and his two associates began offering Sunday Masses in Latin, attracting congregants from that part of the archdiocese. Unlike Saint Francis de Sales, a permanent home could not be found for the west county oratory. Eventually, the Canons Regular left the archdiocese, but Archbishop Burke did not want to abandon their small congregation which had been assembled.

Father Thomas Keller was asked to learn and celebrate the 1962 Mass for the west county congregation while the archbishop sought a more permanent solution. Father Keller worked with Canon Lenhardt, who warned the young priest that the devil would not go easy on him for supporting the ancient Mass. The prediction proved to be true in many ways.

Father Keller continued saying the Sunday Latin Mass until Archbishop Burke arranged with Abbot Thomas Frerking, OSB to convert the lower level of the Saint Anselm Parish Center into a chapel. The new parish was to be called the Oratory of Ss. Gregory and Augustine. It was a propitious decision, as Saint Gregory I was the author of that Mass which was changed only slightly at the Council of Trent; hence the Tridentine Mass. Saint Augustine of Canterbury was a Benedictine missionary sent by Pope Gregory to convert the people of England. The Benedictine community at the Abbey of Saint Mary and Saint Louis, which conducted the Priory

School and pastored Saint Anselm parish, had English roots.

Father Bede Price, OSB was named the first rector of this oratory. It was a good choice, as Father Bede had a deep appreciation for the liturgy, Church history, and Benedictine spirituality. His interest in the oratory and its small congregation was evident, and word got out to others longing for the beauty of the Tridentine liturgy. New parishioners began to flock to the Oratory of Ss. Gregory and Augustine.

Catechism classes were introduced to the children so they might know their Faith better. Eventually, adult classes were also held. Besides celebrating the 1962 Mass with great devotion, Father Bede used his sermons to instruct as well as to preach the Gospel. And the congregation grew larger.

Soon the little chapel was filled, and more Masses had to be added. Other monks learned the 1962 Mass and loved it. Fathers Aidan and Ambrose became regular celebrants of the Mass. Young monks in the monastery were attracted also.

After nine years in the chapel under the Saint Anselm Parish Center, an abrupt about-face occurred in the Benedictine community. Father Bede was sent to England. The Oratory was told it would have to leave by May 2017, just six months away, and after that time, the Benedictines would no longer serve the Oratory's needs.

Lay leaders in the Oratory turned to Archbishop Robert Carlson for help. By now, the parish had over two hundred members. Father Keller was again involved in finding a solution. Evening meetings followed and tempers flared. Nobody wanted to see the Oratory dissolve.

By January, with just four months remaining, it was decided to accept an invitation to share facilities at All Saints Catholic Church in University City. Archbishop Carlson helped with the transition and appointed the All Saints pastor as the new rector of the Oratory.

The people of All Saints were most welcoming, changing their Sunday Mass schedule to accommodate the Oratory's 7:30 and 11:30 Masses. Classrooms in the old school were painted and cleaned for the CCD classes. Ryan Hall became the center of a riotous gathering every Sunday after the last Mass, with parishioners bringing potluck selections every week and kids running wild through the building or across the street at Ackert Park.

Parishioners drove in from as far away as Warrenton and Troy and Bloomsdale. A strong sense of camaraderie grew. A Corpus Christi procession was arranged to circle the neighborhood and go down part of the Delmar Loop. The rector, recovering from knee surgery, watched from the rectory window, as nothing like this had been seen in the Loop for at least sixty years!

On November 26, 2017, Father Keller returned to celebrate the 11:30 Mass for the oratory's tenth anniversary. He delivered the sermon and shared a greeting from Father Bede, who was now in exile. "It was a privilege to be your parish priest. I hope I was a good one, and I will always keep you in my prayers. I would have done anything in the world to offer this anniversary Mass, but God in his providence had other plans. It's a good reminder of something we all know too well, 'thy will, not mine be done.'"[261]

Archbishop Carlson promised to help the pastor of All Saints/ Oratory, who himself had learned the Tridentine Mass. The archbishop was sure that there would be a list of young priests "as long as my arm" to assist him. This was not to be the case. Only a few priests offered to say a few Masses. The extra help fell mainly on Father Keller at first. But he was pastor of a large parish in south county.

In July, providence struck. Monsignor Eugene Morris was basically detached from his duties at Our Lady of Sorrows Parish. He loved the Latin liturgy and was free to celebrate most of the 11:30 Masses. With time, he became the sole celebrant at the later Mass. The congregation came to admire and love him. He took up residence at Saint Luke's in Richmond Heights. The next step was obvious.

In the spring of 2018, Monsignor Morris and the rector of the Oratory met with Bishop Mark Rivituso and Father Michael Boehm, director of Priest Personnel. They presented a plan in which Monsignor Morris would become the rector of the Oratory, and its location would move to Saint Luke's. The plan was accepted. Saint Francis de Sales Parish continued to be conducted by the Order of Christ the King Sovereign Priest. Several other priests offered the 1962 Mass on occasion, or even regularly in their own parishes.

The Oratory of Ss. Gregory and Augustine would be the only Latin Mass parish, conducted under the auspices of the Archdiocese of Saint Louis and led by a priest of the archdiocese. Due to the change in location, close to Highway 64, along which eighty percent of the parishioners lived, and due to the stability of having a full-time rector, the Oratory again flourished, doubling in size in one year.

---

261 Rev. Thomas Keller. "The Tenth Anniversary of the Oratory of St. Gregory and St. Augustine." November 26, 2017.

Another initiative taken by Archbishop Burke was to recruit away from Wake Forest University in North Carolina, Father Samuel A. Weber, OSB. He was given free rein to establish The Institute for Sacred Music in the archdiocese. The object was to provide educational programs for choirs and their directors in Gregorian chant, antiphons for English Masses and Liturgy of the Hours. Father Weber would be in residence at Kenrick-Glennon Seminary and offer courses for the seminarians.

Father Weber's credentials were stellar. After taking a BA and M. Div. at Saint Meinrad Seminary, he studied ancient Greek and Latin for an MA from the University of Colorado, Boulder. Later he took a Licentiate in Sacred Theology from the Pontifical Athenaeum Sant' Anselmo in Rome and studied Gregorian chant for two years, also in Rome.

Father Weber was widely published, respected in Protestant communities as well as Catholic circles, and was an advisor for the International Committee on English in the Liturgy (ICEL).

In making the announcement, Archbishop Burke said, "The concern does not come from a negative judgment on the music presently used for sacred worship, but from the sense of the Church's perennial, that is, constant, responsibility to make the celebration of the Sacred Liturgy as worthy and beautiful as possible. Given that sacred worship is the highest expression of our life in the Church, the desire is to offer every possible help for the most-worthy and most beautiful possible celebration of the Sacred Liturgy."[262]

For the next four years, Father Weber enriched the worship within the archdiocese offering classes and workshops both at Kenrick-Glennon and at various locations. He regularly helped at Saint Francis de Sales Parish and taught many priests the Mass according to the 1962 missal. He influenced the liturgy at the Cathedral and won the admiration of many seminarians who continued to correspond with him and visit him long after he left Saint Louis.

External affairs could not be ignored, and Archbishop Burke found himself in the familiar role of an archbishop defending life. Cardinal Carberry, Archbishop May, and Archbishop Rigali had all taken leading roles in the moral landscape of defending the dignity of human life.

In 2006 a group called Missouri Coalition for Life-Saving Cures pressed for a constitutional amendment which would allow for fetal

---

262 "Archdiocese of St. Louis Opens Sacred Music Institute, Renowned Priest-Musician Takes Helm." *Catholic News Service.* April 7, 2008.

stem cell research and human cloning allowable under federal law. President George W. Bush restricted federal funding that either created or destroyed human embryos.

Six states had laws restricting this research, and the Missouri legislature was active in restricting the research as much as possible. Seven states actually supported the research financially. Claire McCaskill, running for the U. S. Senate as a Democrat, supported the amendment.

Many people had been impressed with the cloning of Dolly the Sheep in Scotland in 1996. This had been done by somatic cell nuclear transfer, that is, combining an egg with a body cell, in this case from the mammary gland. Dolly was euthanized six-and-a-half years later because of advanced lung cancer, not uncommon in sheep, and severe arthritis. The normal life of a sheep is eleven to twelve years.

Opposed to the amendment was Missourians Against Human Cloning. They were supported by the incumbent, Republican Senator Jim Talent. Vitae Foundation ran ads showing the difference between adult and embryonic stem cell research. The campaign was working. The earliest polls showed the amendment had 68% support. Shortly before the election, the latest poll showed 51% in favor and 35% opposed.

As the election day was approaching, Archbishop Burke called for a day of prayer on November 2, All Souls Day. He went to Du Bourg High School and joined the students and faculty to recite the rosary, which was broadcast on a Catholic radio station. In a statement, the archbishop said, "Somatic cell nuclear transfer, that is, human cloning, is the prideful attempt of man to generate human life by himself without God and in defiance of God's plan for us."

He added, "We recognize that the vote of each of us on Amendment 2 will be either a vote for the protection of the right to life of our tiniest brothers and sisters, or a vote to subject them to destruction through scientific experimentation."[263]

The November 7, 2006 vote was a disappointment to the pro-life faction. Amendment 2 passed 51.2% to 48.8%. The senate seat went to the pro-choice Catholic, Claire McCaskill.

Yet, there was something of a victory for pro-life Missouri after all. The close vote and the general pro-life atmosphere of Missouri scared

---

263 "Archbishop Burke Calls for Prayers Prior to Vote on Cloning." *Catholic News Agency*. October 23, 2006.

off Stowers Institute for Medical Research. Originally, they planned a $2 billion facility in Kansas City to proceed with the cloning research. They abandoned the Missouri plan and went to Delaware instead. So, Missourians Against Human Cloning won even in their defeat at the ballot box.

While Archbishop Burke made use of Catholic media to stress the moral dimensions of human cloning, there was a wider consequence to evangelization through the air waves. The Society of Our Mother of Peace used a local Catholic radio station to bring the Catholic message of evangelization into many households in North Saint Louis and north county.

The 1970s and 1980s saw efforts to bring new catechesis to Catholics in the Archdiocese of Saint Louis. The arrival of Father Alberione's Pauline Community and the establishment of Pauline Books & Media was a positive addition to Catholic Supply, Vincentian Press, and Ligouri Press.

Something was missing. Too many Catholics did not know their Faith. They were confused about Catholic doctrine, chose pro-abortion politics, and denied the Real Presence in the Eucharist. There was a constant decline in Mass attendance, a decline in parochial membership. There was too much confusion in Catholic schools, while Catholic colleges and universities marched to their own drummers, adhering to the Land o' Lakes declaration of independence from the hierarchy of the Church.

Yet a marvelous thing was about to happen. A religious, Sister Angelica Rizzo, lay in a darkened hospital room, awaiting an unsure surgery the next day. It was July 31, 1956. She had been told that she had a fifty-fifty chance of never walking again. In prayer, she gave voice to a dream she had been contemplating for three years. "Lord, if you let me walk again, I'll build you a monastery in the South."[264]

The surgery was a success. The sister's community, the Poor Clares, reluctantly agreed to allow the experiment in the South. A positive response came from Archbishop Thomas Toolen of Mobile-Birmingham. Overcoming one obstacle after another, the foundation finally became a reality in 1961.

The monastery was completed and came to house a community of sisters, but after an open house which ran for ten days, Sister Angelica

264 Raymond Arroyo. *Mother Angelica: The Remarkable Story of a Nun, Her Nerve, and a Network of Miracles*. New York: Doubleday. 2005. P. 74.

realized that she had incurred a debt of $90,000 with no way to repay it.

In August 1962 Sister Angelica cut a 45-rpm record, a talk entitled "God's Love for You." It sold over 1,500 copies. She recorded a second one, "The Presence of God," a year later. Yet post-Vatican changes would batter Our Lady of the Angels Monastery, as well as most Catholic institutions. Some sisters abandoned their habits, others their vocations. When Sister Angelica recorded an interview embracing the "spirit of the Council," donations waned.

Things began to change under the influence of Father Robert De Grandis, a young Italian priest who visited the monastery often. He introduced Sister Angelica to the Catholic charismatic movement. Eventually, she developed a style in which she called herself "a conservative liberal who happens to be charismatic."[265]

The charismatic movement deepened Mother Angelica's spiritual life. Her alarm at developments in American society and in her Church made her a conservative liberal. She produced a bumper sticker which read, "Fight Mind Pollution." By that, she meant pornography, indecent living. She spoke out against the Equal Rights Amendment. She adopted a modified, dignified habit for the nuns: a brown tunic, a beige collar, and a veil.

To pay for the monastery, Mother Angelica recorded cassette tapes and sold them for a dollar each. Other schemes were tried. The nuns made fishing lures, but few sold. They established the Li'l Ole Peanut Company, roasting peanuts, packaging them, and distributing them to grocery stores, bars, sporting events, and schools.

In March 1969 Archbishop Luigi Raimondi, the apostolic delegate to the United States, stopped by the monastery and was impressed with the zeal of Mother Angelica and promised continued support. Valuable Vatican support would be needed for future challenges.

Other adventures followed, like a print shop costing over $100,000 which began turning out "mini-books." The Abbess continued to give talks around Birmingham, but also to wider audiences. In March 1978 she spoke at parishes in Chicago, handing out free literature and tapes. When she was invited to visit a television station located in a Chicago skyscraper, she was smitten.

Mother Angelica was told that she could have her own television station for a mere $650,000. By now, she had published fifty-seven books and reached thousands of people. How much more could she

---

265 Ibid. P. 134.

do with a television station?

Mother's visit to Chicago gave her a television inspiration; it also gave her a collaborator who would be with her for years to come. Deacon Bill Steltemeier was visiting when he attended a talk by Mother Angelica. The Nashville lawyer was so impressed that he visited the Birmingham monastery a month later, offering a donation, but more importantly, offering his services.

The first attempt at a television program, entitled *Our Hermitage*, was not a success. Other takes were made between late April and June of 1978. Before a live audience, Mother Angelica's humor and wisdom shined. That was the key to success.

The tape was hand-delivered to Pat Robertson's Christian Broadcasting Network in Virginia Beach, Virginia. It was enthusiastically received, and CBN offered to broadcast it to its three-and-a-half million viewers, if Mother could produce another sixty episodes.

Rising to the challenge, Mother Angelica and her skeleton crew began taping three and four episodes at a time at a nearby studio. It was there at Channel 42, CBS, that she had a rousing confrontation with management. CBS had planned on broadcasting a mini-series entitled *The Word*, which featured newly discovered manuscripts they believed brought into question the divinity of Christ.

When she confronted the general manager, Hugh Smith, she threatened to leave the station. He retorted, "You need us." She replied, "No, I don't. I only need God! I'll buy my own cameras and build my own station." Smith snorted, "You can't do that," to which she replied, "You just watch me."[266]

Cooler heads tried to moderate Mother's enthusiasm, but she told them, "Unless you are willing to do the ridiculous, God will not do the miraculous... When you have God, you don't have to know everything about it; you just do it."[267]

Pure pluck saw her through. On January 27, 1981, the Federal Communications Commission awarded permission to set up a Catholic satellite television station, the first ever. With a grant from the Grace Foundation for over $600,000, Eternal Word Television Network was funded. It was then that Mother Angelica got snagged.

Like Father Placid in Oklahoma City, just as an apostolic work was beginning to launch, an ecclesiastical surface-to-air missile seemed

266 Arroyo. *Mother Angelica*. P. 145.
267 Ibid. P. 146.

to shoot it down. In this case, the Sacred Congregation for Religious discovered this cloistered nun moving about freely, speaking and fund raising. Following the Vatican's lead, Bishop Joseph Vath of Birmingham offered her a bleak choice, either abandon travel beyond the monastery and studio or seek exclaustration, leaving the convent entirely.

True to form, Mother Angelica tried her best to remedy the situation; she wrote to the papal nuncio, Archbishop Pio Laghi, for his permission to continue her vocation and her mission. And she relied on God to save her.

Just then a truck with $600,000 worth of equipment arrived, but the money had to be paid in advance to receive the shipment. The nun went to the chapel to pray when a phone call came from the Bahamas. A voice on the phone told how he had been moved by one of Mother's mini-books and wanted to donate. He was sending $600,000.[268]

Bill Steltemeier solved Mother's cloister situation. He went to New York and planned to meet Cardinal Silvio Oddi, prefect for the Sacred Congregation of the Clergy. He convinced the cardinal to fly on his private plane to visit the Birmingham monastery. After doing so, Oddi was completely won over and returned to Rome as the monastery's cardinal protector. The travel ban was lifted, but success was modest. Only six cable companies carried Mother's programming, reaching only 300,000 households.

Another challenge came when the United States Catholic Conference of Bishops set up their own cable station, the Catholic Telecommunications Network of America, with a backing of more than four million dollars. But CTNA was hobbled by its own bureaucracy and limitations, with liberal bishops looking for one kind of programming and conservatives another. Mother Angelica solved the dilemma by offering free airtime on her network, if she could control the content.

Awaiting a response, Mother played the Roman card. In November 1982 she and Sister Joseph met Pope John Paul II after Mass in his private chapel. She pledged to him the support of EWTN. He accepted. Later, Cardinal Oddi was assured that EWTN would not broadcast any of the USCCB program which did not agree with Vatican teachings.

By late 1983, EWTN was carried on ninety-five cable stations. Mother Angelica was appearing on live broadcasts, proving she was a natural entertainer as well as a font of wisdom. She got sup-

---

268 Arroyo. *Mother Angelica.* P. 158.

port from Harry John of Miller Brewing and received gifts from the Knights of Columbus and from Archbishop Bernard Law of Boston.

On one occasion, an elderly couple visited the monastery of Our Lady of the Angels, and Mother packed them a lunch with bananas and sandwiches for their trip home. Returning to Florida, the couple convinced a foundation they led to send Mother a donation of $150,000 toward the completion of her studio. By 1985, EWTN was found on more than 220 cable stations.

The importance of EWTN was in full view during the ten-day papal visit in 1987. The bishops' conference suggested a joint venture, and it proved to be a win-win for everyone. The bishops got their Catholic Telecommunications Network of America on the air for the first time. EWTN got into twenty million households.

Nonetheless, the coverage disturbed Mother Angelica. The Holy Father was confronted time after time by dissident priests, nuns, laity, and even bishops. He stood his ground, but it enraged the little nun from Birmingham. She was determined not to let her platform be used for attacks on the pope or on Catholic teachings. She was determined to end the honeymoon with CTNA and not broadcast portions of the upcoming meeting of the Bishops' Conference.

A heated phone conversation ensued.

Reverend Robert Bonnot of CTNA called and insisted that the coverage be complete. Mother replied that she would not broadcast comments made by bishops who were not in line with the Magisterium.

Father Bonnot countered, "And who are you to decide which bishop should be aired?" She retorted, "I happen to own the network" to which he responded, "Well, you won't always be there."

That set off this torrent. "I'll blow the damn thing up before you get your hands on it. I've chosen my Magisterium; you choose yours!" With that, the abbess hung up.[269]

Eventually, a compromise was reached in which a review board of five bishops could override decisions made at EWTN about USCCB programming. The compromise was set for two years.

While relations continued to be bumpy, it was the papal visit of 1993 which set off another crisis. Thirty-two million households tuned in to Denver, Colorado where the Stations of the Cross were presented in Mile High Stadium. Pope John Paul II was not in attendance. His representative was Cardinal Eduardo Pironio.

---

269 Arroyo. *Mother Angelica*. P. 211.

The nation was shocked when the Passion was performed by the Fountain Square Fools, a Cincinnati mime group, with a female actor in the role of Jesus Christ.

Spokesmen for the Bishops' Conference reacted weakly, saying the mime was not meant to a historical portrayal. The Archdiocese of Denver tried to get to the bottom of who allowed the fiasco but was frozen out by silence. The secular press crowed as did advocates for female ordination.

Mother Angelica went on the air to counter these deflections. The following Saturday, she was on live and declared, "Yesterday I made a mistake when I was talking to you. I asked you to watch the Holy Father as he made the Stations, but he didn't make the Stations. So, I'm sorry for that error. I'm very happy he wasn't there." She went on to declare the use of a woman to enact Christ was "an abomination to the Eternal Father!" That was just the start.

Clearly animated, Mother Angelica continued, "It's blasphemous that you dare to portray Jesus as a woman. You know, as Catholics we've been quiet all these years. After the Vatican Council – those beautiful documents inspired by the Holy Spirit... they were misrepresented and misportrayed and misinterpreted all these years, and every excuse, like this mime, has been blamed on the Vatican documents... I'm tired, I'm tired of being pushed in corners. I'm tired of your inclusive language that refuses to admit that the Son of God is a man! I'm tired of your tricks. I'm tired of your deceit. I'm tired of you making a crack, and the first thing you know there's a hole, and all of us fall in. No, this was deliberate... You made a statement that was not accidental." She ended the manifesto with "I am so tired of you, liberal church in America."

But she did not end there. Mother Angelica pointed out the abuse of liturgy, disrespect for the Eucharist, mandatory sex education in schools, the precipitous fall in religious vocations, and disrespect for the Holy Father.[270]

Michael Warsaw, a new EWTN producer, saw it as the Catholic equivalent of the 1976 film *Network*, when anchor Howard Beale cried out for the nation, "I'm mad as hell and I'm not going to take it anymore." Archbishop Rembert Weakland, a constant critic of John Paul, said Mother Angelica's comments were a "senseless and heartless condemning of one another" and "vitriolic."[271]

---

270 Arroyo. *Mother Angelica.* P. 241-242.
271 Ibid. P. 243.

Archbishop Weakland and others could wring their hands all they wanted; the numbers were with the nun. Following the Denver World Youth Day, EWTN gained another two hundred cable carriers, adding another two million households in the United States and more than that in foreign lands.

Cardinal Silvio Oddi told Mother Angelica that he had had a conversation with the pope and John Paul told him, "EWTN is the key to restoring the Roman Catholic Church in America."[272]

The Denver show-down would not be the last controversy for Mother Angelica. Later, she locked horns with Cardinal Roger Mahoney of Los Angeles in what should have been an avoidable dust-up, prompting Mother Angelica to look to yet another medium.

By 1996 Mother Angelica's attention turned to radio, and she began encouraging the laity to open up stations in their communities. She used her television programs to recruit them and promised support in programming once they came on board. In Saint Louis, she was to find an eager audience

An elderly priest from the Springfield, Illinois diocese came to Saint Louis to give spiritual direction and preached the virtues of a daily Holy Hour.[273]

One who was attracted to the notion of spending an hour or more with the Lord in the Real Presence of the Blessed Sacrament was Tony Holman. He practiced the discipline for over two years when he was inspired with a deep desire to evangelize on radio. Holman was attracted to the words of Scott Hahn, a convert teaching at Franciscan University of Steubenville who produced scores of talks recorded on cassette tapes. Tony wanted to get these messages out to others to help them deepen their faith, maybe via a radio station. But how?

Not knowing anything about radio, Tony Holman began approaching stations, asking if they were willing to sell. After many rejections, he found one fellow willing to sell his station, AM 1080. The two met at a Denny's east of Saint Monica Parish. Tony asked his fiancée, Teresa, to pray in front of the Blessed Sacrament every time they met while negotiating a deal. The negotiations led to five or six visits to Denny's when the owner offered to sell. He would maintain ownership of the studio building and sell the license and towers to Tony.

---

272 Arroyo. *Mother Angelica*. P. 195.
273 Interview with Tony and Teresa Holman. Covenant Network Headquarters. 16 January 2020.

When the owner named his price, Tony was surprised. It was lower than he had expected. He was nearly in tears as he thought to himself, "This is not good negotiating." The deal went through.

Before beginning broadcasting, Tony and Teresa attended a few Catholic radio conferences in California. The first, in 1996, had only a few in attendance. Three apostolates, Immaculate Heart in Reno, Nevada, Queen of Peace in Jacksonville, Florida, and Covenant Network had already begun broadcasting by the second conference with Jerry Usher and Scott Hahn. It was better attended. Mother Angelica had made programming available for AM and FM stations. The next conference was held in Alabama at EWTN with Mother Angelica. Previously, Tony Holman had thought in terms of primarily airing talks by apologists.

A Catholic radio station for the Saint Louis area was becoming a reality. On May 1, 1997, AM 1080, WRYT, went on the air for the first time. It was the feast of Saint Joseph the Worker in the month dedicated to Our Lady.

Most of the original staff did not want to transition to a Catholic radio station and sought employment elsewhere. This put an extraordinary burden on Tony and Teresa. EWTN provided most of the feeds at first. The couple began some of their own programs, like a series on Catholic Church history, interviews, and added some local "community calendar" events and prayers.

Tony and Teresa were not yet married, and Teresa was staying with her sister in Chesterfield. Each morning she left by 4:45 AM to drive to Glen Carbon, Illinois to open the station. Although Tony dealt with the business side of the station, he was actually more comfortable with its spiritual mission. On one visit to EWTN for a conference, Tony joined the two other radio founders on stage with Mother Angelica.

In 1997 Tony and Teresa were married. On Saint Patrick's Day of 1999, they happily showed their newborn, Clare, to Father Benedict Groeschel at the Covenant Network studio. It was a special moment, as Father Groeschel had given a talk years earlier on the day which happened to be Tony and Teresa's first date together.

Some of the most exciting live broadcasting from WRYT came on April 13, 1998. A violent storm with an accompanying tornado came ripping through Saint Charles County, Missouri. Tony and Teresa followed its progress as it made a beeline for Glen Carbon. Statues of saints and the Blessed Virgin Mary were placed in every window while Teresa broadcast the latest towns damaged and which towns were in the storm's path.

As the tornado continued toward Illinois, Teresa recited 'the storm prayer" on air and everyone ducked under furniture while they heard a roar overhead. Signals were sent from the station to the tower by microwave. Often, even in a rainstorm, the signal was disrupted. Remarkably, throughout this F1 tornado, WRYT continued to broadcast. No one was injured or killed, but some damage was recorded all around the station and tower, neither of which was harmed.

It was the station's mission, simple and straight-forward, which drew others to collaborate in the work. It reflected the fact that Covenant Network was born in and sustained by Eucharistic Adoration which propelled those involved to evangelize, especially using the medium of radio. The mission statement reads, "Through the grace that we have received from Jesus in the Most Blessed Sacrament the mission of this apostolate is simply to evangelize the Catholic faith primarily through radio."

The Catholic Knights of America invited Covenant Network to rent for a nominal fee their building on Hampton Avenue in Saint Louis. An early volunteer, a retired carpenter named Ervin Grassi, built the Hampton Studio and stayed on to volunteer in other ways. He lived a simple life in a small, South Saint Louis bungalow, and when he first visited the fledgling station, he was invited to join the crew for lunch. They served up canned tomato soup, and he thought to himself, "These are my kind of people."

Grassi served even though he was dying of melanoma, and with death made a large donation to the apostolate.

In Illinois, there were other collaborators. Dr. David Mack, an orthopedic surgeon, and his wife Elaine also had a strong devotion to the Blessed Virgin. He helped found the Marian Center in Springfield and later founded a Marian Center in Sioux City, Iowa. Both were very pro-life and saw Catholic radio as a means to get out the Marian pro-life message. As a result, they were responsible for the creation of WIHM (Immaculate Heart of Mary) in Taylorville and WOLG (Our Lady of Guadalupe) in Carlinville.

Tom Shrewsbury, an invaluable collaborator with the network, had been a professional actor, performing with Vincent Price, Lucille Ball, Carol Burnett and others. He returned to Illinois to establish the Springfield Theatre Guild where he starred as Harvey and Mr. Roberts. Shrewsbury served in a consultant status at the United Nations with the U. S. Department of Rehabilitation. In the Dominican Republic he worked with the World Health Organization to bring polio vaccines to all children and served in the Nixon administration on the Committee on Employment of the Handicapped.

But the driving passion in Tom Shrewsbury was devotion to the Blessed Virgin. He established the Marian Center in Springfield, Illinois and became a strong supporter of Covenant Network.

Another collaborator was Msgr. Lawrence Moran in Terre Haute, Indiana. He loaned rooms to Covenant Network in his rectory at Saint Patrick's parish. Over the years he conducted eight hundred interviews for programs. Msgr. Moran was given technical assistance by a retired engineer, Mike Moroz, who ran the station in Terre Haute from 2004 until December 2019.

Covenant Network continued to grow over the years due to countless volunteers, supporters, and contributors. By 2019 Covenant Network had a presence with forty stations as far away as Springfield, Illinois; Atoka, Oklahoma; Garyville, Louisiana; and Terre Haute, Indiana.

A survey showed the impact of Catholic radio. Ninety-four percent of listeners said they were more spiritually engaged and inspired. Thirty-one percent said they came back to the Church because of the programming, and forty-seven percent reported attending Mass more frequently after listening regularly to Catholic radio.[274]

Covenant Network constantly received testimonials. One wrote, "As a Protestant, I greatly appreciate your radio station. Two years ago, I started to look at the Church of Rome, and now I am in the RCIA program." J.G.

Another wrote, "Listening to you daily helps me w/my daily journey of conversion. I stay w/my children so attending workshops, class etc.... is not realistic. RADIO IS Realistic!" L.A.H. Another attested, "It also helps me keep my focus on eternal life." J.R.

Speaking of the witness of something as simple as a bumper sticker, M.A.W. wrote, "The other day a young man came into my store. After talking to him for a while he explained he was going to start RCIA soon. He was quite knowledgeable about the Catholic faith. He said he saw a bumper sticker, "CATHOLIC RADIO AM 1080 WYRT" and started listening especially to Catholic Answers. He is one of many

---

274 National Catholic Radio Listener Survey.

who have started listening and coming back to the faith or are on their way to becoming a Catholic because of your radio station."

Another initiative led by laity and encouraged by Archbishop Burke was the Association of Hebrew Catholics. David and Kathleen Moss met with the archbishop in his office on May 19, 2006. Later that afternoon Archbishop Burke wrote a letter to David welcoming him to transfer the headquarters of the AHC to the Archdiocese of Saint Louis.

The archbishop wrote, "First of all, permit me to express my esteem for the apostolate of the Association of Hebrew Catholics. The mission of your association responds, in a most fitting way, to the desire of the Church to respect fully the distinct vocation and heritage of Israelites in the Catholic Church."[275]

The letter mentioned the recommendation of Bishop Carl Mengeling of Lansing, Michigan in whose diocese the AHC was located at the time, that the Association was faithful to the Magisterium, and that its members exhibited "moral uprightness."

In a most gracious way, the archbishop ended his letter, "I have instructed my staff to give you every possible help in locating a fitting place for the headquarters and your personal quarters."

Archbishop Burke was not unfamiliar with the Association of Hebrew Catholics. While promoting the cause of Father John A. Hardon, Servant of God, Burke came to know Marty Barrack, a member of the AHC. What led to the AHC's move to St. Louis was that after four years of their being housed with Ave Maria College in Ypsilanti, Michigan, the school's founder, Tom Monahan of Domino Pizza fame, moved the college to a Florida location where it became a university.

The inspiration for the Association came from Father Elias Friedman, a Carmelite monk and convert to Catholicism. Born into a Jewish family in South Africa, Friedman converted during the Second World War and joined the Carmelites at Stella Maris monastery in Haifa, Israel. His first book, *The Redemption of Israel*, was followed by *Jewish Identity*.

In a life of prayer and study, and an acute reading of the signs of the times, Father Friedman believed that the world and the Church were entering into an auspicious era. He witnessed the horrors and apostasies of the twentieth century, the return of Jews to their native home-

---

275 Most. Rev. Raymond L. Burke to Mr. David Moss. May 19, 2006. Archives of the Association of Hebrew Catholics.

land, and the reassessment of Judaism by the Catholic Church through the Second Vatican Council. Father Friedman considered the "regime of assimilation" of Jewish converts to Catholicism to be a tragic mistake and lost opportunity. With time, the Jewish identity of the converts would be lost, and their children would be thoroughly gentile.

The other side of the coin was just as destructive. Most often, the Jewish community would shun the converts and consider them traitors. Emblematic was the visit of Cardinal Jean-Marie Lustiger, cardinal-archbishop of Paris and a convert to Catholicism, to Israel in 1995 when he was publicly criticized by Chief Rabbi Meir Lau as a traitor to the Jewish people.

Lustiger gave a strong defense. "Saying that I am not Jewish is a denial of all my family members who died during the Holocaust. I am a Jew, like my father, my mother, my grandfather and grandmother and the rest of my family members who were massacred in Auschwitz and in other camps."[276]

As early as 1979, Father Friedman challenged Msgr. William Aquin Carew, Apostolic Delegate of Jerusalem, to reject the regime of assimilation. Carew responded positively. This gave Father Friedman the courage to approach the Holy See asking for recognition of Jewish converts having a unique status within the Church. This became an ongoing effort parallel to the recognition of the Anglican ordinariate created in 2012.

The effort to create this community within the Church had other effects. Father Friedman convinced Andrew Scholl of Australia to begin publishing a newsletter to help all associates to stay in contact with one another. Eventually, this became the work of David Moss who began to publish a quarterly, *The Hebrew Catholic.*

Another interested party was Msgr. Eugene Kevane, professor at the Angelicum in Rome and former president of the Notre Dame Pontifical Catechetical Institute in Virginia. He, too, approached David Moss who became president of the AHC, as well as Dr. Ronda Chervin, professor of philosophy at the Franciscan University of Steubenville. AHC affiliates are found in Australia, Canada, Great Britain, Ireland, Italy, New Zealand, Poland, Spain, South Africa, and South America as well as the United States.

---

276 "Jewish-Born Cardinal Defends Visit to Israel. Controversy: French Churchman's Participation in Holocaust Seminar was attacked. He said critics discounted his relatives who "were massacred." *Los Angeles Times.* April 27, 1995.

The Association of Hebrew Catholics in Saint Louis is small but has achieved great things. In 1987 it published Father Friedman's *Jewish Identity* and established The Miriam Press. The initial type-setting cost was $4,000, which AHC did not have. Out of the blue, contributions totalling $4,200 found their way into their bank account.

Miriam Press has published nine books, including the autobiography of Ronda Chervin. AHC has sponsored seventeen lecture series by Dr. Larry Feingold, associate professor of theology and philosophy at Kenrick-Glennon Seminary. Among the publications was Dr. Feingold's three-volume *The Mystery of Israel and the Church*.

Members from the Saint Louis AHC attended the 2018 conference in Dallas which brought together around sixty Christian converts who shared their Jewish identity. The dialogue was fruitful, with one member using Zoom to attend from Moscow. David Moss gave a presentation on the Eucharist which was well-received. Mass was celebrated in Hebrew, and many non-Catholics attended.[277]

In a talk delivered at the AHC Conference in Saint Louis in early October 2010, Dr. Feingold outlined the gifts which the Jewish people have to offer to mankind, but particularly to the Church. He grounded his observations in Paul's Letter to the Romans 9: 2-5. It was the Jewish people whom God chose for the privilege of the Incarnation, and the history of Israel shows divine preparation for the event. He noted, "Other religions are products of man's natural religious sense and imagination. They are attempts of man to reach God. However, Judaism – and its fulfillment in Christianity – is the religion formed by God in which God reaches to us, enabling us to reach back to Him."[278]

Dr. Feingold pointed to Romans 11:29 to show that the Covenant God offered to Israel is irrevocable and was stated as such in the Second Vatican Council document, *Nostra Aetate*, Paragraph 4.

The relationship of Hebrews within the Catholic Church was explored in a pre-recorded interview by David Moss with Archbishop Raymond Burke. The Archbishop noted, "... it seems to me that it's a great gift to the Catholic Church that that collective identity as the chosen people would be cultivated, would not be lost, but it would be handed down from one generation to the next."

---

277 Interview with David and Kathleen Moss. AHC Headquarters. January 20, 2020.
278 "You Shall Be My Witnesses…" *Hebrew Catholics and the Mission of the Church*. AHC Conference in St. Louis, Missouri on October 1-3, 2010. P. 8.

Burke mentioned the great appreciation Pope Benedict XVI had for the contribution of Hebrew Catholics, especially regarding prayer and liturgy, and spoke of his own experience attending the AHC Passover Seder meal in Saint Louis. "Hebrew Catholics were bringing through this celebration an ever-deeper appreciation of the meaning of the coming of Christ into the world, of His saving death, and then of the continuation of the fruits of His saving death through the Eucharist."[279]

The interview included some difficult moments in the relationship of Hebrew Catholics in the Church. In some Church circles, Hebrew Catholics are criticized for "judaizing" the Church by such practices as that Seder meal. They point to a medieval condemnation of Coptic Christians by Pope Eugenius IV for practicing pre-Christian observances. Yet 300 years later, Pope Benedict XIV declared, "... it cannot be absolutely asserted that the man judaizes who does something in the Church which corresponds to the ceremonies of the old Law."

Archbishop Burke explained that the development of doctrine shows a greater and greater nuance in our understanding and added, "There should not be anything in Jewish practice which is in itself a denial of the Catholic faith because everything that our Lord revealed to His chosen people was in view of the coming of the Messiah."[280]

The Association of Hebrew Catholics in Saint Louis remains a small but active community. Despite hostility from some quarters and bewilderment from other quarters, AHC provides valuable insight into the Jewish roots of Catholic worship and spirituality, and if Father Elias Friedman is right, the signs of the times make the AHC mission essential to the new evangelization called for by recent popes.

As a providential sign, when AHC found a house near the Saint Louis Cathedral, funding for the purchase materialized within twenty-four hours.

A project near and dear to Archbishop Burke's heart was the archdiocesan seminary. He was a frequent visitor, often seen walking one-on-one with individual seminarians, offering spiritual advice.

Yet Kenrick-Glennon had not had a face-lift since the 1987 merger of the two seminaries on the Glennon campus. Even then, most of the renovations were cosmetic.

---

279 "You Shall Be My Witnesses..." *Hebrew Catholics and the Mission of the Church.* P. 36.
280 Ibid. P. 39.

The archbishop called for a capital campaign called Faith for the Future, a $50 million project with half of the funds going to major building renovations and half into an endowment fund, an area in which the seminary sorely lagged behind comparable institutions. Additional moneys would go to support Catholic Charities and tuition assistance for Catholic schools.

At first, there was some doubt that so much money could be raised. After all, the archdiocese had just conducted its Returning God's Gifts campaign under Archbishop Rigali.

Archbishop Burke retained the services of CCS, Community Counseling Services, to conduct a fund-raising feasibility and planning study. The results were mildly encouraging. Eighty-one archdiocesan priests and one bishop were consulted. Only 33% were positive or very positive, while 48% were doubtful. Of the fifty-six laity and two deacons, 63% were positive or very positive, while only 6% were negative.

Surprisingly, when asked about support for the seminary and seminarians, 52% of the priests gave low ratings, while the laity gave 56% for high ratings. A very positive sign was the strong support for Msgr. Ted Wojcicki's role in the campaign. He was the seminary rector and had the support of 81% of the clergy polled and 93% of the laity.

Archbishop Burke forged ahead, meeting and then surpassing the goal. The renovation plans were changed substantially in 2011 under the leadership of the next archbishop, Robert Carlson. CannonDesign was hired as the architectural firm and BSI, a Saint Louis company, did the construction. The two firms worked well together on this and other major projects.

The final report for the Faith for the Future Campaign confessed that the going was tough. "Another complicating factor was that Archbishop Burke left the archdiocese before he was able to complete the Major Gift effort. As a result of Archbishop Burke's efforts prior to his departure, $13 million of the $22 million major gift goal was raised." Another $6 million was sought in smaller gifts.

The report continued to show the shortfall of parish contributions and added, "CCS collaborated with Frank Cognata and his staff to design a plan to raise more than the original $28 million, which was also flexible enough for the individual parishes."

Interestingly, the report did not mention the financial milieu of the fund-raising period. The United States was undergoing the Great

Recession of 2008-2009, the most severe economic meltdown since the Great Depression of the 1930s.

The report ended on a positive note. "Archbishop Carlson walked into the campaign at a critical juncture and gave a clear message that the campaign was a priority to him. This was not an easy task, but it was an important element in the success of the campaign. More than $45 million has been raised at the parish level, which is a great tribute to the priests and lay people of the Archdiocese."[281]

In July 2006 Archbishop Raymond Leo Burke was called to Rome to assume the second highest office of any American in the curia. He was named head of the Supreme Tribunal of the Apostolic Signatura, the Vatican's Supreme Court.

It was with a heavy heart that the archbishop said farewell to his archdiocese. His last visit to Kenrick-Glennon Seminary was an emotional one. The refectory reception was touching and tearful. As he climbed into his car to drive down to the entrance on Glennon Drive, all the seminarians, dressed in cassocks, lined the road as a tribute to the man they had come to love and admire in the four short years he served as archbishop of Saint Louis.

In Rome, Burke was swiftly made a cardinal, and in May 2008 he became a member of the Pontifical Council for Legislative Texts, the official interpreter of canon law, as well as a member of the Congregation for Clergy, the body which oversaw seminary formation. Later, he was named to the Congregation for Bishops, the department which recommends names to the Holy Father for episcopal ordination.

Cardinal Burke's legacy in the archdiocese was one of creative controversy. Many disagreed with his strong stands, especially regarding politics and life issues. Many others admired him for his clear and strong voice on those very issues. What he left behind as he went to Rome was a pride of lions: seminarians, clergy, and laity eager to defend the Faith, eager to see it grow.

---

281 Patrick Moughan to Archbishop Robert Carlson. Memorandum of January 12, 2010. "Faith for the Future Campaign Summary." Faith For the Future File. Archdiocesan Archives of Saint Louis. The report showed that to date the campaign in six parishes had raised over $1 million, that the average Parish Phase gift was $1,511 per household, that 23% of families had made gifts and that the campaign was already 120% above its goal.

Parishioners received the Eucharist from Archbishop Burke at the communion rail at the Latin mass at St. Francis de Sales Oratory, 2006. From the Archdiocese of St. Louis Archives and Records.

Canon Jason Apple, Vicar of St. Francis de Sales Oratory in South St. Louis, blessed the faithful at Mass March 5, 2010. Photographer Lisa Johnston. Courtesy of St. Louis Review.

Cardinal Raymond L. Burke visited the Oratory of Ss. Gregory and Augustine in 2011 to celebrate the Benediction of the Blessed Sacrament followed by a reception. As Archbishop of St. Louis, Burke canonically established the Oratory on the first Sunday of Advent 2007, the same year as the Holy Father's motu proprio, Summorum Pontificum. Photographer Lisa Johnston | aeternus.com.

Raymond Cardinal Leo Burke took a "family photo" with the clergy and altar boys at the Oratory of Ss. Gregory and Augustine during his first pastoral visit there on January 7, 2011. Cardinal Burke stands center with Fr. Aiden McDermott, OSB (front left), Fr. Bede Price, OSB (front, second from right), and Fr. Thomas Keller (front, far right). Photographer Lisa Johnston | aeternus.com.

On the solemnity of Corpus Christi in 2017, parishioners at Ss. Gregory and Augustine held a procession from All Saints Church in University City. Led by bagpiper Chris Apps, part of the procession's route was in the Delmar Loop. Photographer Lisa Johnston. Courtesy of St. Louis Review.

Father Eugene Morris delivered the homily at an outdoor novena at the Carmelite Monastery in July 2007. From the Archdiocese of St. Louis Archives and Records.

Archbishop Burke posted a sign in the lawn at the archbishop's residence on Lindell in 2006 that rejected Missouri Constitutional Amendment 2, which allows stem cell research and therapy in Missouri. From the Archdiocese of St. Louis Archives and Records.

Mother Angelica spoke at Keil Auditorium in St. Louis in 1985. Photographer Richard Finke. From the Archdiocese of St. Louis Archives and Records.

Archbishop Raymond Burke talked with young men at CBC High School about their faith, 2006. From the Archdiocese of St. Louis Archives and Records.

Archbishop Burke was a frequent visitor at Kenrick-Glennon Seminary. At a Mass at the seminary in 2007, Archbishop Burke celebrated communion with the seminarians. From the Archdiocese of St. Louis Archives and Records.

Students study in the new multi-floor library at the seminary in 2013. Renovations were made possible from the Faith for the Future campaign. Photographer Lisa Johnston. Courtesy of St. Louis Review.

Faith for the Future project renovations at Kenrick-Glennon Seminary were completed in 2013. Kyle Berens, a theology student, read from his Missal along the new rooftop deck area of the seminary. The rooftop is modeled after the one at the North American College in Rome which overlooks St. Peter's Basilica and the Vatican. Photographer Lisa Johnston. Courtesy of St. Louis Review.

Chapter Eleven

THE LONG VIEW

Saint Louis was founded in 1764 as a commercial venture to bring together fur trapping and merchandise trading, a joint effort of French Creole and Native Americans. From its founding, as demonstrated by Pierre Laclède's decision to name the city after Saint Louis IX, king of France, and to set aside the three principle blocks of the village for civic, commercial, and religious purposes, the Catholic Church has played and continues to play a key role in the life of this metropolis and its surrounding region.

The first church and cemetery were constructed in Saint Louis in 1770, six years after the founding. A small log cabin served as the first Catholic church, and a plot of ground was set aside in the block called Place d'Église for a cemetery at the corner of Third and Market. The cemetery was later removed to Seventh and Saint Charles Streets when the city government forbad cemeteries within the city limits. Later the cemetery was again removed to Seventeenth and what is now Martin Luther King Drive. Also, several rural parishes were to establish their own cemeteries, such as Saint Monica in Creve Coeur. In 1866 Archbishop Peter Richard Kenrick developed Calvary Cemetery between Florissant Avenue and Broadway, and in 1869 he added Saints Peter and Paul on Gravois Boulevard.

There were several small cemeteries along Jefferson Avenue, but these were overwhelmed by the Cholera epidemic of 1849 which killed more than 4,000 Saint Louisans. That same year Bellefontaine Cemetery was established as a non-profit, non-denominational cemetery, and Mount Sinai Cemetery was established for the Jewish community.

As of this writing, there are seventeen cemeteries administered by Catholic parishes as well by the Archdiocese of Saint Louis. On occasion, lots are given to the poor as an act of charity upon the death of a loved one. These include Resurrection, Saints Peter and Paul, Mount Olive, Calvary, Sacred Heart, Saint Charles Borromeo, Saint Peter, Saint Ferdinand, Saint Monica, Our Lady of the Holy Cross, Saint Vincent, Sainte Philippine, Saint Mary's, Ascension, and Valle in Sainte Genevieve.

In 1827 Saint Rose Philippine Duchesne established the first orphanage in Saint Louis, housing twenty girls at Broadway and Hickory. In 1832 at Mullanphy Hospital, the Sisters of Charity set aside an orphanage wing for boys, the first west of the Mississippi. In 1843 the Daughters of Charity established an orphanage for forty-three girls. Two years earlier in 1841, the Catholic Orphans Association of Saint Louis was established to help address the needs of parentless children in Saint Louis.

James Neal Primm, in his *Lion of the Valley*, pointed out that at that time there were three Catholic orphanages and two Protestant orphanages in Saint Louis, including the Saint Louis Protestant Orphans' Asylum, founded in 1834.

The first Saint Vincent de Paul Society in America was founded in Saint Louis in 1845 by Dr. Thomas Anderson, John Everhart, Dr. Moses Linton, and Judge Bryan Mullanphy. Its object was to provide charitable relief to families and individuals struggling with economic hardships. The Society provided valuable assistance to victims of the 1849 cholera epidemic and fire that same year which destroyed much of downtown Saint Louis, causing destruction and widespread unemployment.

In 1849 the Sisters of the Good Shepherd came to Saint Louis to establish a house of safety for girls and women who were vulnerable to the harsh realities of a frontier city. At first, they were housed in a home donated through the will of a deceased priest and supported financially by Anne Lucas Hunt. As the need grew, a larger facility known as The Reformatories was built to accommodate around three hundred women and another one hundred and fifty girls. Some sixty of these women pledged to live their whole lives in the convent, calling themselves the Community of Magdalens. As the city grew around the facility, Adolphus Busch donated an eleven-acre farm on Gravois where the facility was relocated in 1895.

In 1906 Father Peter Dunne set up Newsboys Home to give shelter to some thirty-five homeless boys. In 1908 Father Timothy Dempsey set up a "hotel" for the homeless, providing 207 beds in a 68-room facility. The number of "guests" ran from 8,000 to 10,000 a year. Later he established Saint Patrick's Day Nursery and Emergency Home for Women.

In 1993 the Franciscan Sisters of Mary established Almost Home after realizing that homeless teenage mothers, who are legally considered unaccompanied minors, could not be admitted to traditional homeless shelters. These young mothers and their children had access to very few supportive services and had no place to stay. To this day, Almost Home remains the only organization in St. Louis that exclusively houses teenage moms and their children.

The Center assists women in the criminal justice system in making a successful transition to their families and communities through practicing and promoting restorative justice.

Dismas House serves referrals from the U.S. Bureau of Prisons, the U. S. Probation Offices in the Eastern District of Missouri and Southern District of Illinois, the Pretrial Services Office, and direct court commitments. Residents can stay for a few days up to six months or longer, depending on their needs as determined by the referring authority. It is located in the former Brothers' residence at the old McBride High School on North Kingshighway.

Until recently the Little Sisters of the Poor provided more than 110 low-income senior residents with a loving home-like atmosphere where they could live out their days in peace and comfort. In 1868 they came to Saint Louis to care for the elderly poor. Six Sisters began by begging for the needy and establishing a home for the elderly poor where they would be cared for with dignity.

The Mother of Good Counsel Home is a skilled nursing facility in St. Louis and combines loving care and professional service for residents who need total nursing care 24 hours a day. The Sisters of St. Francis of the Martyr St. George and the staff provide a warm home-like environment where residents can feel secure and personally cared for each day.

Our Lady's Inn provides a loving home and an array of services supporting pregnant women and their children who are dealing with homelessness. Since 1982 Our Lady's Inn has served as a life-affirming alternative to abortion for more than 5,000 women who have chosen life for their unborn babies. For more than 30 years these families have been sheltered and supported in their efforts to live healthy and productive lives, attain educational goals, gain employment, and secure stable housing.

Cardinal Ritter Senior Services (CRSS) provides services to improve the quality of life for senior adults by promoting and providing social, health, and housing programs and services in St. Louis City and County, as well as in St. Charles, Jefferson, Franklin, and Warren Counties.

Catholic Charities of St. Louis (CCSTL) has been helping people in need since 1912. Organized as a federation of eight agencies, Catholic Charities assists 156,000 people annually through more than 100 programs at 50 sites. CCSTL serves 11 counties in the St. Louis metropolitan area. These include Cardinal Ritter Senior Services providing a continuum of care to senior adults including social, health, and housing services. Catholic Charities Community Services provides legal assistance, refugee services, housing crisis help, and homeless prevention for individuals and families in need.

Catholic Family Services is a professional counseling agency which provides community-based education and mental health services at numerous outreach locations. Good Shepherd Children & Family Services provides the highest quality foster care, adoption, expectant parent counseling, advocacy, and residential services. Marygrove provides day and residential treatment for children and youth, including diagnosis, therapy and treatment, education, and healthcare. It also provides crisis care, therapeutic foster care, transitional and independent living programs.

Queen of Peace Center is a family-centered behavioral healthcare provider for women with addiction, their children and families. Saint Martha's Hall offers shelter, counseling, and education to battered women and their children. St. Patrick Center provides opportunities for self-sufficiency and dignity to people who are homeless or at risk of becoming homeless.

Father Dempsey's Charity is located in the Grand Center area and affords transitional housing and a safe place to give a fresh start to men without a home. Today there are up to 60 residents with a place to live and who receive help with daily nourishment, getting a job, obtaining needed medical treatment, and accessing government benefits available due to military service, age, or disability. The average length of stay is one year.

Guardian Angel Settlement Association serves those living in poverty by helping them improve the quality of their lives and achieve economic independence. Established in 1859 by the Daughters of Charity as an orphanage for young immigrant girls, they evolved into an agency serving children, teens, families, and older adults. Today they work to educate and empower through appropriate programs and services. Besides a professional staff, they are assisted by numerous volunteers throughout the St. Louis area who devote more than 11,000 hours annually.

Today there are 143 Saint Vincent de Paul parish conferences within the Archdiocese of Saint Louis. Each of these gives assistance to the needy in the form of food, energy assistance, and rental assistance. Some provide bus passes and other services. The Society provides on an archdiocesan-wide basis: crisis intervention, transportation services, health services, and five thrift stores.

The contribution of the Catholic Church to education in Saint Louis is remarkable and began decades before any attempt was made to found a public-school system. In 1823 the City of Saint Louis paid Father Niel's school to educate poor children of the city, since there was as yet no public education available. In 1838 the city of Saint Louis established two elementary schools for the general population. Both were co-institutional, that is, having one section for boys and another for girls, and both charged a small tuition. In 1847 these schools became free public schools supported by tax dollars. This was forty years after Father James Maxwell established Sainte Genevieve Academy in 1808, receiving the first charter for a school from the territorial government.

By 1839 the Diocese of Saint Louis provided Saint Mary of the Barrens Seminary in Perryville, Missouri, a novitiate in Florissant, Saint Louis University, Saint Vincent Academy in Cape Girardeau, seven elementary schools for boys, and ten elementary schools for girls. By the 1840s Catholic schools provided free education to over 3,000 children, while twenty-seven public schools provided free education to 3,791 children. In 1857 the Sisters of Mercy established Saint Patrick Free School in Saint Louis and extended their apostolate to visiting the sick and inmates at the city jail. In 1858 the School Sisters of Notre Dame assumed responsibility for schools at Saint Joseph Parish, Saints Peter and Paul Parish and Saint Liborius Parish, with a combined enrollment of 3,400 children. In 1873 these congregations of Sisters were joined by the Precious Blood Sisters.

The first public high school in Saint Louis was established in 1855 and in five years would have an enrollment of 301 students. The archdiocese was slower in establishing high schools but got serious in 1911 when three archdiocesan high schools were opened at Saints Peter and Paul, Saint Teresa, and Saint Francis de Sales Parishes. In 1913 Rosati-Kain High School opened its doors to girls. In 1935 McBride High School was opened for boys. This school joined Saint Louis University High School and Christian Brothers College

High School and was soon joined by Nerinx Hall in Webster Groves, Villa Duchesne, Ursuline Academy in Kirkwood, Saint Joseph High School for Negroes, Saint Elizabeth's on the South Side, Dominican at Saint Mark's Parish, Incarnate Word Academy in Normandy, and Xavier High School at Saint Francis Xavier Parish. At its high-water mark in 1961, the Catholic community provided for Saint Louis 210 elementary schools enrolling 87,000 children and another 28,000 in the high schools.

Saint Mary's of the Barrens was the first institution of higher learning to receive a charter in Missouri. It was founded in 1818 and chartered in 1822, granting both bachelor's and master's degrees. In 1824 the Society of Jesus founded Saint Regis Indian School in cooperation with the federal government.

The Sisters of Saint Joseph opened Saint Joseph School for the Deaf in 1836, fourteen years before the State of Missouri opened a public school dedicated to educating the deaf. Mother Saint John Fontbonne and six other Sisters founded the school at Carondolet after several Sisters studied in France to perfect the educational methods needed. Classes began in 1837, and Missouri paid part of the tuition until the state opened its own school in 1850.

In 1880 the Oblate Sisters of Providence came to Saint Louis to open a school for black children. Fifty were enrolled in the first year, and an orphanage for black children was founded in 1882. Catholic education took a forward-leaning position regarding racial integration. In 1847 the Sisters of Saint Joseph opened a school for black children but were forced to close it due to violence. In 1943 Father Patrick Molloy helped create the Catholic League to allow his athletes at Saint Joseph High School for Negroes to compete with white athletes from McBride, CBC, and SLUH, opening the way for greater integration of high school athletics.

Cardinal Joseph Ritter ordered the total desegregation of Catholic schools throughout the Archdiocese of Saint Louis in 1947, seven years before the landmark decision of *Brown v. The Board of Education of Topeka*.

The Catholic community in Saint Louis has provided educational opportunities to area girls very early in our history. The Sacred Heart Nuns opened schools in Saint Charles and later in Florissant for girls as early as 1818. These were followed by the Loretto Sisters in 1823, Visitation Nuns in 1833, and Ursuline Nuns in 1845. This continued to be the case with the founding of Nerinx Hall, Villa Duchesne, Saint Elizabeth, Incarnate Word, Xavier High School, and Rosati-Kain.

Saint Louis College, later Saint Louis University, was founded by Bishop William Du Bourg in 1818. It grew as the first university west of the Mississippi under the leadership of the Society of Jesus, opening its doors to all students regardless of denomination. In 1836 the Medical School was founded and opened in 1842 with the Board made up of Dr. B. G. Farrar, Rev. William Greenleaf Eliot, founder of Washington University, philanthropist John O'Fallon and William Ashley of fur-trapping fame. It was one of only eight medical schools in the United States until it was forced to close under threats of violence from Know-Nothing rioters. It would be reopened in 1903.

The SLU Law School opened in 1844 under the direction of Judge Richard Aylett Buckner and opened to all students regardless of denomination. It was forced to close several years later due to enrollment issues. By 1929 Saint Louis University had been joined by other Catholic institutions of higher learning including Christian Brothers College (1855-1917), Kenrick Seminary, Maryhurst Normal, Saint Mary's Junior College, Notre Dame Junior College, Maryville College, Webster College, and Fontbonne College. Saint Louis University was the first American university in a former slave state to integrate its faculty and student body in 1944.

Catholic schools of the Archdiocese of Saint Louis continue to constitute the largest school system in the state of Missouri. Approximately 35,000 students are enrolled in 121 elementary schools and nearly 15,000 students attend 27 Catholic high schools. The Archdiocese of Saint Louis enrolls in its schools a larger percentage of Catholic children, per capita, than any other diocese in the country. In addition, almost 21,000 public school students participate in the Parish Schools of Religion, and 6,000 adults take part in parish faith formation programs. Financial aid is available through the Tuition Family Plan, Today and Tomorrow Education Fund, the Catholic Family Tuition Assistance Endowment Fund, and Parish Employees Endowment Fund, and more recently, Beyond Sunday.

There are ten archdiocesan high schools and two parish high schools. In addition, there are six Catholic high schools for boys run by Religious congregations and nine for girls. Special Education programs include early intervention centers, elementary special education schools, a center for autism, pre-vocation services, and learning centers which partner with parish schools. Saint Joseph Institute for the Deaf provides auditory-oral education. Higher educational institutions include Saint Louis University, Fontbonne University, Maryville University, Aquinas School of Theology, and Kenrick-Glennon Seminary.

In 1828 the Sisters of Charity established a hospital in Saint Louis with the help of the Mullanphy family. It was the first hospital in the city and the first west of the Mississippi. During the cholera epidemic of 1832, the City of Saint Louis made use of the Sisters and their hospital, as they were the only qualified nurses in the city. Two Sisters died treating victims of the epidemic. Federal funds helped sustain the hospital through the crisis. Catholic nuns played a significant role in caring for the wounded in the Civil War.

In 1894 a School of Nursing was added to Mullanphy Hospital. The Sisters of Mary of the Third Order Franciscans came to Saint Louis in 1868 to take up hospital work. In the yellow fever epidemic in the South in 1878, thirteen sisters volunteered to assist the victims. All thirteen contracted yellow fever, and five died. In 1883 smallpox came to Saint Louis. The Health Commissioner gave the "Quarantine Hospital" to the Franciscan Sisters for two years during which time 1,400 patients were treated. From 1884 to 1889, the Sisters ran the Missouri Pacific Railroad Hospital and later oversaw the Terminal Railroad Hospital, the Wabash Railroad Hospital, and the Laclede Gas Hospital.

They established hospitals in Saint Charles and in Cape Girardeau, founded Saint Anthony Hospital on Grand and Chippewa in 1900, and the first tubercular hospital in the Mid-West, Mount Saint Rose, in 1902. In 1904 they founded Saint Vincent Hospital and served Native American patients under federal contract. Saint Louis County sent its sick to Saint Mary's Hospital and Mount Saint Rose, as there was no hospital in the County at the time. A school of nursing was founded in 1907, and African American nurses were trained by 1933. Other Catholic hospitals included Alexian Brothers (1869) for male patients, adding a male nursing school in 1928, Saint John's Mercy Hospital (1871), adding a nursing school in 1905, and De Paul Hospital (1874) under the direction of the Daughters of Charity.

The Catholic community continues to make exceptional contributions to the Saint Louis area by way of health care facilities. These include Cardinal Glennon Hospital for Children, De Paul Health Center, Mercy Hospital, Saint Alexius, Saint Joseph Hill Infirmary, SSM

Saint Clare Medical Health Center, Mercy South, Saint Joseph Hospital in Saint Charles, Saint Louis University Hospital, and Saint Mary's Health Center. Beyond these, Saint Louis has nine other denominational or non-denominational hospitals.

As early as 1844, the Jesuits established a school for the boys of German immigrants. Father Joseph Melcher made three trips to Germany and Austria to recruit over forty priests and seminarians to serve the growing German population in the Saint Louis area. He also brought the Ursuline Nuns to Saint Louis. In 1854 Saint John Nepomuk Parish was founded to serve the needs of the Bohemian population. By 1857 Father John Hogan traveled with Irish railroad workers to serve their needs. In 1866 *Societa d'Unione Fratellanza Italiana* began giving humanitarian aid to poor Italian immigrants as well as to families in Italy. It was the first such society in America.

Many Catholic laity gave extraordinary aid to charitable and educational efforts in Saint Louis. Anne Lucas Hunt gave property to establish the Loretto Academy and gave funding to the Good Shepherd Sisters' work with vulnerable women and girls. John Thornton left $579,000 for "charitable works of the Archdiocese" in his 1858 will. John Mullanphy helped the Sisters of Charity establish the first hospital west of the Mississippi. His son, Bryan Mullanphy, founded the Saint Vincent de Paul Society, gave generous donations to many charities, and established the Travelers' Aid Society, which is still functioning today due to his bequest. Mrs. William Cullen McBride gave $250,000 for the establishment of McBride High School. More recently, Charles F. Vatterott, Jr., a member of the Catholic Interracial Council, used his construction firm to build at-cost housing for Black families, helping to establish Saint Martin de Porres Parish.

There are many other and varied outreaches that the Catholic community provided to the Saint Louis area. Father Ambrose Heim, first chaplain of the Saint Vincent de Paul Society, was acutely aware of the financial woes of his immigrant parishioners. Many were poorly-paid day laborers who feared to put what little money they had into commercial banks which often failed, causing depositors to lose their money. Father Heim founded the "little bank," in which he held the deposits himself, keeping the money secure and paying a small rate of interest to the depositors. In 1850 Archbishop Peter Richard Kenrick took Father Heim's idea and created The Bishop's Bank. Eventually, the bank had nineteen million dollars in deposits. No-interest and low-interest loans were made to parishes and to religious communities doing charitable works. During the Panic of 1857, when commercial banks were closing, the City of Saint Louis turned to The Bishop's Bank for a loan for public works.

One of the saddest events in American history came with the forced displacement of Native Americans in the 1830s. While much is known about the Cherokee Trail of Tears, the story of the removal of the Potawatomi from Indiana and Illinois along the Trail of Death to Kansas is all the more compelling and recalls the efforts of Catholics to ameliorate the tragedy. When the Indiana militia forced the Potawatomi under Chief Menominee to march all the way from Indiana to Kansas, 859 people were displaced, and 150 would die along the way. Father Benjamin Petit shared their hardship and died later due to the privations they suffered. The survivors were cared for at Sugar Creek Mission by Jesuit Fathers. Later, a party of Jesuits and Sacred Heart Sisters, including Saint Rose Philippine Duchesne, would join the Potawatomi to run a school for them and to care for their spiritual needs. The Jesuits included Father Peter De Smet, who would dedicate his life to the protection and promotion of Native Americans, along with Fathers Peter Verhaegan, Christian Hoeckens, John Anthony Elet, and Charles Felix van Quickenborne, all of whom served Native American communities during their careers in America.

There are many contemporary challenges which confront the Catholic community of Saint Louis. Its long and storied history should act to encourage those who carry on this legacy. Archdiocesan historian Rev. John Rothensteiner wrote, "From small, almost insignificant beginnings in the primeval forests and prairies of the Continent of North America, the Church opened a steady advance, slowly. Laboriously, but ever hopefully struggling onward, until the true center was found in the city of the Crusader Saint on the banks of the mightiest river of the world."[282] The sentiment is as true today as it was when he penned those words in 1928.

---

282 Rev. John Rothensteiner. *History of the Archdiocese of St. Louis.* Volume II. St. Louis: Blackwell Wielandy Co. 1928. P. 765.

BIBLIOGRAPHY

Arroyo, Raymond. *Mother Angelica: The Remarkable Story of a Nun, Her Nerve, and a Network of Miracles.* New York: Doubleday. 2005.

Bailey, Beth & Farber, David, ed. *America in the 70s.* Lawrence: University of Kansas Press. 2004.

Barron, Bishop Robert. *Letter to a Suffering Church: A Bishop Speaks on the Sexual Abuse Crisis.* Park Ridge: Word On Fire. 2019.

Berger, Dan, ed. *The Hidden 1970's: Histories of Radicalism.* New Brunswick: Rutgers University Press. 2010.

Bernstein, Carl and Politi, Marco. *His Holiness: John Paul II and the Hidden History of Our Times.* New York: Doubleday. 1996.

Bornstelmann, Thomas. *The 1970s: A New Global History from Civil Rights to Economic Inequality.* Princeton: Princeton University Press. 2012.

Briggs, Kenneth A. *Holy Siege: The Year that Shook Catholic America.* San Francisco: HarperCollins. 1992.

Burkle-Young, Francis A. *Passing the Keys: Modern Cardinals, Conclaves, and the Election of the Next Pope.* Lanham: Madison Books. 1999.

Cannon, Jane. *Legacy of Love and Learning: A History of the Academy of the Sacred Heart in St. Charles, Missouri, from its Founding in 1818, Written for its Bicentennial Celebration in 2018.* St. Charles: Academy of the Sacred Heart. 2017.

Daughters of St. Paul. *Communicators for Christ.* St. Paul Editions. 1972.

Dolan, Cardinal Timothy M. *Priests for the Third Millennium.* Huntington: Our Sunday Visitor. 2000.

Faggioli, Massimo. *Vatican II: The Battle for Meaning.* New York: Paulist Press. 2012.

Flannery, O. P. Austin. *Vatican Council II: The Conciliar and Post-Conciliar Documents.* "Inter Mirifica." Wilmington: Scholarly Resources. 1975.

Fromm, David. *How We Got Here: The 70s*. New York: Basic Books. 2000.

Gordon, Colin. *Mapping Decline: St. Louis and the Fate of the American City*. Philadelphia: University of Pennsylvania Press. 2008.

Greeley, Andrew M. *The Making of the Popes 1978*. Kansas City: Andrews and McMeel, Inc. 1979.

Groeschel, C.F.R., Fr. Benedict J. *From Scandal to Hope*. Huntington: Our Sunday Visitor. 2002.

Gronowicz, Antoni. *God's Broker: The Life of Pope John Paul II as Told in His Own Words*. Richardson & Snyder.

Guste, Placid. *History of the Society of Our Mother of Peace: Written for Cardinal Carberry*. Unpublished. As cited in Br. Peter Sirangelo, SMP. *Why African Converts to Catholicism in Saint Louis, Mo: The Experiences of the Society of Our Mother of Peace*. Master's Thesis. Kenrick-Glennon Seminary. 2005.

Hartman, Andrew. *A War for the Soul of America*. Chicago: University of Chicago Press. 2016.

Hebblethwaite, Peter. *Paul VI: The First Modern Pope*. New York: Paulist Press. 1993.

History of St. Agnes Home: Prepared for the Jubilee Year September 2009 – September 2010. Privately Published.

Horner, OSB, Timothy. *In Good Soil: The Founding of Saint Louis Priory and School, 1954 – 1973*. Saint Louis: Saint Louis Abbey Press. 2001.

Hughes, John Jay. *No Ordinary Fool: A Testimony to Grace*. Mustang: Tate Publishing & Enterprise. 2008.

Jenkins, Philip. *Decade of Nightmares: The End of the Sixties and the Making of Eighties America*. Oxford: Oxford University Press. 2006.

John Paul II: Pastoral Visit to St. Louis. St. Louis: Archdiocese of St. Louis. 1999.

Kengor, Paul, *The Crusader: Ronald Reagan and the Fall of Communism*. New York: Regan. 2006.

Linacre Institute. *After Asceticism: Sex, Prayer and Deviant Priests*. Bloomington: Authorhouse. 2006.

MacNutt, Francis. *The Power to Heal*. Notre Dame: Ave Maria Press. 1977.

May, Archbishop John L. October 16, 1981. *With Pen and Staff*. Ligouri: Ligouri Publications. 1992.

Mother Mary Teresa. Bittle, O.F.M. Cap., trans. *The Servant of God Mother Mary Teresa of St. Joseph: An Autobiography*. Wauwatosa: Carmelite Convent. 2000.

Ponnuru, Ramesh. *The Party of Death*. Washington, D. C.: Regnery Publishing. 2006.

Reese, S. J., Thomas J. *A Flock of Shepherds: The National Conference of Catholic Bishops*. Kansas City: Sheed & Ward. DATE

Rothensteiner, Rev. John. *History of the Archdiocese of St. Louis*. Volume II. St. Louis: Blackwell Wielandy Co. 1928.

Schneider, Monsignor Nicholas A. *Changing Times: The Life of John Joseph Carberry, Cardinal Archbishop of Saint Louis, Pro-Life Pioneer, Mary's Troubadour*. Saint Louis: Independent Publishing Corporation. 2008.

Schulman, Bruce J. *The Seventies: The Great Shift in American Culture, Society, and Politics*. New York: Da Capo Press. 2002.

Schlafly, Phyllis. *How the Republican Party Became Pro-Life*. Dunrobin Publishing. 2016.

Self, Robert O. *All in the Family: The Realignment of American Democracy Since the 1960's*. New York: Hill and Wang. 2012.

Steinfels, Peter. *A People Adrift: The Crisis of the Roman Catholic Church in America*. New York: Simon & Schuster. 2003.

Synan, Vincon. *An Eyewitness Remembers the Century of the Holy Spirit*. Grand Rapids: Chosen. 2010.

Velott, La Rue H. *The Order of Deacon: Past and Present*. Columbus: National Association of Diaconate Directors. 2008.

Weigel, George. *Witness to Hope: The Biography of Pope John Paul II*. New York: HarperCollins. 2001.

Weiner, Tim. *One Man against the World: The Tragedy of Richard Nixon*. New York: Henry Holt and Company. 2015

White, Theodore H. *The Making of the President, 1968.* New York: Simon & Schuster. 1970.

Williams, Daniel K. *Defenders of the Unborn: The Pro-Life Movement before* Roe v. Wade. New York: Oxford University Press. 2016.

Williams, Daniel K. *God's Own Party: The Making of the Christian Right.* Oxford: Oxford University Press. 2012.

Witt, Michael J. *I. Phil: The Journey of a Twentieth Century Religious.* Winona: Saint Mary's Press. 1987.

Zöller, Michael. Trans. Steven Rendall and Albert Wimmer. *Washington and Rome: Catholicism in American Culture.* Notre Dame: University of Notre Dame Press. 1999.

ARTICLES AND UNPUBLISHED PAPERS

Bethell, Tom. "Sex, Lies and Kinsey." *The American Spectator.* May 1999.

Lorilla, S.M.P., Bro. Xavier Ronnie Maldo. *The Shaping of the Charism of the Society of Our Mother of Peace.* Master's Thesis. Kenrick-Glennon Seminary. 2014.

Polizzi, Reverend Sal. E. "The Edward Street Overpass: A Lesson in Political Expediency." Research Paper. Saint Louis University. 1972.

Sirangelo, SMP., Bro. Peter. *Why African Converts to Catholicism in Saint Louis, Mo: The Experiences of the Society of Our Mother of Peace.* Master's Thesis. Kenrick-Glennon Seminary. 2005.

"You Shall Be My Witnesses... Hebrew Catholics and the Mission of the Church." AHC Conference in St. Louis, Missouri on October 1-3, 2010.

INDEX

2001 Eucharistic Congress, 234
60 Minutes, 3, 113, 250
Agca, Mehmet Ali, 140
AIDS, 4, 195–196, 203, 206, 260
Akin, Jimmy, 264
Alinsky, Saul, 23, 156
All Saints Parish, University City, 13, 225
Almost Home, 295–296
Americans for Democratic Action, 232
Ampleforth Abbey, 44–45
Anglican Lambeth Conferences, 26
Archdiocesan Human Rights Office, 156, 162, 171
Archdiocesan Pro-Life Committee, 37, 70–73, 135, 174, 189, 223, 244
Arrowhead Stadium Regional Charismatic Conference, 86–87
Association of Hebrew Catholics, 282, 284–285

Bakke, Allan Paul, 116
Benedict XVI, Pope, 87, 221, 227, 252, 264–265, 285
Biondi, SJ, Father Lawrence, 233, 247
Birthright, 30, 38, 72, 174–175, 223
Bishop Healy School, 110, 122, 167
Blue Notes *(Notanda),* 153, 175–176, 197–198
Bommarito, Monsignor Vincent, 92, 230–231
Bozak, Marek, 263–265
Braxton, Bishop Edward, 220–221, 235, 240
Brezhnev, Leonid, 139, 160, 164
Brothers of Mary, 60–61
Bryant, Anita, 108
Brzeziński, Zbigniew, 129, 138
Burke, Cardinal Raymond Leo, vii, 224–225, 258–267, 269–272, 282, 284–289, 291–292

Calley, Lieutenant William, 11–12
Canons Regular of the New Jerusalem, 267
Carberry, Cardinal Joseph, 14–18, 34–36, 38, 44, 47, 49–50, 53–54, 57, 66, 70–71, 73, 81–82, 84, 87–88, 92–93, 101–105, 107, 109–111, 124–127, 133–136, 152, 169, 179, 183, 217, 222, 229, 270, 305–306
Cardinal Ritter Prep High School, 208, 213

Cardinal Ritter Senior Services (CRSS), 296–297
Carlson, Archbishop Robert, ix, 257, 264, 268–269, 286–287
Carmelite Sisters of the Divine Heart of Jesus, 39
Carnahan, Governor Mel, 237–238
Carter, President Jimmy, 11, 98, 111–112, 114–115, 117–119, 129, 138–143, 159
Casey, William, 138–140, 160, 164
Casti Connubii, 25
Catholic Charities of Saint Louis, 122, 175, 177, 195, 208, 223, 225, 286, 296–297
Catholic Family Services, 297
Catholic Supply Company, 71, 73–74, 95, 272
Catholics in Political Life, 260
Cervantes, Mayor Alphonso, 76, 109
Charismatic Renewal Office, 94, 182
Christian Brothers College High School, 58–59, 61, 292, 298–299
Christifideles Laici, 144–145
Citizens for Educational Freedom, 144
Clark, Judge William, 138
Clinton, President Bill, 230, 236
Coalition for an Open Convention, 1
Cognata, Frank, 199–200, 286
Contemporary Mission, 101, 103–106
Cordero, Mother Paula, 15, 55
Costello, Monsignor John M., 83, 177
Covenant Network, 278–281
Curran, Father Charles, 5, 201–202, 207
Cushing, Cardinal Richard, 26, 56

Daley, Mayor Richard, 1
Dallas Charter, 255–256
Daughters of Saint Paul, 14–15, 54–56
De Lubac, SJ, Henri, 99
De Smet Jesuit High School, 58–59, 198
Deddens, Father Clarence, 81–82, 84, 93
Dismas House, 296
Doe v. Bolton, 31, 70
Dolan, Cardinal Timothy, 200–201, 226–227, 243, 251, 253, 304
Dolan, OP, Sister Mary, 157
Doorways, 195–196
Duggan, Martin, 54, 144
Duggan, Mae, 144
Dunford, SJ, Father Robert, 69

Ecclesia in America, 236
Eckhoff, SSND, Sister Mary Ann, 168, 186, 208, 227
Economic Justice For All, 193
Edward Street Overpass, 76–77, 79, 307
Ehrlich, Paul, 6
Eisenstadt v. Baird, 27, 32
Equal Rights Amendment, 112–113, 143, 173, 273
Ervin, Senator Sam, 96–97, 113, 280
Eternal Word Television Network (EWTN), 235, 275–279
Eucharistic Adoration, v, 43, 228–229, 246, 280
Faith for the Future, 286–287, 293
Federation of Catholic Urban Schools (FOCUS), 168–169, 187, 208
Feingold, Dr. Lawrence, 284
Filipiak, Father Edward, 134–135, 151
Firestone, Shulamith, 8
Foley, SJ, Father John, 69–70
Ford, President Gerald, 98, 111, 113–114, 155
Frankfurt School, 8
Frerking, OSB, Abbot Thomas, 267
Friedan, Betty, 8, 114
Friedman, Milton, 141
Friedman, OCD, Father Elias, 282–285

Gauthe, Gilbert, 218, 249–250, 255
Gaydos, Bishop John, 82, 83, 93, 214, 222, 241
Geoghan, John, 248, 250, 255
Glennon, Cardinal John, 40–41, 75, 151–152
Gorbachev, Mikhail, 146, 164–166
Gore, Vice President Al, 238
Gottwald, Bishop George J., 35, 67, 82, 217, 219, 253
Griesedieck, Monsignor Edward, 88
Griswold v. Connecticut, 7, 27, 29, 32
Groeschel, CRF, Father Benedict, 235, 254, 256, 279, 305
Guste, Father Placid, 49–50, 305

Haig, Secretary of State Alexander, 138
Häring, CSSR, Father Bernard, 6
Harris, III, George, 4
Henry, George, 227, 245
Hermann, Bishop Robert, 82, 84, 87, 95
Holman, Teresa, 278–279
Holman, Tony, 278–279

Horner, OSB, Father Timothy, 44–45, 48, 305
Hughes, Father John Jay, 179–182, 191, 215, 258, 305
Hume, Abbot Basil, 44
Humphrey, Vice President Hubert Horatio, 1–3
Humanae Vitae, 5–6, 99, 136, 201
Hunthausen, Archbishop Raymond, 194, 196, 201, 207
Hyde Amendment, 112, 114

Improvement Association of the Hill, 76
Intercessors of the Lamb, 225

Jaruzelski, General Wojciech, 140, 145–146, 163, 165
Jefferson, Mildred, 29
John Jay College of Criminal Justice, 250
John Paul II, Pope, 86, 128–130, 132–140, 144–147, 153, 159–161,
    163–166, 192, 196, 201–207, 215–216, 234–239, 251, 260,
    266, 275–278, 304–306
Johnson, President Lyndon Baines, 1–3, 12, 22, 154
Johnson, Virginia, 8

Keller, Father Thomas, 267–269, 289
Kennedy, Senator Robert, 1
Kenrick-Glennon Seminary, 50–51, 199, 222–223, 225–226, 242,
    251, 270, 284–285, 287, 292–293, 301, 305, 307
Kertz, Molly, 227, 230, 244
King, Jr., Dr. Martin Luther, 4
Kinsey, Alfred, 8–9, 307
Koop, Surgeon General C. Everett, 143, 173
Krol, Cardinal John, 105, 109, 128, 139, 196
Küng, Father Hans, 98, 136

Lader, Lawrence, 10
Laffer, Arthur, 141
Laghi, Archbishop Pio, 133, 138, 275
Latin Mass, 100, 196–197, 252, 266–267, 269, 288
Léger, Cardinal Paul-Emile, 6
Lenhardt, Canon Karl, 266–267
Liese, Representative Chris, 237–238
Life in the Spirit Seminars, 84
Life-Line Coalition, 175
Little Sisters of the Poor, 296
Lucas, Archbishop George, 225–226, 242

MacNutt, Father Francis, 84–87, 306
March for Life, 230–231, 244
Marianist Apostolic Center, 62–63
Maritz, Young and Dusard, Inc., 41–42
Marx, Father Paul, 8, 29
Mary Teresa of Saint Joseph, Mother, 39–40
Masters, William, 8
Matthews, FSC, Brother I. Philip, 16, 106
May, Archbishop John L., vii, 135, 158, 161, 169–170, 172–173, 175,
      178, 180–181, 183, 186, 188–189, 192–202, 208–212, 214,
      216, 218–219, 222, 242, 262, 270
McCarthy, Senator Eugene, 1, 3
McCaskill, Senator Clare, 259, 271
McCormack, SJ, Father Richard, 6
McHugh, Father James, 17–18, 29
Mercy High School, 13
Meyer, SM, Brother Mel, 63, 67
Millett, Kate, 8
Milliken v. Bradley, 24
Missouri Catholic Conference, 70–71, 174
Mitchell, Attorney General John, 21, 96–97
Montfort Fathers, 101, 120
Morgan v. Hennigan, 24
Morris, Monsignor Eugene, 237, 269, 290
Moss, David and Kathleen, ix, 282–284
Mother of Good Counsel Home, 219, 296
Moynihan, Daniel Patrick, 12–13, 20, 35
My Lai Massacre, 11
Myerpeter, SM, Brother Eugene, 61–62

National Conference of Catholic Bishops (NCCB), 16, 18, 23, 29, 68,
      81, 109, 133, 135, 163, 172, 192–197, 201, 210, 228, 306
National Federation of Catholic Physicians' Guilds, 27
National Mobilization to End the War in Vietnam, 1
National Right to Life Committee, 18, 29
Naumann, Archbishop Joseph, 175, 189, 223–226, 241, 244, 258–
      259
Network, 114
Nixon, President Richard, 2–3, 6–7, 11–13, 19–22, 56, 78, 96–98,
      111–112, 155, 306
No Transfer Policy, 169–170

O'Boyle, Cardinal Patrick, 6
O'Donnell, Bishop Edward J., 71–73, 181, 199, 201, 209, 212, 214, 217–219, 242
O'Reilly, Father John, 102–105, 120–121
Office for Continuing Formation of Priests, 226
Operation Food Search, 207–208
Oppenheimer, Canon Daniel, 267
Oratory of Ss. Gregory and Augustine, 267–269, 289
Order of Christ the King Sovereign Priest, 265–267, 269
Our Lady's Inn, 223, 296

Paul VI, Pope, 4, 6, 16, 57, 70, 98–101, 113–114, 124, 126, 215, 229, 305
Pauline Books and Media, 55, 229, 272
People v. Belous, 28–29
Permanent Diaconate, 80–84, 93, 102, 152, 176–178, 190, 199, 222, 225
Personae Humanae, 107
Pius XI, Pope, 25, 56
Polizzi, Monsignor Sal, 76–79, 149, 307
Populorum Progressio, 4
Potzman, Deacon Ken, 93
Price, OSB, Father Bede, 268, 289
Priests for the Third Millennium, 226, 253, 304
Priory of Saint Mary and Saint Louis, 44, 47

Queen of Peace Center, 297
Quinn, Deacon J. Gerard, 84, 177, 190

Rahner, Father Karl, 98, 100
Ransom, CM, Father Ronald, 200, 210
Ratzinger, Father Joseph, 99, 127, 260
Reagan, President Ronald, 98, 113, 119, 138–144, 146, 153–166, 192–193, 206, 210, 305
Reaganomics, 141, 156
Reconciliation Weekends, 234
Redemptor Hominis, 131, 153
Redemptoris Mater, 145
Religious of the Sacred Heart, 60
Returning God's Gifts – Sharing Our Hope, 229, 286
Rigby, OSB, Father Luke, 44, 65
Rise Up Angry, 10

Rivers, Father Clarence, 68
Rizzo, PCPA, Mother Angelica, 272–279, 291, 304
Rockefeller, Vice President Nelson, 19, 98
Roe v. Wade, 18–19, 25, 27–28, 30–33, 70, 73, 91, 113, 135, 142, 155,
    230, 307
Rogers, Reverend Adrian, 115, 142–143
Rosati-Kain High School, 170–171, 216, 240, 298, 300

Sacerdotalis Coelibatus, 5
Sacram Diaconatus Ordinem, 80
Sacred Heart Academy, 60
Sacred Heart Nuns, 299
Saint Agatha Parish, 263, 265–266
Saint Ambrose Parish, 75–77, 79
Saint Anselm Parish, 48, 176, 195, 229, 267–268
Saint Anthony of Padua Parish, 216, 228
Saint Elizabeth, Mother of John the Baptist Parish, 52
Saint John's Abbey, 249, 253, 255
Saint Louis Association of Community Organizations (SLACO),
    156–157, 185
Saint Louis Review, 16–17, 82–83, 168–170, 172, 174–176, 180–181,
    195, 200, 217, 224
Saint Louis University High School, 14, 58, 171, 298, 300
Saint Louis University Hospital, 231, 234, 302
Saint Mary's High School, 61
Saint Mary's Hospital, 11, 301
Saint Raymond's Maronite Church, 54, 228–229, 251
Saint Roch Parish, 85
Saint Stanislaus Kostka Parish, 236, 261–266
Saint Vincent de Paul Society, 62, 82, 175, 180, 296, 302
Sarpong, Bishop Peter K., 102–103, 105
Schlafly, Phyllis, 112–114, 142–144, 306
Schmidt, Roell Ann, 85–86
Shanley, Paul, 248
Sheridan, Bishop Michael, 222–224, 241, 244
Shocklee, Monsignor John, 81, 171, 184, 188
Shrewsbury, Tom, 280–281
Shrine of Our Lady of Czestochowa, 132, 136, 207
Shrine of Our Lady of Guadalupe, Mexico City, 130
Shrine of Our Lady of Guadalupe, La Crosse, 261
Shrine of Saint Joseph, 134–135
Siri, Cardinal Giuseppe, 125, 128
Sisters of Mary of the Third Order Franciscans, 301

Sisters of St. Francis of the Martyr St. George, 296
Sisters of the Good Shepherd, 295
Snyder, Deacon Robert, 177, 190, 199
Society for Cutting Up Men (SCUM), 9
Society of Our Mother of Peace, 49–54, 65, 272, 305, 307
Solidarity, 138–140, 145, 159–160, 164–165
St. Agnes Home, 39, 41–43, 64, 305
St. Agnes Wonder Salve, 41
St. Louis Jesuits, 68
Stanley v. Georgia, 7
Steib, Bishop J. Terry, 168, 177, 199, 201, 217–219, 242
Strategic Defense Initiative (SDI), 161, 163
Students for a Democratic Society, 1
Summorum Pontificum, 265, 267, 289
Swann v. Charlotte-Mecklenburg Board of Education, 23
Swift, CM, Father James, 236–237

Tenet Health Care, 232, 234
Teresa of Calcutta, Mother, 134, 149
Thalidomide, 26
The Hill, 75–79, 93
The Stonewall, 9
The Ville, 13
Time for Choosing, 154
Today and Tomorrow Educational Foundation, 208–209

Vianney High School, 61–63, 67
Villa Maria Maternity Home, 175
Vincentian Press, 73, 272
Visitation Academy, 84
Visitation Nuns, 84–85, 299
Vitt, OSU, Sister Mary Margaret, 14, 36
Volpe, John, 56, 78–79

Wałęsa, Lech, 137, 145
Wallace, Governor George, 2–3, 11
Walters, General Vernon, 138, 160
Washington University, 4, 8, 48, 61, 300
Watergate Affair, 96
Weber, OSB, Father Samuel A., 270
White House Conference on Families, 118, 142–143
William McBride High School, 61–62, 298–299, 302
Willke, Jack and Barbara, 30, 37, 71–72

Winnipeg Statement, 6
Wojtyła, Bishop Karol, 127–129, 131–133, 136, 138, 236
Women Concerned for the Unborn Child, 30
World Peace Committee, 162–163
WRYT, 279–280

Yippies, 1

Zipfel, Bishop Paul, 219, 242–243

CPSIA information can be obtained
at www.ICGtesting.com
Printed in the USA
BVHW080808291120
594143BV00002B/3